HOW THE
BOND MARKET
WORKS

Staff of New York Institute of Finance

New York Institute of Finance

LIBRARY OF CONGRESS
Library of Congress Cataloging-in-Publication Data

How the bond market works / staff of New York Institute of Finance.
    p.   cm.
    Includes index.
    ISBN 0-13-423310-7 : $30.00
    1. Bonds.   2. Government securities.   I. New York Institute of
Finance.
HG4651.H68 1988
332.63'23--dc19   88-15352
                                                                          CIP

This publication is designed to provide accurate and authoritative information
in regard to the subject matter covered. It is sold with the understanding that
the publisher is not engaged in rendering legal, accounting, or other
professional service. If legal advice or other expert assistance is required, the
services of a competent professional person should be sought.

*From a Declaration of Principles Jointly Adopted by a Committe of the American
Bar Asociation and a Commitee of Publishers and Associations*

© 1988 by NYIF Corp.
A Division of Simon & Schuster, Inc.
70 Pine Street, New York 10270-0003

Printed in the United States of America

10 9 8 7 6 5 4

New York Institute of Finance
(NYIF Corp.)
70 Pine Street
New York, New York 10270-0003

Contents

CHAPTER 6
Inside a Primary Dealer, 95

The Players . . . Primary Dealers . . . Government
Securities Brokers . . . Government Securities Customers
. . . Government Securities Customers . . . Who Does
What Inside a Primary Dealer? . . . The Trading Desk . . .
Treasury Bill Traders . . . Treasury Coupon Traders . . .
Other Trading Desks . . . The Trading Manager . . . The
Sales Force . . . The Economics Department . . . Financing
Government Securities . . . Repos and Reverse Repos . . .
Inside a Financing Transaction . . . Kinds of Financing
Transactions . . . Customer's Money . . . Customer's
Collateral . . . Special Repo . . . A Typical Day

CHAPTER 7
Municipal Debt, 130

What Are Municipal Bonds? . . . The Primary Market . . .
The Municipal Bond Dealers . . . The Financial Advisor . .
. The Bond Counsel . . . The Syndicate . . . Who Does
What Inside a Municipal Securities Dealer? . . . The
Underwriters . . . The Traders . . . The Sales Force . . . The
Public Finance Group . . . Muncipal Research . . . How a
Competitive Underwriting Works . . . After the Offering

CHAPTER 8
Corporate Bonds, 157

How a Negotiated Underwriting Works . . . The Cooling-Off
Period . . . The Investment Banker . . . The Preliminary
Prospectus . . . Due-Diligence Meeting . . . Blue-Skying
the Issue . . . Agreement Among Underwriters . . . The
Public Offering . . . Types of Corporate Bonds . . . Pricing
Corporate Bonds . . . Understanding Bond Quotations

CHAPTER 9
The Secondary Market, 181

Glossary, 201

Index, 269

Introduction

Almost every corporation and government in the world issues bonds. When compared on the basis of dollar volume, the bond market dwarfs the trading done in stocks (which are issued only in the private sector).

Yet, ironically, the stock market enjoys far greater visibility among members of the public, whether or not they are investors. Nightly, we see how the Dow Jones Averages fared, and the financial news repeatedly focuses on the stock market.

One of the effects of the October 1987 Crash, however, is that many former participants in the raging bull stock market are now seeking other vehicles; either as alternative investments or simply for balance. Many are discovering the enormous and diverse world of bonds. Yet, because of the attention historically paid to equity trading, many investors do not understand enough about bonds and their markets.

This book explains, among many other things:

*   Essentially, how does a bond differ from a share of stock?

*   How are the various types of bonds brought to the market?

*   What goes on within the Federal Reserve System—the "Fed"—that affects bond prices every day?

*   What are the relationships between bond prices and interest rates in general?

*   When trading bonds, which is the more important consideration: price or yield?

*   Who does what inside a securities brokerage firm or dealer bank when it brings a bond issue to market?

*   When you buy a bond, how much interest are you entitled to?

Whether or not you are currently an investor, you will find *How the Bond Market Works* an illuminating and intriguing description of the workings of some of the largest markets in the world.

Chapter 1

Riding the Yield Curve

Most people have invested, at one time or another, in U.S. government savings bonds. You buy the bonds at one price, hold them for five years, and then "cash them in" at a much higher value.

As the buyer of a savings bond, you are lending money to the government. For example, when you "buy" a bond at $25, you are extending the government use of that money for at least five years. In return, the government gives you a certificate that acts as an IOU. In the indenture, or trust agreement, on the back of the certificate, the Treasury promises to pay back twice the amount of the loan — in this case, $50.

The series EE savings bond, which is what this type of bond is called, has all the elements of a loan. The "term" is five years, although you can continue to hold the bond and accrue interest for up to 40 years. "Maturity" is at the end of five years. The "principal" of the loan is not $25, as you might think, but $50.

This might be confusing, but here's the explanation. With almost any loan, the borrower pays interest to the lender. But the interest can be repaid in a number of ways.

1. In a home mortgage, the monthly payment consists of part principal and part interest. Usually the payments in the early years of the mortgage are mostly interest.

2. Interest can also be paid in installments over the term of the loan. For example, U.S. government series HH savings bonds make two interest payments a year until maturity, at which time the Treasury repays the entire principal amount to the holder.

Series HH bonds, incidentally, can only be received in exchange for series EE bonds, not bought for cash. They are available in denominations starting at just $500. The rate that newly issued series HH bonds pay is adjusted periodically to reflect the current market rate. However, once a series HH bond is issued, its interest rate never changes.

3. Interest can also be deducted from the principal up front, and this is how series EE bonds work. The principal of the loan — or face amount of the bond — is actually $50. Instead of sending out semiannual checks, however, the Treasury simply deducts what it would pay in interest payments at the beginning of the term. So the bond buyer pays only half of the face amount and is paid the full face amount at maturity. This type of debt instrument is said to be "discounted."

WHAT IS A BOND?

A bond is a long-term debt security. It represents "debt" in that the bond buyer actually lends the face amount to the bond issuer. The certificate itself is evidence of a lender-creditor relationship. It is a "security" because, unlike a car loan or home-improvement loan, the debt can be bought and sold in the open market. In fact, a bond is a loan intended to be bought and sold. It is "long-term" by definition; in order to be called a bond, the term must be longer than five years. Debt securities with maturities of under five years are called bills, notes or other terms.

Since bonds are intended to be bought and sold, all the certificates of a bond issue contain a master loan agreement. This agreement between issuer and investor (or creditor and lender), called the "bond indenture" or "deed of trust," contains all the information you'd normally expect to see in any loan agreement, including the following:

1. *Amount of the loan:* The "face amount," "par value," or "principal" is the amount of the loan — the amount that the bond issuer has agreed to repay at the bond's maturity. A typical face value is $1,000, although some bonds issued by the U.S. government have much larger par values.

2. *Rate of interest:* Bonds are issued with a specified "coupon" or "nominal" rate, which is determined largely by market conditions at the time of the bond's primary offering. Once determined, it is set contractually for the life of the bond.

The dollar amount of the interest payment can be easily calculated by multiplying the rate of interest (or coupon) by the face value of the bond. For instance, a bond with a face amount of $1,000 and a coupon of 8% pays the bondholder $80 a year ($1,000 times .08).

3. *Schedule or form of interest payments:* Interest is paid on most bonds at six-month intervals, usually on either the first or the fifteenth of the month. The $80 of an-

Figure 1-1a. A Corporate Bond Certificate (front).

Figure 1-1b. A Corporate Bond Certificate (back).

W. R. GRACE & CO.
12⅞% NOTE DUE 1990

This Note is one of a duly authorized issue of Notes of the Company designated as its 12⅞% Notes Due 1990 (herein called the "Notes"), limited (except as otherwise provided in the Indenture referred to below) in aggregate principal amount to $100,000,000, issued and to be issued under an indenture (herein called the "Indenture") dated as of September 15, 1980 between the Company and Bankers Trust Company, Trustee (herein called the "Trustee", which term includes any successor trustee under the Indenture), to which Indenture and all indentures supplemental thereto reference is hereby made for a statement of the respective rights thereunder of the Company, the Trustee and the Holders of the Notes, and the terms upon which the Notes are, and are to be, authenticated and delivered.

The Notes are subject to redemption, upon not less than 30 nor more than 60 days' notice by first-class mail, at any time on or after September 15, 1986, as a whole or from time to time in part, at the election of the Company, at a Redemption Price equal to 100% of their principal amount, together with accrued interest to the Redemption Date (but interest instalments whose Stated Maturity is on or prior to the Redemption Date will be payable to the Holders of such Notes, or one or more Predecessor Notes, of record at the close of business on the relevant Record Date referred to on the face hereof), all as provided in the Indenture.

In the event of redemption of this Note in part only, a new Note or Notes for the unredeemed portion hereof shall be issued in the name of the Holder hereof upon the cancellation hereof.

If an Event of Default, as defined in the Indenture, shall occur and be continuing, the principal of all the Notes may be declared due and payable in the manner and with the effect provided in the Indenture.

The Indenture permits, with certain exceptions as therein provided, the amendment thereof and the modification of the rights and obligations of the Company and the rights of the Holders of the Notes under the Indenture at any time by the Company and the Trustee with the consent of the Holders of 66⅔% in aggregate principal amount of the Notes at the time Outstanding, as defined in the Indenture. The Indenture also contains provisions permitting the Holders of specified percentages in aggregate principal amount of the Notes at the time Outstanding, as defined in the Indenture, on behalf of the Holders of all the Notes, to waive compliance by the Company with certain provisions of the Indenture and certain past defaults under the Indenture and their consequences. Any such consent or waiver by the Holder of this Note shall be conclusive and binding upon such Holder and upon all future Holders of this Note and of any Note issued upon the transfer hereof or in exchange herefor or in lieu hereof whether or not notation of such consent or waiver is made upon this Note.

No reference herein to the Indenture and no provision of this Note or of the Indenture shall alter or impair the obligation of the Company, which is absolute and unconditional, to pay the principal of and interest on this Note at the times, places, and rate, and in the coin or currency, herein prescribed.

As provided in the Indenture and subject to certain limitations therein set forth, this Note is transferable on the Note Register of the Company, upon surrender of this Note for registration of transfer at the office or agency of the Company in the Borough of Manhattan, The City of New York, duly endorsed by, or accompanied by a written instrument of transfer in form satisfactory to the Company and the Note Registrar duly executed by, the Holder hereof or his attorney duly authorized in writing, and thereupon one or more new Notes, of authorized denominations and for the same aggregate principal amount, will be issued to the designated transferee or transferees.

The Notes are issuable only in registered form without coupons in denominations of $1,000 and any integral multiple thereof. As provided in the Indenture and subject to certain limitations therein set forth, Notes are exchangeable for a like aggregate principal amount of Notes of a different authorized denomination, as requested by the Holder surrendering the same.

No service charge shall be made for any such transfer or exchange, but the Company may require payment of a sum sufficient to cover any tax or other governmental charge payable in connection therewith.

The Company, the Trustee and any agent of the Company or the Trustee may treat the Person in whose name this Note is registered as the owner hereof for all purposes, whether or not this Note be overdue, and neither the Company, the Trustee nor any such agent shall be affected by notice to the contrary.

The Notes are hereby designated as Superior Indebtedness for the purposes of (a) the Indenture covering the Company's 4¼% Convertible Subordinate Debentures Due March 1, 1990 issued pursuant to the Indenture dated as of March 1, 1965 between the Company and Chemical Bank New York Trust Company, Trustee, within the meaning of, and as defined in, Section 3.01 of such Indenture and (b) the Indenture covering the Company's 6½% Convertible Subordinate Debentures Due 1996 issued pursuant to the Indenture dated as of November 15, 1971 between the Company and The Chase Manhattan Bank (National Association), Trustee, within the meaning of, and as defined in, Section 3.01 of such Indenture.

Terms used herein which are defined in the Indenture shall have the respective meanings assigned thereto in the Indenture.

ABBREVIATIONS

The following abbreviations, when used in the inscription on the face of this Note, shall be construed as though they were written out in full according to applicable laws or regulations:

TEN COM—as tenants in common
TEN ENT —as tenants by the entireties
JT TEN —as joint tenants with right of survivorship and not as tenants in common

UNIF GIFT MIN ACT—........ Custodian........
(Cust)   (Minor)
under Uniform Gifts to Minors
Act...............
(State)

Additional abbreviations may also be used though not in the above list.

FOR VALUE RECEIVED, the undersigned hereby sells, assigns and transfers unto

PLEASE INSERT SOCIAL SECURITY OR OTHER
IDENTIFYING NUMBER OF ASSIGNEE

PLEASE PRINT OR TYPEWRITE NAME AND ADDRESS OF ASSIGNEE

the within Note of W. R. GRACE & CO. and does hereby irrevocably constitute and appoint

_____Attorney
to transfer the said Note on the books of the within-named Corporation, with full power of substitution in the premises.

Dated_____

nual interest on the bond in the previous example would probably be paid in two installments of $40 each.

4. *Term:* A bond's "maturity," or the length of time until the principal is repaid, varies greatly but is always more than five years. Debt that matures in less than a year is a "money market instrument" — such as commercial paper or bankers' acceptances. A "short-term bond," on the other hand, may have an initial maturity of five years. A "long-term bond" typically matures in 20 to 40 years. The maturity of any bond is predetermined and stated in the trust indenture.

5. *Call feature (if any):* A "call feature," if specified in the trust indenture, allows the bond issuer to "call in" the bonds and repay them at a predetermined price before maturity. Bond issuers use this feature to protect themselves from paying more interest than they have to for the money they are borrowing. Companies call in bonds when general interest rates are lower than the coupon rate on the bond, thereby retiring expensive debt and refinancing it at a lower rate. (This is analogous to a homeowner's refinancing a house when mortgage rates drop.) The former issue is then said to be "called for refunding."

For example, let's say a 10¾% $1,000 bond is currently yielding a full 2 percentage points more than general interest rates, (that is, the rates of interest being paid on other types of debt) and the issuer wants to take advantage of the call feature in the bond's indenture. In this case, the call price is "110" (that is, $1,100). The issuer calls the bond at $1,100, at the same time selling a new issue at 9%. The proceeds of the new issue are used to pay off the old issue. The issuer now enjoys a lower cost for its borrowed money.

Some bonds offer "call protection"; that is, they are guaranteed not to be called for five to ten years. Call features can affect bond values by serving as a ceiling for prices. Investors are generally unwilling to pay more for a bond than its call price, because they are aware that the bond could be called back at a lower call price. If the bond issuer exercises the option to call bonds, the bondholder is usually paid a premium over par for the inconvenience.

(Sometimes if bonds are trading below their face amount, the issuer might go into the open market and buy back its own bonds. This transaction is called an "open market purchase.")

6. *Refunding:* If, when bonds mature, the issuer doesn't have the cash on hand to repay bondholders, it can issue new bonds and use the proceeds either to redeem the older bonds or to exercise a call option. This process is called "refunding."

7. *Collateral:* If the loan is secured by collateral, the indenture will specify its nature.

DIFFERENT TYPES OF YIELDS

Although the indenture describes the terms of the loan implied in bond ownership, it says nothing about the value of the security. To know that, you must understand the three basic types of yield.

1. *Coupon (Nominal) Yield.* As we have seen, if a bond has a face value of $1,000 and pays interest at a rate of 8%, the coupon, or nominal, yield is 8%. This comes to $80 a year ($1,000 times .08). Because the coupon percentage rate and principal don't change for the term of the loan, the coupon yield doesn't change either.

But the second type of yield can.

2. *Current Yield.* Suppose you could buy an 8% $1,000 bond for $800. Regardless of what you paid, you are still entitled to the $80 annual interest. Yet the $80 represents a higher *percentage* yield than the 8% coupon rate. Since you paid only $800 (not $1,000) and still receive $80 return

a year, the actual yield is 10% ($80 divided by $800). This is the bond's "current yield."

Because this bond is selling at less than its face value, it is said to be selling at a "discount."

The discounted bond would be quoted at "80," which means $800. To translate the quote into a dollar price, simply multiply it by $10. So a quote for 80½ means $805, that is, 80.5 times $10. A quote of 90⅞ would be $908.75, or 90.875 times $10. As you can see, each eighth in a bond quote is equal to $1.25 (whereas an eighth in stock trading is equal to 12.5 cents). So:

Dollar Values of ⅛ Increments in Bond Quotes

1/8	$1.25
1/4	$2.50
3/8	$3.75
1/2	$5.00
5/8	$6.25
3/4	$7.50
7/8	$8.75

If the bond were selling for more than its face value, it would be trading at a "premium." For example, suppose the 8% bond were selling for $1,100 (110). In that case, the current yield would be 7.3% ($80 divided by $1,100) — lower than the coupon rate. In general, therefore, discounts mean an increased current yield, and premiums mean a lessened current yield.

3. *Yield to Maturity (YTM)*. Current yield does not take into account the difference between the purchase price of the bond and the principal repayment at maturity. Someone who pays $800 for a $1,000 bond will receive $1,000 —$200 more than the purchase price — at maturity. That $200 is also considered yield and must be included in yield calculations. For instance, let's say the 8% $1,000 bond has five years left to maturity, when it is bought for $800.

To include the $200 discount in the yield calculation, divide it by the number of years remaining to maturity. There's a rule-of-thumb formula to calculate this yield which is referred to as "yield to maturity" (or YTM). (Actually, the formula for yield to maturity is a bit more complicated than the one we're giving you.)

$$\text{Yield to maturity} = \frac{\text{Coupon} + \text{Prorated Discount}}{(\text{Face Value} + \text{Purchase Price}) \div 2}$$

In this case, the only piece of information not immediately available is the "prorated discount." To get that, divide the discount by the number of years to maturity: $200 divided by 5 years equals $40 per year. Let's plug the numbers into the formula and work it out:

$$\text{YTM} = \frac{\text{Coupon} + \text{Prorated Discount}}{(\text{Face Value} + \text{Purchase Price}) \div 2}$$

$$= \frac{\$80 + \$40}{(\$1,000 + \$800) \div 2}$$

$$= \frac{\$120}{\$900}$$

$$= 13.3\%$$

Thus this discounted bond has a:
* Coupon yield of 8% ($80 divided by $1,000).
* Current yield of 10% ($80 divided by $800).
* Yield to maturity of 13.3% ($120 divided by $900).

The same yield to maturity formula can be applied to bonds trading at a premium, with two slight changes.

$$\text{YTM} = \frac{\text{Coupon} - \text{Prorated Premium}}{(\text{Face Value} + \text{Purchase Price}) \div 2}$$

Suppose the same 8% $1,000 bond were selling for $1,100 with 5 years to maturity:

$$\text{YTM} = \frac{\text{Coupon - Prorated Premium}}{(\text{Face Value + Purchase Price}) \div 2}$$

$$= \frac{\$80 - (\$100 \div 5 \text{ years})}{(\$1,000 + \$1,100) \div 2}$$

$$= \frac{\$80 - \$20}{\$1,050}$$

$$= 5.7\%$$

This bond, selling at a premium, has a:
* Coupon yield of 8% ($80 divided by $1,000).
* Current yield of 7.3% ($80 divided by $1,100).
* Yield to maturity of 5.7% ($60 divided by $1,050).

Yield to maturity is generally what bond traders are referring to when they use the word "yield." Of the three, it is the one type of yield that assesses the effect of principal, coupon rate, and time to maturity on a bond's actual yield.

WHAT DETERMINES BOND PRICES?

While yield to maturity enables traders and investors to compare debt securities with different coupon rates and terms to maturity, it does not determine price.

Bond prices depend on a number of factors, such as the ability of the issuer to make interest and principal payments and how the bond is collateralized. Later chapters cover issuer-related influences on prices.

An across-the-board factor that affects bond prices is the level of prevailing interest rates. In previous examples, an 8% bond yielded different rates depending on whether the bond sold at a premium or discount. What was not explained was *why* the bond should sell for more or less than its face value. The reason has to do with interest rates.

Assume the 8% bond was issued 5 years ago, when prevailing interest rates (on other investment vehicles) were about 8%. Further assume that current prevailing interest rates are about 9%. Why should investors buy a five-year-old bond yielding 8% when they can buy a newly issued 9% bond? The only way the holder of an 8% bond can find a buyer is to sell the bond at a discount, so that its yield to maturity is the same as the coupon rate on new issues.

For example, say interest rates increase from 8% to 10%. With 15 years to maturity, an 8% bond has to be priced so that the discount, when amortized over 15 years, has a yield to maturity of 10%. That discount is a little under $200:

$$\text{YTM} = \frac{\text{Coupon Rate} + \text{Prorated Discount}}{(\text{Face Value} + \text{Purchase Price}) \div 2}$$

$$= \frac{\$80 + (\$200 \div 15 \text{ years})}{(\$1{,}000 + \$800) \div 2}$$

$$= \frac{\$93.33}{\$900}$$

$$= 10.4\%$$

The 8% bond with 15 years to maturity must sell at a little over $800 to compete with 10% issues.

The possibility that interest rates will cause outstanding bond issues to lose value is called "interest rate risk."

Yet there is an upside to this risk. If interest rates decline during the five years that the 8% bond is outstanding, the holder could sell it for enough of a premium to make its YTM rate equal to the lower yields of recent issues.

For instance, should interest rates decline to 7%, the price of the 8% bond with 15 years to maturity will increase by about $100.

$$\text{YTM} = \frac{\text{Coupon} - \text{Prorated Premium}}{(\text{Face Value} + \text{Purchase Price}) \div 2}$$

$$= \frac{\$80 - (\$100 \div 15)}{(\$1,000 + \$1,100) \div 2}$$

$$= \frac{\$73.33}{\$1,050}$$

$$= 7.0\%$$

All other influences aside, the general principle is that bond prices tend to increase when interest rates fall, and to decline when interest rates are rising.

As a corollary, the prices on longer-term bonds fluctuate more than those of shorter-term bonds in response to interest rate changes. For example, we know that the 8% bond with 15 years to maturity has to adjust nearly $200 in price to accommodate a rise in rates to 10%.

Under the same circumstances, an 8% bond with five years to maturity requires less of a discount — $80 to be exact.

$$\text{YTM} = \frac{\$80 + (\$80 \div 5)}{(\$1,000 + \$920) \div 2}$$

$$= \frac{\$96}{\$960}$$

$$= 10\%$$

Thus, the shorter the term to maturity, the less volatile the price adjustment to a change in interest rates.

There is a great deal more to bond pricing, as we'll see in later chapters. But the intimate relationship with interest rates is the key to understanding what drives bond prices. When the U.S. Treasury, a municipality, a corporation, or any other issuer decides on a primary offering of bonds, it must weigh, among other things, the effect of interest rates.

When bonds start trading in the "secondary" market (after they are initially brought to market), they are subject to ongoing interest rate risk. That is, bond prices react to the same factors acting on interest rates. These factors are generally recognized to be the following:

1. *The Business Cycle.* During an upswing, American businesses start borrowing money to buy equipment or raw materials, to build plants, or to develop new services. Would-be borrowers (the demand side) compete for diminishing funds (the supply), driving the cost of money (interest) up. Banks start raising their lending rates. To attract money into the bond market, yields have to rise. As a result, the generally accepted principle is that, as economic activity picks up, interest rates tend to rise.

2. *Inflation.* When the costs of goods rise, lenders have to increase their rates of interest to offset their loss of purchasing power. Borrowers pay the higher rates because they expect to use the money profitably and pay back the loan with future dollars of reduced purchasing value. Consequently, interest rates are thought to include borrowers' expectations with respect to inflation. Whether or not that assumption is valid, most economists agree that interest rates (the cost of money) rise with the inflation rate.

3. *Flow of Funds.* At most brokerage firms, economists analyze how capital is flowing through the economy and try to project the future amount of borrowing. In so doing, they are attempting to gauge the supply side (amount of credit available) and the demand side (future borrowing) of interest rates. If their analyses are correct, they may be able to project future interest rates.

When it comes to interest rates, the Federal Reserve System plays a major role, as it sets and executes the fiscal policy of the U.S. government. (See Chapter 3.)

INTEREST ON INTEREST — TOTAL RETURN

Fluctuating interest rates also affect a bond's "total return," which is the return based on the reinvestment of interest payments over the term to maturity.

Up to the 1950s and '60s, many bond owners — such as university or foundation endowments — simply took their coupon interest payments and spent them. At that time, many bond certificates were printed with coupons attached, each coupon representing an interest payment. To receive your interest payment on this type of bond, known as a "bearer" bond, you had to cut off a coupon and present it to the issuer, usually through a financial intermediary such as a bank or brokerage firm. This practice, known as "coupon clipping," became associated with affluent investors, the perception being that the wealthy could afford to buy enough bonds to live off the coupons.

Coupon clipping also reflected a form of simple interest. If a person buys a bond and does not reinvest the coupon payment dollars, then the principal remains constant — whether the price paid for the bond was at face value, a premium, or a discount. The preceding examples of coupon rate and current yield were examples of simple interest because they assumed that the interest was not reinvested.

Once interest dollars are reinvested, however, the bondholder starts receiving "interest-on-interest." For example, suppose a pension fund portfolio manager (PM) has in the fund's holdings 25 $1,000 8% bonds. Every year these bonds earn $2,000 in interest (.08 times $1,000 face value times 25 bonds). With that $2,000, the manager buys two more of the same type of bond. In so doing, the PM has converted the $2,000 interest payment into $2,000 of additional principal — on which interest will be paid. The portfolio now contains $27,000 worth of these bonds, and the following year's interest will be $2,160 ($27,000 times .08). If the $2,160 is used to buy additional bonds, then the next year's principal becomes $29,160. (This example, of course, ignores commissions, other costs, and tax obligations.)

Interest-on-interest is a form of "compounding." Compound interest can dramatically increase the total return to the bondholder, typically over half of a bond's total compounded return. For example, suppose our 8% $1,000 bond were bought for $1,000 (face value) at issuance and held for 20 years to maturity. If the bondholder were to "clip coupons" for 20 years, the total dollar return would be $1,600 ($80 times 20 years). This would be an example of simple interest. On the other hand, if for that same term the bondholder reinvests all interest payments for a return also of 8%, the return is much greater. Without going into the somewhat complicated math, the *additional* dollar return over 20 years would be $2,201, for a total compounded return of $3,801 ($1,600 simple interest plus $2,201 interest-on-interest).

This is not to say that interest has to be reinvested in the same bond. If other investment opportunities present themselves as interest payments are received, all the better. For instance, if the $1,600 in coupon payments were consistently reinvested in an instrument that returned 10%, the total compounded return would be $4,832 — $3,232 of that being interest-on-interest.

Understandably, the value of interest-on-interest diminishes with the time left to maturity. In the preceding example, the interest-on-interest for an 8% bond held for 20 years was 58% of the total return: $2,201 of $3,801. If the bond were held for ten years under the same conditions, the interest-on-interest would represent only 33% of the total compounded return: $800 simple interest plus $394 interest-on-interest for a total of $1,194. For five years, the total compounded return is only $482: $400 simple and $82 compound. For one year, the interest-on-interest is only $1.63: 2% of the total compounded return.

As you can see, the total compound return, or "total rate of return," is not the same as yield to maturity. YTM is simply a number that can be calculated from the bond's principal, coupon rate, and time left to maturity. It expresses only the present value of the bond's cash flow. Total return is calculated from principal, coupon rate, and interest-on-interest. It assumes that the coupon dollars will be put to work earning additional dollars. While the dollar yields for the two types of calculations may differ — and usually do — the percentage rates of return may be the same under one or more of the following conditions.

First, suppose the bond has a "zero coupon." In other words, the interest is deducted from the face value up front, as in the case of series EE savings bonds. Since no coupon dollars are received, there is no opportunity to reinvest them. In such cases, the yield-to-maturity rate on a zero coupon bond would be the same as the rate of total return because the interest has, in effect, already been "reinvested" at the YTM rate.

Second, if only one payment period is included in the calculation, then there is no opportunity for reinvestment. This would be the case if you were to make a YTM calculation on a bond with only six months to maturity (that is, one interest-payment period). Since there is no opportunity for reinvestment, the two rates are the same.

Third, if all coupons are reinvested at the YTM rate, then it would, of course, equal the rate of total return. Again, the dollar yield for total return would be higher than that for YTM, but the rates would be the same.

Of the two types of return, the rate of total return is generally regarded as a better gauge of market value than yield to maturity for two reasons.

First, the total rate of return is more realistic in that it takes into account future changes in reinvestment rates. For instance, if future coupons are reinvested at less than the YTM rate, the rate of return will decrease. If future reinvestment rates are higher than YTM, then the rate of total return rises. Yield to maturity accounts for none of this.

Second, it enables investors and traders, given a reasonable assumption about future reinvestment rates, to more accurately forecast total return. For example, suppose a portfolio manager expects bond rates to decline over, say, the next year, and he decides to invest some of the portfolio's funds in bonds at an 8% yield to maturity. Given his reinvestment rate assumptions, he knows that the actual total return will be less than 8%, and he can adjust his expectations accordingly.

THE YIELD CURVE

Given an assumption about reinvestment rates, how *do* professional traders and portfolio managers make their buy and sell decisions? What general principles do they use with respect to yields, prices, and risk? In brief, their thinking and actions are based on their analysis of what is known as the "yield curve."

To explain the yield curve and its implications, let's assume that the reinvestment rate will stay fixed at 8% until maturity. Given that assumption, the yield to maturity can be depicted simply in a graph as follows:

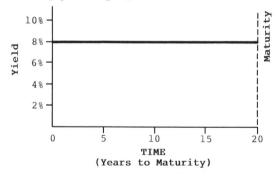

The horizontal line extending from the tic mark for 8% represents the anticipated "yield curve" for this bond. (It's called a "curve" even though it's straight.) If the coupons are reinvested consistently at 8% for 20 years, then at maturity the *actual* yield curve will look just like that line. Also, the actual total rate of return will be the same as the yield to maturity, because all reinvested interest will earn interest at 8%. But what if the coupons were reinvested at different rates of return? As soon as that happens, the line

for total rate of return diverges from that for yield to
maturity. If the coupon reinvestment rate is higher than
the YTM rate, the total rate of return will be higher. Given
a lower-than-YTM rate of reinvestment, the total rate of
return will be lower. The varying rates of return can be
depicted as follows:

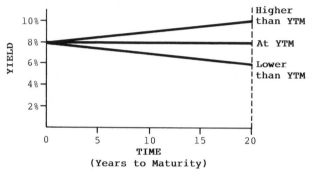

In this figure, the line above the one for the anticipated
YTM assumes that the bondholder was able to put coupon
dollars to work in such a way as to earn a rate greater than
8%. Perhaps he bought other bonds or preferred stock with
higher YTMs; investing in another investment vehicle does
not lessen the compounding effect.

The lower line demonstrates the total rate of return if
the bondholder was unable to reinvest at the YTM rate.
Maybe some of the coupons had to be applied toward a
down payment on a car, in which case the yield on those
dollars drops to zero. Perhaps some coupon dollars were
put into a 5% or 6% certificate of deposit, in anticipation of
paying a tuition bill. In such cases, the total rate of return
diverges downward from the YTM rate.

The yield curve is therefore a depiction of bond market
rates over time. The curve is supposed to represent the net
result of all the buying and selling in the market — and
therefore reflect the net effect of supply and demand pressures. The curve demonstrates graphically what market
participants are willing to pay for short-term, intermediate-
term, and long-term debt instruments.

A typical yield curve therefore looks like this:

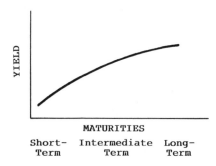

This graph is known as the "indifference curve," since it shows that the market is collectively "indifferent" to accepting one yield at a given maturity along with a different yield at another maturity. (This coexistence of various yields at different yields is referred to as the "term structure" of rates.)

As an example, let's take the preceding yield curve and assign some values to it:

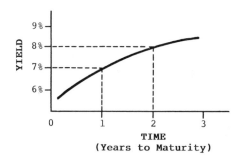

One-year securities are yielding 7% and two-year securities 8%. The market is indifferent to 7% one-year and 8% two-year instruments in the same market.

That seems strange, but there is a theory that attempts to explain this attitude on the part of investors. The "expectations theory" views the yield curve as a function of buyers' expectations of future interest rates. In our example, the holders of a one-year 7% security are content because they expect rates to increase, thereby enabling them to reinvest at maturity in another one-year security at 9%. Their two-year yield would therefore be:

$$7\% \text{ (1 year)} + 9\% \text{ (1 year)} = 8\% \text{ (2 years)}$$

Similarly, holders of the 8% two-year security can hold the instrument till maturity, and then sell it at the expected YTM of 9%. The two-year rate would then be:

$$8\% \text{ (2 years)} + 1\% \text{ (1 year)} - 1\% \text{ (1 year)} = 8\% \text{ (2 years)}$$

Yields on shorter-term securities are generally more volatile than those on longer-term ones. Given terms to maturity of only several years, changes in price are not drastically amortized and therefore have significant effects on yield to maturity.

An upward-sloping yield curve reflects higher future rates. The underlying reasoning is that investors tend to sell longer-term securities and buy shorter-term ones. This is another way of saying that they have a greater "liquidity preference." This theory holds that investors attach greater value to shorter-term securities because they are "closer to cash." The horizontal yield curve has buying pressure (demand) on it short-term and selling pressure (supply) long-term.

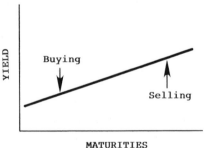

The curve rotates, under the pressures of supply and demand, until market equilibrium is restored. This straight-line yield curve therefore represents the effects of investors' expectations with respect to yield and their collective preference for more liquid, short-term instruments.

But it does not show the effect of investors' assessment of risk. The working principle with respect to risk is that prices become more volatile as the term to maturity increases. Thus, to reflect this risk, and assuming interest rates are expected to rise, the prices of longer-term securities tend to be lower than those of shorter-term ones. Inasmuch as lower bond prices increase yield to maturity, longer-term maturities are associated with lower prices and higher YTMs.

In addition, changes in price have a lessened effect on longer-term yields. For example, a $100 change in the price of a one-year bond affects the yield by the full amount. For a two-year bond, the annual yield is affected by $50. As the term to maturity increases, a price change is more and more amortized, and its effect increasingly diluted. Therefore, prices must change dramatically on long-term securities to have any significant effect on yield. As a result (the mathematical reasons being set aside), the actual yield curve is indeed a curve:

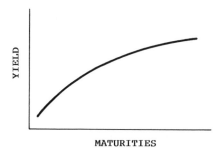

MATURITIES

This is not to say, however, that all yield curves are upward-sloping. The assumption in all our examples has been that rates are expected to be higher for longer-term securities. When future rates are expected to decrease, the yield curve descends.

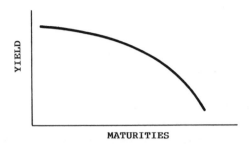

In such a case, reinvestment rates and total return are going to decrease.

Yield curve analysis extends *far* beyond these rudimentary concepts. Professional traders and portfolio managers must understand in complex detail the relationships among price, yield, liquidity, and risk. They must be able to "ride the yield curve," that is, buy and sell debt securities so as to obtain the greatest total return.

In "riding the yield curve," professional traders must be sensitive to many forces at work. Not only must they have sound working assumptions about the future level of interest rates, but they must be aware of the returns available on other nonbond debt securities. Chapter 2 briefly covers the huge array of "fixed-income" instruments, and Chapter 3 presents the role of the Federal Reserve System in regulating interest rates.

The Fixed-Income Marketplace

The fixed-income market is so huge and so dynamic that its actual scope is difficult to estimate. Each year:

* U.S. corporations bring dollars worth of "corporate" debt to the market. This figure does not take into account short-term corporate debt, such as commercial paper, or bank issuances, such as bankers' acceptances.
* State and local governments issue about three-quarters of a trillion dollars in "municipal" debt.

  * The Treasury and federal government agencies create over a trillion and a half dollars worth of debt.
  * In the so-called "Eurobond market," overseas companies, western governments and government agencies, and supranational institutions (such as the World Bank, the European Investment bank, and others) issue another trillion and a half dollars.

CAPITAL MARKETS AND MONEY MARKETS

This global arena, in which bonds play a major role, is divided into two markets: the capital market and the money market.

In the *capital market* are traded long-term debt instruments (that is, bonds), along with stocks (common and preferred). These are vehicles by which capital is raised. The bonds traded in this market may be issued by:
  * The U.S. Treasury, through the Federal Reserve System and a group of "primary dealers."
  * Federal agencies, such as the Government National Mortgage Association and others.
  * State and local governments — municipal issuers.
  * Corporations, both domestic and overseas.
  * Foreign governments.

Chapters 4-9 cover the capital markets in detail.

The rest of this chapter focuses on the money market, which consists of short-term fixed-income vehicles, that is, those with less than one year to maturity. This market includes bonds whose maturity is less than one year away, as well as such vehicles as:
  * Treasury bills.
  * U.S. government agency notes.
  * Municipal notes.
  * Bank certificates of deposit (CDs).
  * Commercial paper.
  * Repurchase agreements ("repos").
  * Bankers' acceptances (BAs).

MONEY MARKET PARTICIPANTS

The money market has no specific location. Rather, it is a collection of markets comprised of:
* Banks in the large money centers — New York, London, Tokyo, and so on.
* About 40 or so government securities dealers, known as "primary dealers."
* Roughly a dozen commercial paper dealers.
* A few banker's acceptance dealers.
* A number of money brokers specializing in finding short-term funds from money market lenders and placing the funds with money market borrowers.

The most important money market brokers are based in New York and deal in "federal funds," which represent "surplus reserves" or money that banks do not need to meet the Fed's reserve requirements. These funds are available for short-term (usually overnight) loans.

Money market participants are any political or corporate entities that need to ensure having enough cash on hand to meet their expenses and to operate normally — independently of their cash flow. Participants who at any time need cash may borrow from those who have too much cash for their current needs. Thus the money market provides a pool of cash that, through its trading mechanisms, flows to those participants in need of it. The market is particularly valuable in that the instruments are perceived to entail very little risk of default.

At one time money market investments were available to only the largest financial and commercial institutions. The high interest rates of the early 1980s, however, were too good to ignore. Now, through money market (mutual) funds, individual investors may enjoy the benefits of the money market: short maturities, high liquidity, and relatively low risk.

MONEY MARKET PRODUCTS

The diverse products traded in this market have one characteristic in common: They all mature in less than one year. Let's look at the various short-term instruments traded in this market.

Call Loans

These are short-term loans that banks extend to securities dealers and brokers. These loans are considered safe because the brokerage firms put up securities as collateral. Their name derives from the fact that either the lender or the borrower can terminate them — that is, "call" them in — simply by giving one day's notice.

Federal Funds (Fed Funds)

Member banks of the Fed hold their required reserves as deposits with the district Federal Reserve Bank. On any given day, a bank may be over or under its reserve requirement. Since the Fed itself does not pay interest on the deposited reserve funds, banks with an excess of such funds can lend part or all of the excess to a bank that needs funds to reach its reserve requirement. Because of the supply/demand dynamics, a market has developed for these "federal funds."

The sale of fed funds is called a "straight transaction," and it is made on a one-day, unsecured basis. The bank selling the funds instructs the Federal Reserve Bank to charge its account and credit the account of the buying (that is, the borrowing) bank. On the following day, the transaction is reversed. The exchange is made electronically through the Federal Reserve System's communication network, known as the "Fed wire." No physical delivery is made.

Repurchase Agreements (Repos)

In addition to unsecured loans (such as call loans or borrowing Fed funds), money market participants can engage in "repurchase agreements." In such agreements, the owner of securities for "same-day" or "cash" settlement sells them with the understanding that the seller will buy them back very soon thereafter. A repo is therefore a way of financing securities that are owned or of converting them temporarily into cash. The buyer of the securities is, in effect, lending the seller cash, on a short-term basis (usually overnight). By repurchasing the securities, the original owner "repays" the loan.

Of course, the buyer/lender is compensated for the loan. The "interest" on the cash delivered for the securities is the difference between the price of the first purchase and the price of the resale to the original owner.

A "reverse repo" is a purchase and resale of securities. The purpose of it might be to put cash to work for a short while or to "borrow" securities for delivery in a short sale.

Bankers' Acceptances (BAs)

This credit instrument is used to finance both domestic and international self-liquidating transactions.

Here is how a bankers' acceptance is created. An American importer buys raw material from an overseas exporter. If the exporter were to ship the goods without a "BA," he or she would be paid only when the shipment arrives. Instead, the importer arranges for an American commercial bank to issue, in the name of the exporter, an "irrevocable letter of credit" which specifies the details of the shipment. The exporter can then draw a draft on the American bank and take it to an overseas bank for immediate payment. Once the exporter is paid, the bank forwards the draft to the United States for presentation to the bank that issued the letter of credit. The bank stamps the draft "accepted" and thereby incurs the liability to pay the draft when it matures. Thus a "banker's acceptance" is created.

The shipping documents are released to the U.S. importer against a "trust receipt," which allows the importer to obtain and sell the imported goods. The importer is then obligated to deposit the proceeds of the sale at the accepting bank in time to honor the acceptance at maturity (usually 90 to 180 days).

Typically, the accepting bank discounts the new acceptance for the foreign bank and credits the proceeds to the account of the foreign bank. The cost of acceptance financing is the discount charged plus the commission paid to the accepting bank. This cost can be paid by either of the commercial parties involved in the transaction.

The accepting bank may either sell the acceptance to a dealer in bankers' acceptances or hold it in its own portfolio. Because a banker's acceptance is an irrevocable primary obligation of the accepting bank, it is considered an extremely safe form of investment. The bank is protected not only by the customer's agreement to pay but also by the pledge of all documents evidencing ownership. In fact, in the 71 years that banker's acceptances have been used in the United States, there has been no known case of principal loss to investors.

Commercial Paper

This short-term, unsecured promissory note is issued primarily by corporations needing to finance large amounts of receivables on their books. It is sold on a discount basis with maturities, specified by the buyer, available on any business day, ranging from three to 270 days. Customers can thus choose investments that fit their needs.

Virtually all commercial paper is rated by at least one of the major rating agencies (Moody's or Standard & Poor's, for example). This form of debt is generally considered a safe investment, although not as safe as Treasury bills or banker's acceptances, whose rates of return tend to be lower.

Certificates of Deposit (CDs)

These certificates are issued by commercial banks and thrift institutions against funds deposited for specified periods to earn fixed rates of interest. Although many banks use the acronym "CD" to refer to savings certificates available in modest denominations, money market CDs are negotiable instruments issued in denominations of $100,000 or more. When CDs are traded, the normal round-lot trading unit is $1 million or more.

The minimum maturity of a CD is seven days. Although most CDs mature in a year or less, there is no maximum limit on their maturity. In fact, some banks are now offering variable rate CDs (rates adjusted periodically) for up to five years' maturity.

Treasury Bills

Probably the best-known money market instrument, these bills are short-term discount obligations of the U.S. Treasury. They are popular investments for institutions because of their short maturities and ready marketability. The market for them is so large and efficient, and Treasuries are so liquid, that they are frequently said to be "cash equivalent."

We will talk more about T-bills in Chapter 4.

Municipal Notes

These municipal securities have maturities of less than one year. State and local governments use such short-term municipal borrowing to bridge gaps in financing. Municipalities usually issue notes at discounts from face value (like Treasury bills), with the interest paid at maturity. The types of notes frequently issued by state and local governments are:

*   *Tax anticipation notes* (TANs), issued in anticipation of tax receipts and paid from those receipts.
*   *Revenue anticipation notes* (RANs), issued in anticipation of other sources of future revenues, usually either federal or state aid.
*   *Bond anticipation notes* (BANs), considered the least secure type of short-term note. Because they provide financing until a future bond offering is made, they are only as secure as the ability of the local government to gain voter approval for issuing those bonds.
*   *General obligation* (GO) notes, relatively secure because they are backed by the general credit of the issuing municipality. GO notes are often used for the same purposes as BANs and TANs.
*   *Project notes,* issues of the U.S. Housing and Urban Development Department (HUDs). These notes are issued to fund local housing and urban renewal projects, and are backed both by the revenues from these projects and by the full faith and credit of the federal government. Because of these guarantees, project notes are considered to be very safe investments.

The bond market is only a part of a vast, global trading arena, in which many types of financial instruments are traded. Central to fixed-income trading in the United States — and to one degree or another throughout the world — is the Federal Reserve System. This major player, the "Fed," is the subject of the next chapter.

Chapter 3

The Fed

On the eighth floor of the New York Federal Reserve
Bank at 33 Liberty Street in Manhattan, traders work at
rows of desks clustered in front of a large display board.
On that board are bids for all of the U.S. government's outstanding debt securities. Through telephone consoles at
their desks, these traders deal with securities firms,
securities dealer banks, money market players, overseas
financial organizations, and the Federal Reserve's
securities and foreign departments. Computer screens at

31

Figure 3-1. The New York Trading Desk

their desks give "Fed" traders access to hundreds of pages of quotation information.

This is the trading room of the Federal Reserve System, where the traders perform a number of functions. For one thing, on behalf of foreign central banks, they execute trades in U.S. Treasury debt instruments, bankers' acceptances, and other financial vehicles. They also provide a day-to-day flow of information to the U.S. Treasury on activities in the U.S. government securities market.

Their chief role, however, is to carry out the Federal Reserve's instructions with respect to monetary policy — that is, the policy regulating the money supply in this country. In this role, they exert a strong and pervasive influence on the pricing of bonds and other fixed-income instruments.

THE RICH MAN'S PANIC OF 1907

The trading desk, however, was not part of the Fed as originally created. At the turn of the century, banks in the United States were hardly systematized and largely unregulated. In the case of a "run" on one or more banks, there was no central bank to provide reserve capital and to help absorb the shock. Then, in 1907, there was a "rich man's panic," a crash in the securities market that affected only the wealthy. But it was severe enough to cause Congress to act. In 1917, it founded the Federal Reserve System for the purpose of guaranteeing the soundness of American banks by holding a reserve of capital against all deposits in national banks. Since its inception, however, the Fed's power, position, and influence have expanded until today it has six functions:

1. *It is the commercial and investment banker for the U.S. Treasury.* As *commercial banker*, it provides the U.S. Treasury with essentially the same services as "banks" do for individual customers: taking money on deposit, making loans, and so forth. In fact, over the years, the Fed has taken control of all the avenues by which the Treasury interacts with the world. A Federal Reserve bank handles all payments made by the Treasury, drawing all its checks and conducting all money transfers by the "Fed wire." It also takes deposits of all tax collections, through Treasury Tax & Loan Accounts (TT&Ls).

As *investment banker*, the Fed assists the Treasury in bringing new debt securities — that is, primary offerings — to the market. It provides the same service for the Treasury that brokerage firms do for corporations or municipalities when they wish to offer a bond issue. The Fed is an intermediary between the Treasury, the issuer, and the "primary dealers," which are securities dealers or dealer banks authorized to engage in "primary" offerings of U.S. government securities.

In addition to assisting in primary offers, the Fed takes payments for sales of Treasury securities and makes pay-

Figure 3-2. The Federal Reserve System

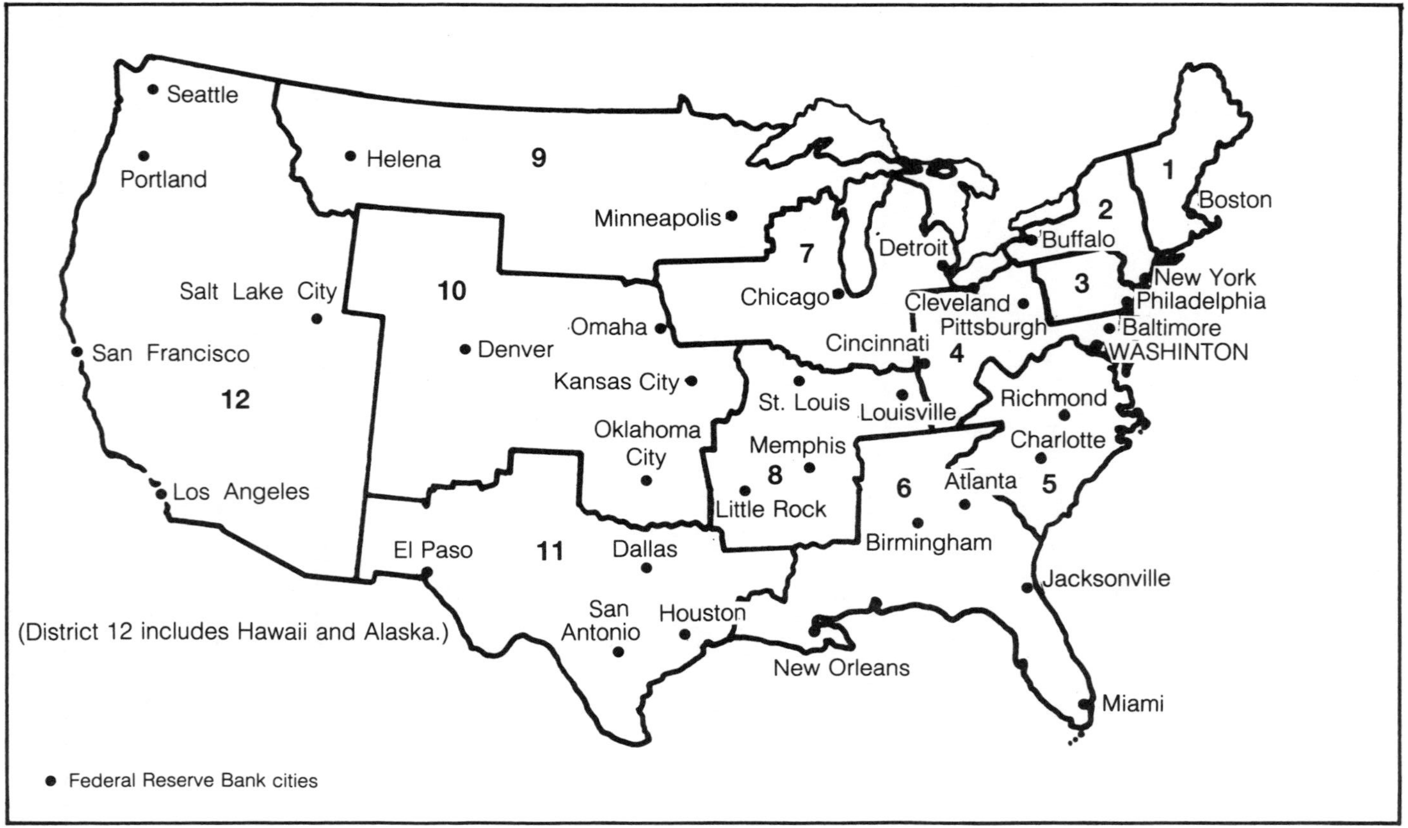

Boston
New York
Philadelphia
Baltimore
WASHINTON
1
2
Buffalo
3
Richmond
Charlotte
Jacksonville
Miami
Cleveland
Pittsburgh
4
Atlanta
5
Detroit
Cincinnati
Louisville
St. Louis
Birmingham
6
Chicago
Memphis
Little Rock
8
New Orleans
7
Minneapolis
Kansas City
Oklahoma City
Houston
Omaha
Dallas
San Antonio
Denver
9
El Paso
11
10
Salt Lake City
Helena
Seattle
Portland
San Francisco
12
Los Angeles

(District 12 includes Hawaii and Alaska.)

• Federal Reserve Bank cities

ments for their purchase. All interest and principal payments on U.S. government securities are made by checks drawn on Federal Reserve Banks.

2. *The Fed is the dealer/manager for portfolios of securities owned by a special list of investors.* A number of large portfolios of dollar-denominated securities are administered by the Fed. That is, the Fed executes transactions for these investors, either by dealing directly with the portfolio or by executing transactions in the market on behalf of these portfolios. Most of the portfolios consist of government trust funds (which are pools of money waiting to be spent for specific purposes) or of the dollar holdings of foreign central banks.

3. *It is the administrator and regulator of the U.S. government securities market.* Since Treasury and government agency securities are exempt from both the Securities Act of 1933 and the Securities Exchange Act of 1934, no regulatory body has power over dealers in this market. Since virtually all government securities trading is over-the-counter, no exchange has authority either. In that vacuum, the Federal Reserve has evolved as the regulator of the government securities market. Thus all "primary dealers" must report daily to the Fed not only their positions and trading volume, but also the methods by which they finance positions. In addition, all U.S. government securities and some agency securities exist not as pieces of paper, but rather only as entries on a computer at the Fed. So the Fed has also become the de facto clearing house for the government securities market.

Since the Fed's control is restricted to primary dealers, a large segment of the market, the non-primary dealers, operates without regulation or oversight. The mid-1980s financial collapses in the unregulated sector, however, have prodded Congress into action. It is conceivable that either the Fed or the SEC could become the statutory regulator of the government securities market.

4. *It is the defender of our national currency.* Ever since the United States went off the gold standard, the Fed has been instrumental in maintaining the value of the dollar in the world currency markets. At times, when demand for the dollar exceeded supply, that task has been very easy. At other times, the world market has been flooded with dollars, pushing their value down. The growth of pools of currencies, called *Eurocurrencies,* held outside their countries of origin has complicated this task. The Fed's role has expanded to include balancing the domestic monetary policy with the value of the dollar in world currency markets.

5. *It is the guardian of the national banking system.* This was the original function of the Fed. Fed examiners still go over the books of each member bank every year, as well as monitoring the activities of its trust department. National banks must still get approval from the Fed to do such things as open new branches or take over another bank. When a bank or a group of banks gets into financial trouble, or when financial uncertainty sweeps the country, the Fed is still the lender of last resort, standing by to help its member banks weather the storm. In this capacity, the Fed fulfills the role of a traditional central bank.

6. *It is the setter and implementor of the national monetary policy; that is, it regulates how much money is available in the U.S. economy.* The Board of Governors of the Fed sets the nation's monetary policy, which in turn determines the availability and cost of credit. As such, the Board plays a major role in setting the economic course of the nation, and occupies a hot political seat.

This last function, as we shall see, has the greatest effect of all on the bond market.

HOW MONETARY POLICY IS EXECUTED

Monetary policy is "executed" by regulating the availability and flow of money through the banking system.

If the Fed acts in such a way as to make money available, then banks have more funds to lend and lending rates tend to drop. Corporations can borrow more for growth and development. Securities houses can borrow more for trading and for extending credit to their own customers. And individuals find it relatively inexpensive to borrow money to buy cars, houses, and other items.

When the Fed slows down the flow of money — or even takes money out of circulation, interest rates tend to rise. The supply of money is scarce, and so its price — in the form of interest rates — goes up. Companies have to delay building programs. Securities firms carry less inventory and tighten up margin requirements. The rates on mortgage and car loans go up.

These are the effects of "loosening" and "tightening" monetary policy.

Executing monetary policy is accomplished through two seldom used vehicles and one often used one. The least used method is the changing of *reserve requirements*, which is the portion of each deposit dollar that must be kept at the district Federal Reserve Bank. The next least used method is the changing of the *discount rate*, which is the rate that the Fed charges on loans to its member banks. The most common method is *open market operations*, which are the transactions that the Fed initiates in the government securities market.

1. *Reserve Requirements.* Commercial banks are required by law to refrain from lending a specified percentage of their funds; these funds are instead held in reserve as a measure of protection for depositors. This percentage, called the "reserve requirement," is dictated by the Fed. To tighten the availability of credit and to slow down the economy, the Fed may increase the reserve requirements of banks, taking money out of circulation. To loosen credit and to stimulate growth, the Fed lowers reserve requirements, thereby putting money into circulation.

2. *Discount Rate.* The Federal Reserve lends funds to member banks through what is called the "discount window." The "discount rate" — the interest rate the banks pay to borrow money — is adjusted from time to time by the Fed in response to changing economic conditions and to complement its monetary policy. A rise in the discount rate, for example, can enhance the restraining effect of the Fed's other policy actions. Since the amount of money borrowed at the "window," as well as the rate at which it is borrowed, influences lending throughout the country's banking system, changes in the discount rate can have a ripple effect on the economy as a whole.

3. *Open Market Operations.* The Federal Reserve Bank of New York, under the direction of the Federal Open Market Committee (FOMC), buys or sells U.S. Treasury securities. To stimulate the economy, the Fed buys the securities, paying for them with reserves that the banks then use to increase their capacity to lend money. Credit becomes "easy." To put the brakes on the economy, the FOMC sells government securities in the open market. Because banks pay for the securities with reserves, they have less money to lend. Credit gets "tight."

Of the three methods, the one that has the greatest, most immediate effects is open market activity, which is the responsibility of the Federal Open Market Committee.

THE WORK OF THE FEDERAL OPEN MARKET COMMITTEE (FOMC)

The FOMC is composed of the seven members of the Board of Governors and five of the twelve Federal Reserve presidents. This committee meets regularly to discuss the general state of the economy, overall monetary policy, and the role of the FOMC in promoting monetary goals. The president of the Federal Reserve Bank of New York is a permanent member of this committee with the title of Vice Chairman. The chairman of the board of governors is selected as chairman of the FOMC. The other Federal Reserve Bank presidents serve on the committee in rotation but the importance of the meetings requires all presidents to attend, whether or not they are voting members.

Figure 3-3. Federal Reserve System Organization

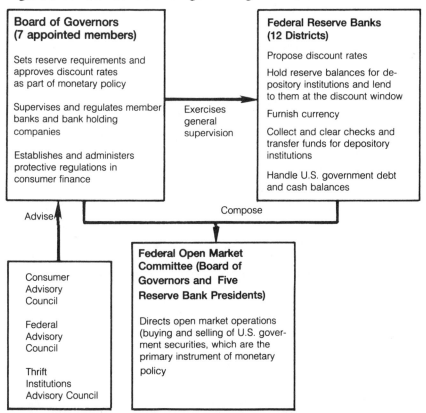

The two key meetings of the Federal Open Market Committee are held each year before the twentieth of February and the twentieth of July. A few days before the February meeting, three documents are circulated among the participants. A "green book" contains an appraisal by the Board's staff of the forces at work in the major economic sectors and financial markets, along with an economic prognosis for the upcoming two to three years. The "red book" is a report from the 12 Federal Reserve Banks across the United States on current and possible future developments. The "blue book" offers an array of short-run "what-if" scenarios for various elements of the monetary situation. Using these documents and other information, each of the 12 Federal Reserve Bank presidents reviews policy options with his staff.

The meeting itself is necessarily a formal one, if the seven Board members and 12 presidents are to be able to address the issue before them. They hear reports on foreign exchange and domestic operations. Following these reports is a statement by the Board's staff as to prevailing credit flows and interest rates, and a presentation of several simulations of the effect of credit growth changes on prices, unemployment, and interest rates. Finally, the staff presents monetary policy options.

At that point, the setting of policy is thrown open to general discussion. At the heart of the discussion is a dual assumption: First, that rapid growth in the availability of money and credit, if sustained long enough, leads to inflation; second, that a prolonged decline in such growth results in recession and deflation. Thus the attendees at this meeting are engaged in a balancing act; too heavy-handed an approach in either direction could lead to undesirable economic consequences.

By the end of the meeting, a policy has been set that the Chairman of the Board must report to Congress by the twentieth of the month.

Setting the policy is one thing. Making it work, however, is another. Every six or seven weeks between the February and July policy-setting meetings, the FOMC meets to reassess the effectiveness and relevance of operations. Is the policy having the desired effect of encouraging steady economic growth while neither overheating the system nor allowing it to cool down?

THE MANAGER OF OPEN MARKET OPERATIONS

The day-to-day execution of policy falls to the open market operations manager. This is the person who attends the FOMC meetings and who supervises the Fed's trading operation on the eighth floor of the New York Federal Reserve Bank at Liberty Street. Under his direction, the Securities Department of the New York Fed handles purchases and sales of U.S. government securities for the System Account (the twelve Federal Reserve Banks), the U.S. Treasury, foreign central banks, and international organizations.

Each day, the manager must gain a "feel" for the money markets. He follows rate changes in money market instruments closely, receiving a constant stream of information from traders. Nonbank dealers make a daily report as to the degree of success they are having in locating short-term loans or repurchase agreements to carry their inventory of government securities. Fed traders telephone dealers to obtain information on the availability and cost of credit in the market.

The manager must also keep alert to the flow of funds in the long-term capital markets. Are corporate bonds selling well on a particular morning or are they in trouble? Are municipal bond dealers able to hold their price levels from the previous day? Is the dollar under foreign exchange pressure? What is the attitude of dealers and customers toward the condition of the market?

The manager receives daily reports on all factors that might have a bearing on the markets and on bank reserves. Reports from dealers on their previous day's activity are checked.

After accumulating this data and developing a feel for the market, the manager must choose a course of action for the day. Aside from doing nothing, the Fed may opt to do one of four things:

1. It can *buy securities* for the System Account. This action adds reserves to the banking system on a permanent

basis, because the Fed buys the securities from member banks and pays for them by crediting the banks' reserve accounts.

2. It can *sell securities* for the System Account. This action drains reserves from the banking system on a permanent basis, since the Fed collects payment for its sales by debiting the reserve accounts of its member banks.

3. It can *do repo* for the System Account. This action also adds reserves to the banking system, but only on a temporary basis, since the dealers have to buy back the securities sold to the Fed a day later or not very long thereafter.

4. It can do *reverse repo* for the System account. This action drains reserves from the banking system on a short-term basis, since the Fed, again, repurchases the securities from the dealers in a day or so.

As you can see, the aim of any one of these FOMC operations is either to put money into or take it out of circulation through the member banks.

A DAY AT THE FED

The workday at the New York Fed centers around the eighth-floor trading room.

9:00 A.M.: The Daily Dealer Meeting

Shortly before 9 a.m., several officers of the securities department go up the back stairs from the eighth to the tenth floors. At the same time, a senior officer or trader of one of the government securities dealers (the so-called "primary dealers") and a couple of colleagues pass under the large wrought iron candelabra at the bank's entrance, through the vaulted ceilinged lobby, and into the elevator that takes them to the tenth floor. There they join the Reserve Bank officers at a rectangular table, where press briefings are also held for reporters on Friday afternoons.

Every weekday morning, representatives of several dealers arrive to speak with desk officers. These daily meetings with members of the dealer community keep the manager and desk officers up-to-date on the forces at work in financial markets. New York-based dealers send representatives to Liberty Street once every two weeks on a predetermined schedule; out-of-town dealers phone in on a similar schedule.

These conversations cover many areas, and they are peppered with the specialized market jargon on prices and the market. To insiders, the lexicon is an efficient way to communicate information, even though the desk officers must remain silent on policy.

These face-to-face meetings demonstrate that the markets are composed of real people. There are only a few hundred of them at most. Yet desk officers have to know who the major players are and how they're likely to react.

A dealer's representative may open the meeting by explaining the firm's expectations with respect to the Federal funds rate, usually elaborating if it expects rates to change in coming weeks. The firm's money market economist analyzes the interest rate outlook of the firm. Desk officers listen — studiously noncommittal — as dealers outline alternative scenarios trying to get each visitor's assessment of the general market and interest rates.

Dealers' comments are most helpful to the Fed officials who need to stay in touch with the market:

* Are dealer's clients taking money out of the fixed-income market or buying short-term instruments?
* Are longer-term securities getting bought?
* In the dealer's opinion, is the brokerage community as a whole positioned short- or long-term?
* How are recently issued Treasury securities faring in the marketplace?

Dealers also provide desk officers with current information on bank activities:
* What securities are banks trading?
* What is the strength of business loan demand?
* Are there CD issuances on the horizon?
* What are banks doing in the foreign exchange market?
* What is the activity in commercial paper and bankers' acceptances?

Day after day these meetings provide the Fed's desk officers with the feedback and input that keep them in close touch with the marketplace.

The morning sessions also enable dealers to discuss areas of interest to them. Senior management may report plans for shuffling manpower or breaking into new areas of activity. Questions may be posed about problems with the Fed's wire transfer network. Desk officers, for their part, may bring up the need for a dealer to be more responsive to bidding when the desk or the Treasury is selling securities. They also may ask about a dealer's position, recent profit experience, or the present state of industry plans for self-regulation.

10:00 A.M.: The Treasury Call

Dealer meetings end at 10 a.m. or before. The officers hurry back to the eighth-floor trading room, where Federal funds brokers have opened trading for the day and are quoting bids and offers to the customers they are bringing together. Desk traders have clipped news items from the news tickers and are checking the information screens for the opening quotes on the most actively traded government securities and for the latest money market analyst opinions. After a few calls to dealers through the direct lines of the telephone console, each trader records the opening prices on the ruled tablets used to track each day's market movements. Meanwhile, the clerks chalk in the price quotes for yesterday's close on the long blackboard that wraps around part of the room. When the desk officers arrive, they catch up with what is happening and quickly report any significant information gained from the dealer meetings.

The daily call from the Treasury occurs pretty close to 10:15. Before that call, the manager goes over how much the day's bank reserves and borrowings differ from what was forecast yesterday. He is also briefed on how the difference between the forecast and actual figures may affect reserves for the next day or so, and for the upcoming week.

Inasmuch as the Fed acts as banker for the U.S. Treasury, the Treasury call every day is one in which banker and "customer" decide on the disposition of the customer's funds. As tax revenues flow from taxpayers, they pass into designated depositories across the country. These depositories may forward the money to the Treasury immediately, or they may hold it, in effect "borrowing" it from the government. The rate is 25 basis points below the Federal funds rate. The Treasury may then transfer — that is, "call" — funds from depositories to its checking accounts at the twelve Federal Reserve Banks so as to be able to write checks and keep an aggregate "minimum balance" of about $4 billion.

When the Treasury issues new securities in excess of those maturing, more cash flows into the Fed Reserve accounts than is paid out for maturing securities. In such cases, the Treasury can move funds out of the Federal Reserve Bank accounts and into the depositories, where the money is invested on behalf of the government.

The tremendous amount of money flowing among these reserve accounts and depositories provides a buffer for bank reserves, protecting them from sudden and massive in- and outflows.

In the daily call from the Fiscal Assistant Secretary, the basic decision is whether to "call" funds out of the depository or place them in the "direct investment facilities" associated with the depositories the next day. In addition to this basic decision, the New York desk officers may pass on information regarding the fixed income market, the foreign exchange, and other areas of interest. Sometimes, the Deputy Assistant Secretary for Debt Management will discuss plans for upcoming issues of Treasury securities.

After the phone is hung up, the New York desk officers formulate an action plan for the day. The aim of the program is, of course, to maintain the reserve requirement levels needed to execute policy. In their planning, the big question is how close their forecast of reserves will be to actual reserves. The difference can be substantial in that banks do not always behave as expected. For example, when a holiday falls around a weekend, banks "play it safe" by keeping excess reserves. As a result, borrowing at the Reserve Bank and the Federal funds rate both tend to rise. Conversely, if the major banks expect the Fed funds rate to drop, perhaps because of a sluggish economy, they will accumulate deficiencies, expecting to cover them later in the week at the by-then-decreased rate.

The officers discuss forecasts, discount window rates, and a number of other factors affecting their goal of maintaining the policy-driven reserve levels. If they forge ahead unthinkingly to do whatever is necessary — react too quickly — they can send disparate and confusing signals to the market. If they allow variances from the forecasted levels to go unchecked too long, their delay can have serious effects on rates throughout the fixed income market. Usually the manager tries to take a middle-of-the-road course that balances attentiveness to policy with stability.

As the desk officers discuss the day's program, the amount of reserves that must be added or withdrawn is usually clear enough. But recommendations to the manager may reflect varying degrees of confidence in the forecast and in the expectations of bank behavior during the week. Market considerations are also talked about — for instance, are securities available for purchases or repos? Yet, in ten minutes the most promising courses of action are presented to the manager. Usually there is general agreement on what needs to be done, but sometimes the manager has to defer the decision until they can get a better reading on what is happening with reserves.

10:30 A.M.: In the Trading Room

Shortly after 10:30, the desk officers are back in the trading room, where they must now catch up on developments. Senior traders report prices on key Treasury securities, why they feel the prices are where they are, and the interaction between the government securities market and those for corporate and municipal debt. One senior trader reports on developments in the federal funds rate, others on the foreign markets. The desk officers also take reports on borrowed and nonborrowed reserves — actual versus estimated.

Taking in a great deal of information quickly, the desk officers evaluate their plan for the day. The manager writes a program of action for the day, while elsewhere in the room preparations are under way for the staff "pre-call" to the Board and to the Reserve Bank president designated to sit in on the 11:15 telephone conference call. In this pre-call, one of the traders provides a highly standardized presentation of all the relevant information gathered up to this point.

11:15 A.M.: The Conference Call

At a quarter after eleven, a conference all is convened. The attendees are:

* At the New York Federal Reserve, the manager, other desk officers, and senior staff members, all gathered in the manager's office.
* In Washington, the Board's staff director for monetary policy and his staff.
* Elsewhere, the Reserve Bank presidents currently serving on the FOMC.

During this 15- to 20-minute call, the market review, reserve situation, and plan of action are presented to the

Board staff (and the Board in turn has a report on each Governor's desk by mid-day). Occasionally one or more of the presidents has a question on operations. If they are concerned with developments in general, they are likely to call later in the day to talk with the manager. By the same token, if the manager needs to discuss developments further, he will conclude the call first, commence operations for the day, and then call the president back. Of course, the New York bank president is kept up-to-date on everything on a regular basis. In addition, when large open market transactions are in the offing, the manager notifies the chairman, who is otherwise kept in touch with all open market operations in general.

11:30 A.M.: Putting the Program into Action

Shortly after all parties hang up on the conference call, the desk officers in New York put the program into effect. While there is typically activity all day long in Federal funds operations, the desk focuses on the Fed's program for *reserve management* operations between 11:30 A.M. and 12:15 P.M. (with rare exceptions for extreme circumstances). All the contra parties in the Fed's open market operations know that this is the time of day that the Fed initiates its program, and they can usually guess the Fed's intentions as soon as the government's traders start making calls.

Once the desk enters the market, two officers take charge of the trading room. If, for example, the desk is making repos or matched sale purchases, six or eight traders start calling the primary dealers in what is called a "go-around" of the market. All the calls often take place in less than a minute, and the whole plan executed in under 45 minutes. Other operations, involving coupon securities or T-bills, can take one or two hours to conclude, because participants must evaluate complicated yield curve possibilities.

While an operation is in progress, the trading room is busy. The buttons on all the telephone turrets light up as the traders place calls to dealer firms. Then there is a lull, while the dealers' salespeople contact customers and their traders decide what they want to do for the firm's own account. Then phones start ringing off their hooks as the dealers contact traders at the Fed to take down their propositions.

Traders record dealer bids or offerings on strips preprinted with two dealer names at the top of each strip. The issues involved have already been posted on each strip so that the amounts and prices bid for, or offered, can be listed quickly. To preclude error, traders repeat each dealer's propositions. When the propositions are in, the officers compare the go-around strips for rates or prices being quoted for various maturities.

After selecting the better propositions, the officers return the strips to the traders, who then notify the dealers as to which propositions were accepted and which rejected. The traders next write tickets on the transactions they handled.

The tickets go to the accounting unit in the adjoining room where the transaction information is entered into the computer. The completed transaction form is then whisked by pneumatic tube to the second floor's government bond department. There the actual exchange of securities and payments takes place through the Fed's computerized system.

Cash transactions — those that are settled the same day — affect the reserves of the banking system almost immediately. For example, securities purchased from the dealers, either outright or under repos, are paid for by immediate credit directly to the reserve accounts of bank dealers and to the accounts of non-bank dealers at the commercial banks that clear for them.

When a dealer has served as an intermediary (or agent) for a customer, the dealer's clearing bank tells the Federal Reserve Bank the name of the institution that will deliver the securities and receive payment over the Federal Reserve wire network.

Through all this activity, the manager has to keep the rest of "the System" informed. The chief means for doing so, in addition to the 11:15 conference call, are the daily wires and written reports sent from New York to the Board and the Reserve Banks. Daily wires from the trading desk, at mid-morning and late afternoon, let everyone know of developments in the money and government securities markets.

Also, on Friday of each week the trading desk mails a complete report on operations for the period ended the prior Wednesday. This report details:

* The daily operations and tracks.
* The reserve measures compared to their desired paths.
* The latest data on the monetary aggregates, as well as the projections being made by the Board and New York Bank staffs.
* Financial markets.
* Bank reserves and money market situations.
* Corporate and municipal securities markets conditions.
* Statistical appendices.

Before each FOMC meeting, the desk also prepares a brief summary report of operations and financial markets since the last Committee meeting. Annually, the officers most closely involved with the reports prepare a comprehensive report for the year, which analyzes policy implementation and financial market developments from this longer perspective.

The eighth-floor trading room is the central focus of the fixed-income trading, not only in the United States but around the globe. Some of the most direct and powerful influences on bond prices emanate from this room, affecting initially the U.S. government securities market and ultimately every debt instrument in the world. In Chapter 6, we will explain how, in executing policy, the Fed interacts with the "so-called" primary dealers. Before doing that, we have to describe, in the next two chapters, the wide array of U.S. government securities issued by the Treasury and federal agencies.

Chapter 4

The U.S. Government
Securities Market: Treasuries

Some of the most influential money decisions in the
world are made every day in the U.S. government securities
market. Billions upon billions of dollars change hands
against a background of staccato, deal-making phone conversations, ringing phones, and chirping automated quotation and trading systems.

Before seeing how trading in this vast market is conducted, however, you must be acquainted with the array of

government instruments offered. These fall into three categories:
* Treasury securities.
* Government agency issues.
* Derivative instruments.

From time immemorial, governments have had to borrow money to get by. It's not that they are more profligate than the rest of us; it's just that large masses of people, or their elected representatives, have always found it easier to spend money for the public good than to pay the necessary taxes. In time past, such lenders and investment bankers as the Rothschilds have financed the public debt privately, and this gave them inordinate political power. Fortunately, the United States has taken a different track in funding the public debt.

In this country more than any other, evidence of the government's indebtedness has become legal tender, a reservoir of savings, and the basis of the largest securities market in the world. By preserving political stability, and by giving the Federal Reserve the power to oversee the government securities market, the U.S. government has found itself in the enviable position of being regarded as the premier issuer of debt securities, even though it has no demonstrable ability to repay them and no collateral behind them.

For whatever reason, the Treasury is able to issue many billions in new securities every year and refund countless billions more, all at yields below those on the highest-quality corporate securities. With all this issuing to do, the Treasury has had to adopt a regular schedule of auctions, so that the market can prepare itself to absorb each issue in turn. The regular rhythm of Treasury auctions is one of the most important constants in the government securities market.

The Treasury issues a very wide range of securities, maturing from a few days after issue to thirty years. By tradition, Treasury issues are grouped into three classes:

bills, notes, and bonds. Let's look at these three classes of securities in detail.

TREASURY BILLS

Treasury bills (T-bills) are securities issued with a year or less to maturity. Bills are issued without coupons; the interest paid to the holder comes from the fact that bills are sold at a *discount* and redeemed at par. The *yield* is determined by the amount of discount and the term to maturity.

Treasury bills have no coupon rate. Instead, they are sold at a "discount from par value." That is, they are sold at a dollar price that is less than the redemption value at maturity. The difference between what investors pay (price) and what they receive when the bill is redeemed (face value), the discount, constitutes the interest payment. The amount of the discount varies at the time of issuance.

For example, investor Starr buys a $100,000, 13-week bill priced at a discount of 10%. She pays approximately $97,500 for the T-bill. After 13 weeks, she redeems it for $100,000. The $2,500 difference represents interest of $10,000 *annually*. If Starr held a $100,000, 10% debt instrument for one full year, she would be paid $10,000 in interest ($10,000 times 10%). Since she held the bill for only a quarter of the year (13 weeks), she is entitled to a quarter of the annual interest ($10,000 times 0.25), or $2,500.

Given the discount in dollars, you can calculate the yield, which is simply the discount expressed as a percentage. To make this computation, dealers use the actual number of days to maturity based on a theoretical 360-day year:

$$\text{Discount (per \$100 of maturity value)} = \frac{\text{Days to maturity}}{360} \times \text{Rate (\%)}$$

To find the price, use the following formula:

Price ($) = $100 – Discount (per $100 of maturity value)

As an example, let's find the dollar price for a T-bill that is due in 147 days and trades on a 9% discount basis. First find the discount:

$$D = M \div 360 \times R\,(\%)$$
$$= 147 \div 360 \times 0.09$$
$$= 3.6750\% \text{ full discount}$$

In other words, the investor receives a discount of $3.675 per $100 of maturity value. For a $100,000 bill, the discount is $3,675.00 ($3,675 times 1,000).

The next step is to calculate the price:

$$P = \$100 - D$$
$$= \$100 - \$3.675 \text{ per } \$100$$
$$= \$96.325$$

The dollar price of the T-bill is equal to $96.325 for every $100 of face (or redemption) value. So a $100,000 bill sold on a 9% basis would cost $96,325.00 and be redeemed for $100,000 after 147 days.

The discount is the pricing mechanism for T-bills. For example, a discount of 12% on a one-year bill would produce a price of 88 (100 – 12), but the same discount on a 13-week bill would produce a price of 97 [100 – (12 ÷ 4)]. (It matures in one quarter of the year.) The yield on each of these bills, however, would be higher than the discount rate, because the buyer received the discount rate on less than the par amount of cash. Thus the yield on our hypothetical year bill would be 13.64% (12% divided by .88), and the yield on the 13-week bill would be 12.37% (12% divided by .97).

See Figure 4-1. On March 6, a T-bill with a face value of $100,000 and a maturity of September 4 is quoted as follows:

	Bid	*Asked*	*Yield*
Discount	6.61%	6.59%	6.91%
Dollar price	$96,695	$96,705	

Figure 4-1. T-Bill Quotations

U.S. Treas. Bills Mat. date	Bid	Asked Discount	Yield	Mat. date	Bid	Asked Discount	Yield
-1986-				-1986-			
3-13	5.52	5.38	5.46	7-10	6.70	6.66	6.91
3-20	6.12	6.04	6.13	7-17	6.70	6.66	6.92
3-27	5.67	5.55	5.64	7-24	6.70	6.66	6.93
4- 3	6.19	6.13	6.24	7-86	6.70	6.68	6.97
4-10	6.14	6.08	6.20	8- 7	6.78	6.74	7.03
4-17	6.44	6.40	6.53	8-14	6.69	6.65	6.94
4-24	6.46	6.40	6.54	8-21	6.70	6.66	6.96
5- 1	6.61	6.55	6.70	8-28	6.68	6.64	6.95
5- 8	6.68	6.64	6.81	9- 4	6.61	6.59	6.91←
5-15	6.68	6.66	6.83	10- 2	6.67	6.63	6.96
5-22	6.67	6.63	6.81	10-30	6.67	6.63	6.97
5-29	6.71	6.67	6.87	11-28	6.68	6.64	7.00
6- 5	6.61	6.59	6.79	12-26	6.66	6.62	7.00
6-12	6.60	6.56	6.77	-1987-			
6-19	6.65	6.61	6.83	1-22	6.66	6.64	7.04
6-26	6.51	6.45	6.67	2-19	6.63	6.61	7.04
7- 3	6.70	6.66	6.90				

The asked dollar price ($96,705) was computed as follows, using 180 days as the time between March 6 and September 4.

Discount = M ÷ 360 × R × Face value

     = 180 ÷ 360 × .0659 × $100,000

     = $3,295

Price ($) = Face value discount

     = $100,000 − $3,295

     = $96,705

Underlying this pricing system is a system of "basis points." There are 100 basis points in each percentage point. For example, a 13-week Treasury bill's discount drops from 7.17 basis to 7.10 basis, a decline of 7 basis points. The dollar value of the decline is $175 per $1 million, or $175 per $10,000.

The Treasury usually issues bills in three maturities: 13 weeks, 26 weeks, and 52 weeks. The first bill is known, when it is issued, as the "three-month bill," the second as the "six-month bill," and the third as the "year bill," although they conform to those exact time periods for only one day.

Thirteen-week and *26-week* bills are auctioned every Monday at all of the Federal Reserve banks. Bids, or tenders, must be submitted by 1:30 p.m. Eastern Time. All bills auctioned on Monday are delivered and paid for the following Thursday, and mature on Thursday the specified number of weeks hence. In the event that a bank holiday falls on a Thursday, the bills are delivered or mature on the following Friday. This regular issuing procedure has been going on for years and is ingrained in the market.

Fifty-two week bills, auctioned monthly, have the same delivery and maturity (Thursdays) as the 13-week and 26 week bills.

Occasionally the Treasury issues bills that mature at other times, often on dates of expected tax receipts, and these are called *cash management bills*. There is no regularity about the issuance of cash management bills.

The buyer of a bill does not receive a certificate, but their ownership is recorded on the computer at the buyer's clearing bank, whose ownership in turn is recorded on the computers at the Federal Reserve. This *book entry system* means that billions of dollars worth of bills can trade every day without the shifting of countless pieces of paper. Instead, the Fed computer records every sale and the bank acts as custodian for the new owner.

Because of the intense interest in Treasury bills, they actually trade before they are issued by the Treasury. From around 4:00 pm on the Tuesday of the week before they are auctioned, when the amount of next week's three- and six-month bill actions is announced, the next week's bills are traded on a "when-issued" basis. These *when issued* bills are very important, because traders in the bill market use them to offset positions in bills that have already been issued. When-issued bills are also important because they don't have to be paid for until Thursday of the following week. Depending on the customer's margin arrangements with a Primary Dealer, when-issued bills give the opportunity to participate in the market on very high leverage.

Bills are traditionally purchased and traded by large investors, either institutions or very wealthy individuals. They are also traded in very large volume. At least half of each day's trading volume in the Treasury securities markets is in bills, about $10 billion each day. In addition, each individual transaction is usually very large. In fact, the usual round lot in the bill market is $5 million. Bills are issued in amounts as small as $100,000, but those amounts are odd lots in the market, and they trade at decidedly disadvantageous prices when compared to round lots. Investors who get quotes on round lots and then try to execute an odd lot order are in for a rude surprise.

TREASURY NOTES

Any securities issued by the Treasury with from one year to ten years to maturity are defined as *notes*. Unlike bills, notes have coupons and pay interest twice a year. All notes are noncallable by the Treasury for their life. There is a very wide range of note issues outstanding, with maturities of from a few days to ten years, and with coupons ranging from 6⅛% to 16¼%.

The Treasury issues notes in regular cycles, like bills, but much less frequently. For many years the Treasury sold only notes and bonds that matured during the months of February, May, August, and November; as these securities matured, they had to be refunded. This most important cycle in the Treasury note market is know as the *quarterly refunding*. Thus, on the last Wednesday of January, April, July and October, at about 4:00 p.m., the Treasury announces the sizes and maturities of the issues to be sold the next week for delivery on the 15th of February, May, August, and November. These issues partly refund the ones maturing, and partly raise the new money the Treasury needs to borrow. As the borrowing needs of the Treasury have grown, it has added more note cycles, including a "mini-refunding" late in the months of March, June, September, and December. In 1985 the Treasury's note cycles looked like this:

* *The two-year note* — auctioned monthly, late in the month, to be delivered and mature on the last business day of the month.
* *The three-year note* — auctioned in February, May, August, and November as part of the quarterly refunding.
* *The four-year note* — auctioned in March, June, September, and December as part of the mini-refunding.
* *The five-year note* — auctioned in February, May, August, and November, but not part of the quarterly refunding.
* *The seven-year note* — auctioned in March, June, September, and December as part of the mini-refunding.
* *The ten-year note* — auctioned in February, May, August, and November as part of the quarterly refunding.

All Treasury notes are quoted in prices denominated in percentage points and 32nds of a percentage point. Although prices are written using a decimal point, the number to the right of the decimal point is expressed in 32nds. Thus a price of 98.16 would be equivalent to 98½% of par, or $985,000 per million dollars par amount. Each 32nd is equivalent to $312.50 per million dollars par amount. Occasionally issues are quoted in 64ths of a percentage point, which is equivalent to $156.25 per million dollars par amount. That million-dollar par amount is considered a *round lot* in the Treasury note market, just as $5 million is in bills.

Most Treasury notes are owned by commercial banks, Federal Reserve banks, U.S. government agencies, and trust funds. These notes permit holders to arrange their portfolios with coupons and maturities spaced over a limited period of years, giving automatic liquidity and attractive average yields.

Even though Treasury notes (and bonds) pay holders interest semiannually, usually on the anniversary of the issue date, interest accrues on them during the period between payments. The buyer of a note or bond pays, and the seller receives, the *accrued interest* when the securities are sold. Thus an investor who buys notes or bonds after a coupon payment date and sells them before the next one receives the bond interest for the period during which he held it.

For example, on June 15 you bought one million dollars par amount of a 10% note, with coupon dates of May 15 and November 15, and held it until October 15. When you bought the notes you would pay 31 days of accrued interest at $273.22 per day, or $8,469.94. When you sold the notes you would receive 153 days of accrued interest at $273.22, or $41,803.27. The person who bought it from you, assuming he held it until November 15, would receive from the Treasury a check for $5,000, half a year's interest.

Thus we can see that no matter when you buy a note or bond, or how long you hold it, the next owner will always get the accrued interest due upon sale.

TREASURY BONDS

All Treasury securities issued with maturities longer than 10 years are called *bonds* (or T-bonds). Bonds are very much like notes, except for a few important differences.

For one thing, some bonds are callable at 100 by the Treasury five years before they mature. Thus you can assume that, if a bond is trading substantially above 100, it may well have a maturity five years shorter than the stated one. That change in maturity can affect the bond's price performance, making it less volatile than it otherwise would be.

Another difference is that Congress passed a law long ago that the Treasury cannot issue bonds that yield more than 4¼%. For many years that has meant that the Treasury has effectively been precluded from issuing bonds. Rather than repeal the law, Congress has chosen to give the Treasury limited authority to issue bonds yielding more than 4¼%. As the Treasury's appetite for money has grown, it has had to go back to Congress repeatedly for more and more authority. When Congress engages in a political battle with an Administration, it sometimes withholds the bond authority.

That action has in the past, and may in the future, upset the Treasury's bond issuing cycles, but generally the Treasury has two bond cycles:

The *twenty-year bond* — auctioned in March, June, September, and December as part of the mini-refunding.

The *thirty-year bond* — auctioned in February, May, August, and November as part of the quarterly refunding.

The fact that T-bonds can be easily and quickly converted to cash at a low transaction price is reflected by the slight "spread" between the bid and the asked prices, often very small. Treasury bonds are, therefore, like T notes, quoted in 32nds of a point. For example, a $1,000 government bond is quoted at 96.6. This quotation means 96 ⁶⁄₃₂% of the bond's par value. The price is figured as follows:

96 = 96 % of par value		$960.000
.6 = ⁶⁄₃₂ or (³⁄₁₆) of $10	+	1.875
Dollar price		$961.875

Figure 4-2. Treasury Bond Quotations

TREASURY BONDS, NOTES & BILLS

Friday, March 7, 1986

Representative mid-afternoon Over-the-Counter quotations supplied by the Federal Reserve Bank of New York City, based on transactions of $1 million or more.

Decimals in bid-and-asked and bid changes represent 32nds; 101.1 means 101 1/32. a-Plus 1/64. b-Yield to call date. d-Minus 1/64. k-Nonresident aliens exempt from withholding taxes. n-Treasury notes. p-Treasury note; nonresident aliens exempt from withholding taxes.

Treasury Bonds and Notes

Rate	Mat.	Date	Bid	Asked	Bid Chg.	Yld.
14s,	1986	Mar n	100.11	100.15	- .1	5.13
11½s,	1986	Mar n	100.7	100.11	....	4.97
11¾s,	1986	Apr n	100.19	100.23	....	6.24
7⅞s,	1986	May n	100.3	100.7	+ .1	6.48
9⅜s,	1986	May n	100.11	100.15	....	6.54
12⅝s,	1986	May n	101.4	101.8	- .1	6.43
13¾s,	1986	May n	101.3	101.7	....	6.83
13s,	1986	Jun n	101.22	101.26	....	6.79
14⅞s,	1986	Jun n	102.8	102.12	- .1	6.77
12⅝s,	1986	Jul p	102.2	102.6	....	6.81
8s,	1986	Aug n	100.10	100.14	+ .1	6.92
11⅜s,	1986	Aug n	101.24	101.28	+ .1	6.87
12⅜s,	1986	Aug p	102.11	102.15	....	6.93
11⅞s,	1986	Sep p	102.15	102.19	....	7.03
12¼s,	1986	Sep n	102.22	102.26	+ .1	7.00
11⅝s,	1986	Oct p	102.21	102.25	....	7.10
6⅛s,	1986	Nov	99.21	100.21	+ .3	5.13
10⅜s,	1986	Nov p	102.3	102.7	+ .2	7.18
11s,	1986	Nov n	102.12	102.16	+ .1	7.18
13⅞s,	1986	Nov n	104.10	104.14	+ .2	7.09
16⅛s,	1986	Nov n	105.24	105.28	....	7.14
9⅞s,	1986	Dec p	101.31	102.3	+ .1	7.16
10s,	1986	Dec n	102.1	102.5	....	7.21
9¾s,	1987	Jan p	102.1	102.5	+ .1	7.22
9s,	1987	Feb n	101.14	101.18	....	7.24
10s,	1987	Feb p	102.13	102.17	+ .2	7.25
10⅞s,	1987	Feb n	103.3	103.7	+ .1	7.25
12¾s,	1987	Feb n	104.29	105.1	....	7.09
10¼s,	1987	Mar n	102.30	103.2	+ .3	7.19
10¾s,	1987	Mar p	103.13	103.17	+ .2	7.22
9¾s,	1987	Apr p	102.18	102.22	+ .2	7.25
9⅛s,	1987	May p	102	102.4	+ .2	7.28
12s,	1987	May n	105.5	105.9	+ .3	7.26
12½s,	1987	May n	105.22	105.26	+ .3	7.28
14s,	1987	May n	107.11	107.15	+ .2	7.29
8½s,	1987	Jun p	101.14	101.18	+ .2	7.23
10½s,	1987	Jun n	103.26	103.30	+ .1	7.29
8⅞s,	1987	Jul p	101.30	102.2	+ .4	7.29
8⅞s,	1987	Aug p	102.2	102.6	+ .5	7.28
12⅜s,	1987	Aug p	106.20	106.24	+ .4	7.33
13¾s,	1987	Aug n	108.15	108.19	+ .4	7.33
9s,	1987	Sep p	102.12	102.16	+ .5	7.27
11⅛s,	1987	Sep n	105.15	105.19	+ .5	7.26
8⅞s,	1987	Oct p	102.6	102.10	+ .1	7.35
7⅝s,	1987	Nov n	100.11	100.19	+ .6	7.24
8½s,	1987	Nov p	101.25	101.29	+ .4	7.30
11s,	1987	Nov p	105.17	105.21	+ .4	7.36
12⅝s,	1987	Nov n	107.31	108.3	+ .2	7.42
11¼s,	1987	Dec n	106.12	106.16	+ .3	7.35
7⅞s,	1987	Dec p	100.22	100.26	+ .2	7.39
8⅛s,	1988	Jan p	101.8	101.10	+ .5	7.37
12⅜s,	1988	Jan n	108.12	108.16	+ .2	7.38
10⅛s,	1988	Feb n	104.24	104.28	+ .2	7.38
10⅜s,	1988	Feb p	105.6	105.10	+ .4	7.38
8s,	1988	Feb p	101.9	101.11	+ .5	7.26
12s,	1988	Mar n	108.18	108.22	+ .6	7.37
13¼s,	1988	Apr n	111.2	111.6	+ .6	7.39
8¼s,	1988	May n	101.24	102	+ .5	7.24
9⅞s,	1988	May n	104.24	104.28	+ .7	7.41
10s,	1988	May p	105.1	105.5	+ .4	7.40
13⅝s,	1988	Jun n	112.20	112.24	+ .4	7.51
14s,	1988	Jul n	113.17	113.25	+ .3	7.50

A plus sign means that the quote is to the next highest 64th. As an example, a $1,000 Treasury bond is quoted at 98.8+. This quote is equivalent to:

98 = 98 % of par value	$980.00000
.8 = 8/32 of $10	2.50000
+ = 1/64 of $10	.15625
Price	$982.65625

T-bonds are quoted in the financial news (see Figure 4-2), but professionals in the market use special quote sheets. Figure 4-3 presents part of a quote sheet published every day by several government securities dealers. This sheet lists all Treasury securities in existence on Tuesday, January 21, 1986. The group of securities at the top are bills, and are listed by maturity. The quotes for bills are

Figure 4-3.

UNITED STATES TREASURY SECURITIES
U.S. Treasury Bills

Maturity	Bid	Asked	Chg.	Eq. Bd. Yld.	Amt. of Issue	Days to Maturity	Value per 1.01
1-30-86	7.00	6.50	0.00	6.60	7200	7	1.94
2-6-86	6.785	6.65	0.10	6.76	7200	14	3.89
2-13-86	6.75	6.65	0.00	6.77	7200	21	5.83
2-20-86	6.90	6.80	0.00	6.93	8604	28	7.78
3-6-86	6.92	6.80	0.00	6.95	7700	42	11.67
3-13-86	6.92	6.88	0.00	7200	7.04	49	13.61
3-20-86	6.94	6.90	0.00	7.07	8606	56	15.66
3-27-86	6.94	6.90	0.00	7.08	4500	63	17.50
4-3-86	6.96	6.92	0.00	7.11	7000	70	19.44
4-10-86	6.97	6.93	0.00	7.13	7000	77	21.39
4-17-86	7.01	6.99	0.00	7.20	8337	84	23.33
4-24-86	6.99	6.97	0.00	7.19	6900	91	25.28

Maturity	Bid	Asked	Chg.	Eq. Bd. Yld.	Amt. of Issue	Days to Maturity	Value per 1.01
5-1-86	7.00	6.96	0.00	7.19	7100	98	27.22
5-8-86	7.05	7.01	0.00	7.28	7200	105	29.17
5-15-86	7.07	7.03	0.00	7.29	8500	112	31.11
5-22-86	7.10	7.06	0.00	7.33	7300	119	33.06
6-5-86	7.04	7.00	0.00	7.29	7600	133	36.94
6-12-86	7.00	6.96	0.00	7.35	8600	140	38.89
6-19-86	7.08	7.04	0.00	7.35	7600	147	40.83
6-26-86	7.06	7.02	0.00	7.34	7200	154	42.78
7-3-86	7.18	7.14	0.00	7.48	7600	161	44.72
7-10-86	7.16	7.12	0.00	7.47	8500	168	46.67
7-17-86	7.14	7.12	0.00	7.48	7400	175	48.61
7-24-86	7.15	7.11	0.00	7.48	7200	182	50.56
7-31-86	7.13	7.11	0.00	7.48	7200	189	52.50
9-7-86	7.17	7.13	0.00	7.50	8750	196	54.55
9-4-86	7.22	7.18	0.00	7.57	8750	224	62.22
10-2-86	7.25	7.21	0.00	7.62	8500	252	70.00
10-30-86	7.25	7.21	0.00	7.64	8500	280	77.78
11-28-86	7.26	7.22	0.00	7.68	9000	309	85.83
12-26-86	7.21	7.19	0.00	7.68	9000	337	93.61
1-22-86	7.23	7.21	0.00	7.74	9000	364	100.16

Amounts in millions. Minimum denomination $10,000. All earnings on Treasury bill are subject to Federal income tax, but exempt from state and local income tax.

U.S. Treasury Notes and Bonds

Coupon	Maturity	Bid	Asked	Chg.	Yield to Mat.	Corp. Tax post Tax	Yield Value Equiv.	1985 Par 1/32	Range High	Amt. Pub. Low	Dated Held	Date
N 10 5/8	1-31-86	100-2	100-3		...6.00	3.24	6.00	1.3689	101-30	96-26	9228	1-31-84
N 9 7/8	2-15-86	100-2	100-3		...8.02	4.33	8.02	.4812	101-16	95-12	8116	2-15-86
N 13 1/2	2-15-86	100-10	100-11		...7.53	4.07	7.53	.4729	110-8	95-23	3186	12-8-80

given in the form of a discount rate. The sheet also tells you what the bills yield at that discount. The sheet does *not* tell you the actual dollar price at which the bills are quoted.

The lower section of the sheet lists all the Treasury coupon securities that existed on September 13th. It lumps notes and bonds together, but you can tell which is which by the initial "N" or "B" accompanying each issue. It tells you the coupon and maturity of each issue, an approximate price (bid and offer), and the yield to maturity at the offered price. Some other very interesting columns are included, such as the after-tax yield, and the full coupon that would be necessary to give you the same after-tax yield as this security does. This is called the *taxable equivalent yield.* For issues trading near 100, the yield to maturity and the taxable equivalent are very close together, but for bonds at lower prices, the actual and taxable equivalent yields are often quite far apart.

Obviously, each issue on the list has a different bid and offer and a different yield to maturity. Yield to maturity is the common denominator for comparing different Treasury securities, as well as securities issued by other bodies. What causes different issues to have different yields to maturity? Perhaps the most common reason is differences in perceived credit quality; the higher the perceived quality, the lower the yield. Thus one would expect Treasuries to yield less than agencies, agencies to yield less than AAA-rated corporates, and AAA-rated corporates to yield less than lower-rated corporates.

Sometimes, however, that expectation isn't quite valid. We then need to explain yield differences between securities issued by the same body, like the Treasury. In these cases, we need to look for other reasons.

One such reason could consist of *differences in maturity.* This reason is so common that it has given rise to the term *yield curve*, which describes the changes in yield to maturity as the maturity of like issues increases. When the yield increases as the maturity lengthens, the yield curve is called *normal.* When the yield decreases as the maturity lengthens, the yield curve is called inverted. Some traders are so concerned with the shape of the yield curve and the exact yield differences between maturities that it is virtually the only thing that dictates their trading.

Another factor that can explain yield differences, especially between issues with identical, or nearly identical, maturities, is *coupon and dollar price.* Generally speaking, the higher the coupon — and thus the higher the dollar price — the higher the yield. This is partly because this factor tends to bring the after-tax yields closer together, and partly because of compounding considerations, but it is almost universally true.

That universal yield relationship has given rise to a new kind of security, the *zero coupon* issue. The calculation used to determine yield to maturity does *not provide* for compounding coupon payments as they are received over the life of the issue. It *does*, however, calculate the effect of compounding in determining the premium or discount necessary to achieve a specified yield to maturity, and it assumes that the compounding would have occurred at the yield to maturity.

This "guaranteed compounding" feature of zero coupon securities is attractive enough that buyers are willing to pay prices for those generating lower yields to maturity than full coupon securities. The demand has given rise to two kinds of issues: original issue discounts (OIDs) and stripped issues.

Original issue discounts (OIDs) are issued by the borrower with a coupon below the market rate of interest and at a price below 100. The IRS requires that a taxpayer amortize the discount over the life of the issue and pay taxes on it, which makes OIDs unattractive to accounts that are taxable, but very attractive to pension funds and other investors who do not pay taxes.

Stripped issues are securities issued with current coupons, which are held by a trustee. The trustee issues securities, which are claims on the stream of coupon payments and the principal payment at maturity. This process "strips" the coupons off the security and makes a separate zero coupon security out of each one of them. The Treasury has recently issued securities that are strippable directly, instead of going through the trustee procedure. The stripping of existing long-term Treasury issues has become so popular that the available supply of some issues has been reduced to a mere fraction of the original issue size.

The last reason for yield differences is the *technical condition of the securities*. An issue in which a dealer has a large short position (which he is trying to cover) will often trade at a lower yield than one in which a dealer has a large long position (which he is trying to sell).

A special case of the technical condition aspect has to do with the Treasury's auctions of securities. Since the Treasury does not pay Primary Dealers a selling concession to market its issues, and since the Primary Dealers must bid on all Treasury auctions, dealer activity in the days before the auctions is concentrated in going short the existing issues surrounding the ones to be auctioned. This short position allows the dealer to show his customers swaps out of these issues into the ones he expects to buy in the auction, and also protects the dealer against a fall in general market prices while he is long the securities he just bought. It also has the effect of making the existing issues yield more, temporarily, than they otherwise would.

A great deal of trading in the marketplace, by both customer and Primary Dealers, is based on the idea that there is an equilibrium yield spread between any two issues. Whenever that spread gets out of line, one issue is sold and the other is bought. Then the trader waits for the spread to go back to its equilibrium level. That is good trading strategy, as long as the equilibrium spread is not in the process of changing. If it is, one can be left standing on the dock watching the ship pull away.

Generally, the interest income paid to investors by U.S. government securities — whether Treasury bills, notes, or bonds — is subject to federal taxation, but it is exempt from all state and local income taxes. The exemption from state and local taxes applies only to "direct" obligations of the U.S. government. Certain obligations of federal agencies and government corporations may qualify (see Chapter 5).

Some outstanding issues of Treasury bonds, if held by an individual at the time of death, can be redeemed at face amount to pay estate taxes, even if they were purchased at a discount. Because of this unique feature, these bonds have come to be called "flower bonds." Although such bonds are still in existence and will be around until 1998, they are no longer issued.

While Treasury securities make for a huge market, they are not the only ones related to the federal government. A wholly different trading arena consists of securities issued by federal government agencies and others backed by mortgage pools. These are explained in the next chapter.

Chapter 5

The U.S. Government Securities Market: Agency and Mortgage-Backed Securities

The American voter, and thus the American government, have had longstanding commitments to two sectors of the economy: the family farmer and the family homeowner. A contrary, but equally longstanding perception is that direct government assistance to these or to any other sectors is unfair and undesirable. When both the family farmer and the family homeowner were unable to prosper in the early eighties, the dichotomy between these two viewpoints gave rise to a separate class of securities — those issued or guaranteed by *agencies* of the federal government.

Agencies are not part of the federal government and are often owned by the constituencies they serve. Yet they perform the governmental functions of providing assistance and regulation to their constituencies.

Agencies are generally divided into two categories:

* Those who assist the *farming sector;* the Federal Intermediate Credit Banks, the Banks for Cooperatives, and the Federal Land Banks.
* Those who assist the *homeownership sector;* the Federal National Mortgage Association, the Federal Home Loan Banks, the Federal Home Loan Mortgage Corp., and the Government National Mortgage Association.

Two other agencies occasionally issue or guarantee securities: the Export-Import Bank and the Tennessee Valley Authority. These agencies, however, represent a very small part of the market.

Agencies assist their constituencies in two ways. Some agencies borrow in the marketplace by issuing securities themselves and lending the proceeds to their constituents. In so doing, they substitute their high-quality credit for the lower-quality credit of the farmer or homeowner. Other agencies guarantee the timely payment of principal and interest on securities used by their constituents, thereby enhancing their credit. Some agencies do both. Some agency-guaranteed issues incorporate the full faith and credit of the Treasury, and some do not.

In terms of diversity, quality, liquidity, and trading volume, agency securities fall between the homogeneous world of Treasury issues and the heterogeneous world of corporate issues. Some of the diversity in the agency securities market was eliminated when the agricultural agencies banded together to issue securities under the umbrella of the Federal Farm Credit System, incorporated as Federal Farm Credit Funding Corporation, New York, Fiscal Agent.

In method of issuance, agency securities also fall into two broad classes. *Direct agency issues* use a procedure that falls between a Treasury auction and a corporate underwriting, while *mortgage-backed securities* are issued in a totally uncontrolled process (covered in detail later). Direct agency issues are handled by each agency's *Fiscal Agent*, who occupies a position akin to that of a corporate treasurer. Unlike the Treasury, agencies pay the Primary Dealers (and a few other participants) a commission to market their securities, giving the dealers an exclusive franchise to do this job. The dealers know well ahead of time which agency will be issuing securities and when. They therefore vie with each other to market the largest amount of securities for each agency, thereby hoping to increase their allotment and the resulting total commission. The obvious difference between this process and the Treasury auction is one reason that the spread between Treasury and agency issues with like characteristics has fallen from over .50% to about .20%.

THE FARM CREDIT AGENCIES

1. The *Banks for Cooperatives* (Co-ops) were created by the Farm Credit Act of 1933 for the purpose of supplying credit to eligible agricultural cooperative associations owned and controlled by farmers. One bank was established in each of the twelve Farm Credit districts, and a central bank was established in Washington, D.C. The function of district banks is to make seasonal and term loans available to eligible cooperatives to aid in the production and merchandising of various agricultural products. The principal lending operation of the central bank is to participate in the larger loans of each of the district banks. As with the Federal Land Banks and the Federal Intermediate Credit Banks, the twelve district Banks for Cooperatives and the central bank operate under the supervision of the Farm Credit Administration.

Initially, the Banks for Cooperatives were wholly owned by the U.S. government, but the Farm Credit Act of 1955 provided for the gradual retirement of the government's investment and conversion to private ownership. The last of the government's capital stock was retired by December 31, 1968, and the banks are now wholly owned by the private cooperative associations they serve. To make this conversion to private ownership, each borrower was required to purchase at least one qualifying share in his or her district bank.

In addition, borrowers were required to invest in such stock an amount equal to an established percentage of the interest payable on their loans, with this percentage ranging between 10% and 25%. Additional stock may be acquired by the cooperatives when a bank makes a patronage refund of net savings.

2. The *Federal Intermediate Credit Banks* (FICBs) were created by the Agricultural Credits Act of 1923 to provide a dependable source of funds for institutions that lend to farmers. One bank was established in each of the twelve Farm Credit districts, to operate under the supervision of the Farm Credit Administration. These banks serve primarily as discount banks for institutions that finance agricultural and livestock products, including the production credit associations organized under the Farm Credit Act of 1933. The banks may also make direct loans to qualified farm financial institutions, and they provide supervisory services to the production credit associations upon request.

The Federal Intermediate Credit Banks were organized as wholly owned government corporations. From their inception in 1923 until December 31, 1956, the government held all capital stock. The Farm Credit Act of 1956 provided for the gradual retirement of capital stock. In December 1968, $108 million was transferred by the banks to the Treasury as payment in full for the remaining government-held capital stock, and the agency become privately owned.

3. The *Federal Land Bank* system was created by the Federal Farm Loan Act of 1916, which established one

Federal Land Bank in each of twelve farm districts across the country. The Federal Farm Credit Act of 1933 transferred control of the Federal Land Banks to the newly created Farm Credit Administration, and the farm districts became known as Farm Credit Districts. Although the banks are operated under the close supervision of the Farm Credit Administration, they are now wholly owned by farmers through local Federal Land Bank associations. The last of the government equity was retired in 1947.

The Federal Land Banks' function is making long-term first mortgage loans on farm properties within their respective districts. Such loans were originally made directly to the farmer, but they are now closed through one of the nearly 700 local associations. These loans may not exceed 65% of the appraised value of the land mortgaged as security, and the local association must endorse each loan note. In addition, each borrower must purchase stock in his or her local association in the amount of five percent of the loan, which is held by the association as collateral for the loan. The local association then subscribes to an equal amount of stock in the district Federal Land Bank, which holds the stock as collateral on the loan. All of this stock is retired when the loan is paid off.

Although the *farm credit agencies* used to issue separate securities, they now issue only under the umbrella of the Federal Farm Credit system. Each of the system's securities is the joint and several liability of all the agencies. They are sold throughout a nationwide network of dealers, in a selling group managed by the Fiscal Agent in New York, Federal Farm Credit Funding Corporation. The Fiscal Agent receives daily input as to the market levels for securities that are comparable to the ones he is issuing, and he prices his securities accordingly.

Like many corporations, the Farm Credit system borrows short-term money on a regular basis. Instead of commercial paper, the system issues *discount notes*, which are the agency equivalent of Treasury bills. Unlike bills, though, these notes are not sold at auction, but are sold to dealers, and by dealers to customers, as the system needs to raise the money. Thus discount notes are truly a hybrid of bills and commercial paper. They have higher credit quality than commercial paper, but decidely less liquidity than bills.

The Farm Credit system has regular issuance of *six-month* and *nine-month bonds* through the selling group. These issues are such a regular event that they are comparable to the Treasury refundings. Their liquidity is fairly high in the week or two after they are issued, but it gradually decreases and then drops off sharply when the next six- and nine-month bonds are issued. Then the old bonds become *off the run* securities, signifying that they have much less liquidity and trading volume than the active issues.

The system also has irregular issues of *longer-term bonds*, usually to fund loans made by the Federal Land Banks. These issues are useful because they can be compared to, and swapped against, both longer-term Treasuries and corporates. Their liquidity, however, is not usually as high as the regular system issues.

All Farm Credit system securities are issued in *book entry form* only, which means that buyers do not receive certificates. Instead, their ownership is recorded on the computers at their clearing banks and at the Federal Reserve. Interest and principal payments are made based upon those computer records, not upon presentation of a coupon or certificate.

System securities are legal investments for trust funds, insurance companies, most public pension funds, and most other regulated bodies. They are acceptable as collateral for fiduciary, trust, and public deposits at intermediaries, Treasury tax and loan accounts, and repurchase transactions with the Federal Reserve Bank of New York.

As for *tax treatment*, interest on system securities is exempt from state and local income taxes, but not from federal income tax. Gains from sale, transfer, or inheritance of system securities are subject to federal, state, and local taxes.

MORTGAGE CREDIT AGENCIES

Three mortgage credit agencies have developed over the fifty or so years since the Great Depression.
* The *Federal Home Loan Bank* (FHLB) system oversees the federally chartered thrift institutions in the United States, and assists them in fulfilling their mortgage lending responsibilities.
* The *Federal National Mortgage Association* (FNMA) provides direct assistance to the market for conventional mortgages.
* The *Government National Mortgage Association* (GNMA) provides assistance to the market for federally insured mortgages.

Both the FHLB system and FNMA issue securities directly, and all three guarantee issues of mortgage pass-through securities.

1. The *Federal Home Loan Bank* system was created by authority of the Federal Home Loan Bank Act of 1932 for the purpose of stabilizing and strengthening institutions that promote thrift and individual home ownership. One Home Loan Bank operates in each of the twelve geographic districts designated by the Federal Home Loan Bank Board. The banks are owned entirely by their members.

Savings and loan associations, savings banks, and insurance companies are eligible to become members of the system, and Federal savings and loan institutions are required to join. About 3,000 savings and loan institutions belong to the system, and they hold approximately 90% of the combined resources of all operating savings and loan associations in the country. Each member institution must purchase and maintain holdings of capital stock in its regional bank equal to at least one percent of the aggregate unpaid principal of its home mortgage loans, with a minimum subscription of $500.

The main purpose of the Federal Home Loan Banks is to make loans to member institutions to accommodate unusual credit demands arising from seasonal and cyclical factors. Advances to members are made strictly on the basis of loan requests, with the maximum any one member can borrow limited to twelve times the amount of Federal Home Loan Bank capital stock it holds. Advances to members are secured by the bank's capital stock owned by the member, plus the assignment of a stipulated amount of home mortgages or obligations of the United States.

The principal source of funds for the lending operation of these banks is the sale of consolidated bonds to the public. All twelve banks are jointly and severally liable for any such obligations issued, and the total amount outstanding may not exceed twelve times the combined capital and surplus of all the Home Loan Banks. In addition, the banks must maintain qualified collateral in an amount equal to any outstanding debt. Such collateral may consist of cash, U.S. government obligations, secured advances, or mortgages guaranteed by any government agency. By statute, the Secretary of the Treasury is authorized to purchase obligations of the banks at his discretion in an amount up to $4 billion.

By statute, these debentures are a lawful investment for any U.S. government trust fund, and they may be used by commercial banks as collateral for Treasury tax and loan accounts. National banks and state member banks may invest in them without regard to statutory limitations, and they are eligible as collateral for advances by Federal Reserve Banks to member banks.

Federal Home Loan Banks have issued notes with maturities of less than a year and bonds with maturities of over a year. Both notes and bonds are issued in bearer form only in denominations of $10,000, $50,000, $100,000, and $1,000,000. None are callable prior to maturity. Interest on bonds is payable semiannually, and interest on notes is payable at maturity at any Federal Reserve Bank or branch. Sales of these debentures are made through a fiscal agent and a nationwide syndicate of dealers.

Federal Home Loan Bank discount notes have recently been offered on a continuing basis through a selling group of Primary Dealers. These are notes whose maturities, not to exceed one year, are designated by the buyer at time of purchase. Prices are subject to frequent adjustment much like commercial paper.

As for *tax treatment*, interest income is subject to taxation under the Internal Revenue Code but is specifically exempted from state or local taxation. Capital gains may be subject to state and local taxation, depending upon varying state and local laws.

2. The *Federal National Mortgage Association*, popularly known as *Fannie Mae*, was originally chartered under the National Housing Act of 1938 for the purpose of creating a secondary market for Federal Housing Administration-insured mortgages. In 1950, the activities of Fannie Mae were transferred to the Housing and Home Finance Agency. During this period of its existence, Fannie Mae was a wholly owned government corporation, and all operating funds were borrowed from the U.S. Treasury.

Fannie Mae was reorganized by the National Housing Act of 1954, better known as the Federal National Mortgage Association Charter Act. Under the reorganization, three separate operational entities were created, each with its own assets, liabilities,and borrowing authority. The three divisions were labeled Secondary Market Operations, Special Assistance Functions, and Management and Liquidating Functions.

Under its *Secondary Market Operations Division*, Fannie Mae was authorized to provide a degree of liquidity for government-insured mortgages, thus improving the distribution of investment capital available for home mortgage financing. This liquidity was to be provided by the purchase and sale of mortgages insured by the Federal Housing Administration or guaranteed by the Veterans Administration or rural housing loans insured by the Farmers Home Administration. The Special Assistance Functions Division was to supply special assistance for the financing of mortgages originating from special housing programs which might be established by the President. The Management and Liquidating Functions Division was to serve as a fiduciary with respect to mortgages or other obligations that Fannie Mae had acquired prior to the Charter Act.

All three Fannie Mae divisions were initially capitalized by the issuance of preferred stock to the Treasury. The Charter Act contemplated that the Secondary Market Operations Division would ultimately be completely owned and financed by private investors, while the other two divisions would remain wholly owned by the government. The Secondary Market Operations Division was initially capitalized by the issuance of $92.8 million of Federal National Mortgage Association preferred stock to the Secretary of the Treasury. Additional preferred stock subscriptions by the Secretary of the Treasury were authorized under subsequent acts,with the total of such authorizations aggregating $317.8 million. This authorized preferred stock was issued only as needed to support Fannie Mae's borrowings. The outstanding preferred stock was to be retired as rapidly as possible. To this end, Fannie Mae purchased from the Treasury the portion of stock that was not needed to finance operations and held it as FNMA treasury stock.

To transfer the Secondary Market Operations Division from government to private ownership, sellers of mortgages or loans were required to subscribe to common stock in an amount equal to one percent to two percent of the unpaid principal amounts of the mortgages and loans involved, with the exact amount to be determined from time to time by Fannie Mae. Borrowers were required to purchase stock equal to not more than one-half of one percent.

The Housing and Urban Development Act, effective September 1, 1968, partitioned Fannie Mae into two separate and distinct corporations. The Secondary Market

Operations Division was converted into a privately owned corporation called the Federal National Mortgage Association. The Special Assistance Functions Division and the Management and Liquidating Functions Division were transferred to a newly created government-owned corporation called the Government National Mortgage Association (Ginnie Mae). The outstanding common stock, which was previously nonvoting stock, was converted into no-par common stock with voting privileges. This common stock is now freely transferable and actively traded.

Although all government equity was eliminated, Fannie Mae will continue to be closely controlled by the government through the Secretary of Housing and Urban Development. The regulatory power of the Secretary of Housing and Urban Development continues for the life of the corporation. This is very broad authority, since the 1968 Charter Act states that the Secretary "shall make such rules and regulations as shall be necessary and proper to insure that purposes of this title are accomplished." The Act further states, "no stock, obligations, security, or other instrument shall be issued by the corporation without prior approval of the Secretary."

The functions of the new, privately owned Fannie Mae are identical to the functions previously conducted by the Secondary Market Operations Division of the government-owned Fannie Mae. However, since its activities now fall outside the constraints of the federal budget, it can fulfill the liquidity function more efficiently. Basically stated, Fannie Mae buys government-insured or guaranteed mortgages when investment funds are in short supply and sells these mortgages when funds are in abundance. Originally, Fannie Mae would set a rate at which it would buy or sell obligations and then fill all orders submitted at that rate. This system was replaced in 1968 by the free market system, whereby Fannie Mae announces the volume it wishes to buy or sell and then fills the lowest or highest bids submitted to make up that predetermined volume.

To finance these activities, Fannie Mae was given the authority to borrow money from private sources by any of three different methods:

* It may issue subordinated capital debentures in an amount not to exceed twice the net equity.
* It may issue securities, guaranteed by Ginnie Mae and backed by pools of mortgages. This type of borrowing is limited only by the size of Fannie Mae's mortgage portfolio.
* Fannie Mae has the right to borrow as long as the amount outstanding does not exceed a certain multiple of the sum of net equity and outstanding subordinated capital debentures. This borrowing authority has so far been in the form of debentures, short-term discount notes, and bank loans, and it supplies the bulk of the funds needed.

The short-term discount notes are similar to commercial paper. They are available in bearer form in denominations of $5,000, $10,000, $25,000, $100,000, $500,000, and $1,000,000, with a minimum allowable purchase of $50,000. Discount rates are established by Fannie Mae, and maturities are selected by the investor to fall within 30 to 270 days.

The debentures are sold through a fiscal agent and a nationwide network of dealers. The rate, maturity, and time of each offering must be approved by the Secretary of the Treasury. Various maturities have been offered. These noncallable debentures are available only in bearer form in denominations of $5,000, $10,000, $50,000, and $100,000. Interest on short-term debentures is payable at maturity, while interest on the intermediate and long-term debentures is payable semiannually at any Federal Reserve Bank or the Treasury. Denominational exchanges may be made only through the Federal Reserve Bank of New York.

By statute, these obligations are a lawful investment for any U.S. government trust fund, and they may be used by commercial banks as collateral for Treasury tax and loan accounts. National banks and state member banks may invest in them without regard to statutory limitations, and they are eligible as collateral for advances by Federal Reserve Banks to member banks. They are not guaranteed by the government either directly or indirectly for either principal or interest.

As for *tax treatment*, interest income and any capital gains or losses are subject to taxation under the Internal Revenue Code. Unlike other federal agency securities, however, they contain no specific exemptions from state or local taxation.

3. The *Government National Mortgage Association*, popularly known as *Ginnie Mae*, came into corporate existence on September 1, 1968, pursuant to the terms of the Housing and Urban Development Act of 1968. The purpose of Ginnie Mae was to assume the Special Assistance Functions Division and the Management and Liquidation Functions Division of the Federal National Mortgage Association. Ginnie Mae is wholly owned by the government.

The Special Assistance Functions Division retains the same character that it had under Fannie Mae. Originally, this division could operate only under Presidential authority to purchase selected types of home mortgages, pending the establishment of their marketability. The division was later authorized to purchase selected types of home mortgages, as designated by Congress from time to time. An example of the latest Congressional authority is the temporary allocation of funds for purchase of mortgages to finance the rehabilitation of deteriorating housing for subsequent resale to low-income home purchasers.

Funds for the operation of these programs are obtained by borrowing from the Treasury and by the sale of participation certificates to private investors under the Participation Sales Act.

The Management and Liquidating Functions Division of Ginnie Mae also retained the original functions it had under Fannie Mae, although these were broadened by the Housing Act of 1964, the Participation Sales Act of 1966, and the Housing and Urban Development Act of 1968. The original functions of this division were to manage and liquidate a mortgage portfolio consisting of mortgages acquired from authorized sources. Liquidation is accomplished through regular principal payments, prepayments, or foreclosures, and by sales of mortgages to private investors without disrupting normal market conditions. These functions are financed principally by Treasury borrowings, portfolio liquidations, and sales of participations in mortgage pools.

The Management and Liquidating Functions Division is most important because it acts as a fiduciary to substitute private funds for government financing of mortgages or other obligations acquired by various Federal agencies. The Housing Act of 1964, and later the Participation Sales Act of 1966, specifically authorized Ginnie Mae, under its Management and Liquidating Functions Division, to create trusts consisting of pools of mortgages and loans, from which participations may be sold to private investors. A trust fund is created to receive as trust assets the various mortgages or other obligations of an agency. Thus when the participations are sold, the investor does not acquire a participation in a pool of mortgages, but rather a participation in a trust fund. As trustee, Ginnie Mae still holds the loans in which the investor is theoretically participating. If collections on any pooled obligations from which participations were sold after June 3, 1966, are insufficient to cover required distributions, the trust or agencies must reimburse Ginnie Mae for the difference.

When Fannie Mae was converted to private ownership in 1968, all of its outstanding participation certificates were transferred to Ginnie Mae's Management and Liquidating Functions Division. Since this conversion, Ginnie Mae has not issued any new participation certificates under its own name.

All participation certificates issued by Fannie Mae or Ginnie Mae are guaranteed by Ginnie Mae as to both principal and interest. These certificates do not carry any guarantee by the government, although the Secretary of the Treasury has stated that the Treasury would make any loans necessary to Ginnie Mae to enable it to meet its obligations. The United States Attorney General issued an opinion in November 1966 stating that Fannie Mae's guarantee of certificates issued by its Management and Liquidating Functions Division imparts the moral backing of the full faith and credit of the U.S. government.

Each issue of these participation certificates was issued through a syndicate of underwriting dealers. The certificates are not callable. The early issues were available only in registered form, but the later issues were registered at the option of the buyer. Most issues offered denominations of $5,000, $10,000, $25,000, $100,000, $500,000, and $1,000,000. Interest is payable semiannually.

By statute, these certificates are a lawful investment for any U.S. government trust fund, and they may be used by commercial banks as collateral for Treasury tax and loan accounts. National banks and state member banks may invest in them without regard to statutory limitations, and they are eligible as collateral for advances by Federal Reserve Banks to member banks.

The Housing and Urban Development Act of 1968 gave Ginnie Mae the authority to graduate the timely payment of principal and interest on trust certificates or other securities that are issued by Fannie Mae or by other approved financial institutions and that are based on a trust or pool composed of FHA-insured or VA-guaranteed mortgages.

As for *tax treatment*, these certificates are not exempt from any provision of the Internal Revenue Code. Participation certificates, unlike most Federal agency obligations, carry no specific exemption from state or local taxation.

*Mortgage-Backed Securities Guaranteed
by Ginnie Mae*

When the Housing and Urban Development Act was passed in 1968, it established the Federal National

Mortgage Association's Secondary Market Operations as a private corporation under the name of FNMA. It also set up the Government National Mortgage Association, called GNMA, whose purpose is to make real estate investments attractive to institutional investors.

The most attractive security offered is called the *fully modified pass-through.* FHA and VA mortgages represent an asset pool behind these securities, on which timely payment of principal and interest is guaranteed by GNMA. In turn, the GNMA guarantee is backed by the full faith and credit of the U.S. government.

The securities are issued in denominations of $25,000, $30,000, and $10,000 increments thereafter.

Because of their full faith and credit guarantee, the mortgage-backed securities are eligible as collateral for Treasury tax and loan accounts and for Federal Reserve bond advances and discounts. They are also eligible for national banks to purchase without being subject to the legal limitations placed on investment securities. Since the IRS has ruled that owners of such securities have an undivided interest in the mortgage pool backing them, savings institutions can purchase these securities without jeopardizing their tax status.

MORTGAGE-BACKED PASS-THROUGH SECURITIES

Perhaps the most spectacular development in the government securities market since the early seventies has been the growth in mortgage-backed pass-through securities. During the late 1960s the thrift industry, which had been the primary source of single-family mortgages, was apparently subject to too many pressures and fluctuations to be counted on to supply the necessary funds. With the creation of GNMA in 1968 came an entirely new security, a cross between a publicly traded bond and a single-family mortgage. It was a security, like a note or bond, representing an interest in a pool of mortgages and bearing the guarantee of GNMA. These were called *mortgage-backed pass-through securities* (MBSs) because they were backed by federally insured single-family mortgages, on which the principal and interest payments were "passed through" to the holder of the security. The actual issuer of the MBS is a *mortgage banker*, perhaps a small company that the security owner never heard of. The mortgage banker services all the loans in the pool, collecting the individual monthly payments and passing the funds along, minus a servicing fee, 45 days later.

There are currently over 50,000 pools of GNMA pass-throughs in existence, representing a principal of over $70 billion. Since these pools are issued by a large number of mortgage bankers, the only thing giving the market any homogeneity is the presence of GNMA's guarantee of timely payment of principal and interest, which incorporates the full faith and credit of the Treasury.

Within the first five years of the eighties, both the Federal Home Loan Mortgage Corporation (FHLMC) and FNMA began to issue and guarantee MBSs. Theirs, however, are backed by conventional mortgages, and their guarantees do not incorporate the full faith and credit of the Treasury. As one might expect, their securities carry a higher market yield than do GNMAs, and the market is less liquid. Yet both of their markets are growing all the time.

Because of their mortgage-like nature, the market for pass-through securities has some distinct differences from the market for other debt securities. Traditionally, mortgage trades have been done for settlement several months in the future, when the mortgages are available for delivery. Pass-through securities are traded for settlement from a few days to six months in the future, with the vast majority settling from one to three months after the trade.

TBA Confirmation

With such a long period between a trade and its settlement, the trade must be executed with some inherent uncertainties. Although both parties can determine the approximate size of the security traded and usually the coupon of the pool, they do not know any of the other things necessary to settle the trade. They do not know the exact pool number, the exact principal amount, the issuing mortgage banker, or the exact maturity. Thus the confirmation issued is known as a *TBA (to be announced) confirmation.* This confirmation records the approximate trade agreed to, with exact information to be exchanged as late as forty-eight hours before the settlement is to occur.

Twelve-Year Average Life Assumption

Even when the information is exchanged, some important things are unknown. One is the final maturity of the pool. Each month the principal payment is passed through, along with an interest payment. Some part of this is the regular monthly payment, but part is unscheduled, as a result of such things as prepayments or foreclosures. So we can see that each pool has a different actual maturity and that no one can predict what it will be. Since the maturity is crucial to the derivation of yield to maturity, pass-through traders had to adopt a convention for determining price and yield.

The convention, called the *twelve-year average life assumption,* is based on the FHA's experience of over thirty years of single-family mortgages. The FHA found that the average mortgage in its study lasted twelve years before it was paid down. Thus pass-through traders have adopted the convention that the securities will make 143 regular monthly payments of principal and interest, and then pay off completely in the 144th month. Although its unlikely that any pool, among the over 50,000 created, has ever had that exact history, the market has accepted the convention.

Settlement

One needs to make other adjustments to deal in pass-throughs. For example, unlike notes and bonds, pass-throughs pay interest and principal monthly, instead of semiannually. As a result, pass-through securities transactions settle on only one day each month, usually the third Wednesday. Since the marketplace is very large and trading volume is relatively high, compressing a month's worth of settlements into one day can create a logjam. As if that weren't enough of a problem, pass-through settlement entails physical delivery, not wire transfer. So once a month you have the makings of an explosion. Dealers try to reduce the paperwork by *pairing off transactions*, that is, by eliminating the delivery of offsetting purchases and sales to the same party. In spite of that effort, as many as 20% of each month's pass-through trades fail to settle on the third Wednesday of the month. By the end of that week, though, most of the failed trades have settled.

The monthly payment of principal and interest has another serious implication. In all securities, some dividends or interest payments are sent to the wrong party, because the names in the computer don't reflect a recent change of ownership. Those payments are usually held in escrow by the receivers until their rightful owners claim them. For securities that pay interest twice a year, this is a small annoyance. For a security that pays interest and principal twelve times a year, tracking down dividends owed you but paid to someone else can be thoroughly aggravating.

A final caveat to anyone wanting to trade pass-throughs: Because the monthly payment of principal reduces the remaining principal on the security, the lending and borrowing of pass-throughs to facilitate deliveries is very rare. This would make the shorting of pass-throughs very difficult, and affect the liquidity of the market, were it not for the availability of the forward market. This means that virtually all dealer short sales are concentrated in the delivery months further out, instead of the ones closer in.

As time marches on, and those further-out months become closer in, dealers who are short must do something about making delivery. Since borrowing pass-through securities is not really feasible, they will offer to buy securities for immediate delivery and sell the same coupon security for a later month, using a TBA confirmation for the sale. This is called a dollar roll, and it can provide a very attractive financing vehicle for the pass-through owner.

To understand dollar rolls, you must understand the mathematics of forward delivery prices. The relationship of prices for current delivery to those for later delivery is a function of yields on the security in question and on short-term investments. For example, if pass-throughs yield 11% and short-term instruments yield 8%, the price for the security should decline as the delivery is postponed, to compensate the buyer for the interest lost in the interim. How much should it decline? In this case, ¼ point a month, which is the 3% yield difference divided by 12. Thus, if the price for immediate delivery is 100, the price for delivery one month later should be 99¾.

The need to find securities for delivery can distort this relationship. A dealer who is short may be willing to pay 100¼ for immediate delivery and sell for one-month-later delivery at 99¾. That extra ¼ point may not seem to make much difference, but it has the effect of raising the owner's annualized yield to 14% (the 8% annual rate on the short-term investment plus 6%, the ½ point multiplied by 12). Dollar roll transactions have become so popular that some of the regulatory agencies have issued rules covering their use by such institutions as commercial banks and savings and loan associations.

The issuance of pass-through securities differs significantly from the issuance of Treasuries of direct issue agencies. Instead of an announced issue or auction by a centralized entity, pass-throughs are sold by each of the originating mortgage bankers, without any control by the guaranteeing agency. Furthermore, they are often sold many months before they are delivered and before they even exist. As a result, the availability of figures from GNMA, FHLMC, and FNMA as to how many pass-throughs were *created* during a certain month may bear no relation to the numbers that were *sold* during the month. To complicate matters, mortgage bankers may not know exactly how many mortgages are going to close during the month, and they may sell more or fewer securities than they think they will create. The supply of pass-throughs being sold at any one time, therefore, is virtually impossible to know. Since mortgage bankers may be correcting the number of securities they need to sell up to the last minute, the pass-through market can be much more volatile than the Treasury market, and price relationships between the two securities can swing wildly. Substantial fortunes have been made and lost in arbitraging those price relationships.

DERIVATIVE PRODUCTS

One of the characteristics of the fixed income markets since the late sixties has been a high degree of interest-rate volatility. Who is to blame for that volatility has been a subject of endless debate — as well as more than a few political campaigns — but the markets have had to adapt to it nonetheless. Along with the volatility have come large budget deficits and a large volume of Treasury securities issues.

The Primary Dealer community has limited capital with which to distribute this large volume of securities, and that shortage of capital has been exacerbated by the volatility. Clearly, the dealers had somehow to lay off part of their very high risk.

The solution turned out to be *derivative products*, or investment products whose price performance is derived from another instrument. The best known derivative product is financial futures, but the market has also developed options, both exchange-traded and over-the-counter. Collectively, derivative products have changed forever the face of the fixed income markets — especially the government securities market.

Financial Futures

The original derivative product in the fixed income markets was a financial futures contract. *Futures contracts*, which have traded for many years in the agricultural arena, are bilateral agreements to make and take delivery of a physical item at some point in the future. Originally, agricultural products traded for future delivery on an over-the-counter basis. However, because of the predictable seasonal nature of agricultural demand and supply, trading for future delivery became larger than trading for immediate delivery. Futures exchanges were founded to bring order to a chaotic marketplace and to standardize the contracts, thereby enabling buyers to unwind their positions without going back to the original sellers.

What worked for wheat and pork bellies would also work for debt securities. In 1970 the Chicago Board of Trade began trading in futures on GNMA pass-throughs, and in 1975 the same exchange began trading in futures on Treasury bonds. If the daily trading volume in Treasuries is so much larger than the trading volume in GNMAs, why was the GNMA contract started first? Simply because there was already a liquid market in GNMA securities for forward delivery, and the CBT wanted to give a new concept every chance to succeed.

Succeed it did, beyond their wildest imaginations. In 1985, the bond futures contract traded a larger volume than any other futures contract, between 100,000 and 200,000 contracts a day. In terms of representative dollar volume, it traded more than any other single exchange-traded instrument. Stock index futures and options, which were introduced in the early eighties, trade more contracts on a daily basis, but each contract represents only a fraction of the principal, and risk, of the CBT bond contract.

Often the liquidity provided by the traders in the CBT bond pit has been essential to the smooth functioning of the bond market itself.

The primary reason for its trading success is that the CBT contract is a proxy for the entire long-term bond market. That is, at expiration, any Treasury bond with more than 20 years to maturity can be delivered in satisfaction of the contract. Obviously, some mechanism was needed to equate, for delivery purposes, all the deliverable issues, with a variety of coupons, maturities, and yields.

The mechanism chosen by the CBT was the creation of an imaginary bond that the futures contract represented: an 8%, 20-year bond. Thus the price at which the futures contract trades is the one at which an 8%, 20-year bond would be delivered when the contract expires. Other coupons and maturities are equated to the imaginary security through the use of *conversion factors*, which adjust the principal amounts of bonds to be delivered. Bonds with coupons higher than 8% and maturities longer than 20 years have conversion factors higher than 1. When $100,000 is divided by the conversion factor, the deliverable amount of securities is determined, and that amount can be delivered at the futures price.

As an example, an 11¼% bond with 29 years and 9 months to maturity has a conversion factor of 1.334. You could deliver $74,399.23 of this security per contract sold ($100,000 ÷ 1.334). By itself, that doesn't help us much, but the contract price, multiplied by the conversion factor, gives us the equivalent delivery price for the security. For our 11¼% bond, assuming a futures price of 75½, the equivalent delivery price would be 100.717, or 100 $^{23}\!/_{32}$ (75.5 × 1.334). The equivalent delivery price can be compared to the current price for the security to see if it makes sense to select this security for delivery. Among all the deliverable securities, one is, by this calculation, the *cheapest to deliver*, and that is what the futures contract follows.

The equivalent delivery price and the current price for the security are almost never the same, even for the "cheapest to deliver" security. Why? When bonds can be carried at a profit, the futures price is always lower than the equivalent delivery price, and when the yield curve is inverted, the futures contract is always higher. This phenomenon, called *convergence*, is purely a function of the cost of carry.

If you could buy a bond to yield 12%, finance it at 8%, and sell it in three months for today's price, you could lock up a 4% profit per year, or 1% per quarter. In such a case, the futures contract should decline in price for each quarterly expiration, by approximately the cost of carry divided by the conversion factor. In the case of our 11¼% bond, the next delivery contract should be trading at about 74¾ (75.5 ÷ ¼.334). If you were to buy the bond, finance it, sell the futures contract, and deliver the bond at futures expiration, you should realize 8%, the short-term yield. This relationship, which is basic to the futures markets, is still not yet comprehended by many bond market participants, who still think that they can buy bonds, sell futures, and realize the full bond yield.

Interest Rate Options

If the theory surrounding financial futures is relatively straightforward, the theory surrounding options is anything but simple. Whereas a futures contract is a bilateral agreement requiring both sides to perform at expiration, an option is the right to institute a transaction at any time before expiration. If the buyer and seller of a futures contract share equal status, the buyer of an option has decidedly better position than the seller.

Not surprisingly, then, the option buyer pays the seller a price for that better position. That price, called the premium, is a function of several factors:

* *Strike price*: The price at which the option buyer can execute the transaction.
* *Term*: The number of days until the option expires.

* *Investment yield:* The yield to the holder of the security that underlies the option.
* *Alternative yield:* The yield to the holder of an instrument that matures at the same time as the option expires.
* *Price volatility:* The historical or implied volatility of the price of the item that underlies the option.

Based on this information, you can calculate (or buy a computer program to calculate) the "theoretical value" of any option. *Theoretical value* is the premium level at which a theoretical investor would be indifferent between owning the option and the equivalent position in the underlying instrument. For a call, or the right to buy the instrument, the equivalent position would be owning the instrument itself. For a *put*, or the right to sell the instrument, the equivalent position would be short the instrument itself.

Obviously, however, from even this basic information, the risk inherent in the positions isn't at all the same. When you buy the instrument and the price falls 10 points, you are out the full 10 points. Had you bought a call on the instrument for 2 points, you could lose only those 2 points, no matter how far the instrument itself fell. On the other hand, should prices remain relatively the same, the option's value would most likely decline until, at expiration, most or all of the 2 points would have disappeared.

This property has caused options to be termed *wasting assets*, which has given them a connotation that they do not deserve. Options have often been regarded by regulators as speculative, or inherently inferior, investment vehicles, for two reasons:

* They afford higher leverage than is currently available in common stocks (but lower leverage than is generally available in government securities);
* they are wasting assets.

This image has probably done more to obscure the true nature of options than any other possible misconception. The true value of options — and of futures, for that matter — is that they can change the nature of the underlying instrument, and thus afford the portfolio manager a much wider arsenal of management weapons.

Used in conjunction with positions in the underlying instrument, derivative instruments can add or subtract volatility, increase or decrease risk, and enhance or reduce total return. Certain combined positions have become relatively well known among options professionals:

* *Covered call:* This is the sale of a call against the holding of the underlying instrument. Here the manager is selling the potential for large gains in the future in exchange for cash today.

* *Married put:* This is the purchase of a put against the holding of the underlying instrument. The manager is buying insurance against catastrophic market decline, with the cost to be subtracted from the instrument's total return.

* *Cash-secured put write:* This is the sale of a put against the holding of a cash-equivalent instrument. The manager is selling the potential to profit from a rise in rates in exchange for cash today.

* *Money market call (90/10):* This is the purchase of call against the holding of money market instruments. The term "90/10" comes from the practice of investing 90% of the funds in short-term instruments and 10% of the funds in calls, but that description is somewhat outdated. Here the manager reduces substantially the risk of owning the underlying instrument, with the cost of that risk reduction being subtracted from the total return of the short-term portfolio.

Other option strategies may be appropriate, depending on the manager's market outlook and the relative cost of various options. Choosing among them requires you to know some basic rules about options and options markets.

An option's theoretical value is made up of two parts:

* *Intrinsic value*, or the option's value if exercised immediately, and

* *Time value,* or the value of being able to delay the decision to exercise or not.

Intrinsic value can be positive if, for example, a call has a strike price of 70 and the underlying instrument is trading at 80. Or it can be negative, as in the case of the same call, but with the instrument trading at 65. But time value is never negative. An option with positive intrinsic value is called *in-the-money;* one with zero intrinsic value is called *at-the-money;* and one with negative intrinsic value is called *out-of-the-money.* Time value is made up of the premium minus the intrinsic value. Obviously, when an option is out-of-the-money, the negative intrinsic value is added to the premium to derive the time value.

It is important to remember that:

* *The higher the intrinsic value, the lower the time value.* In other words, the options with higher premiums, and thus higher intrinsic values, will hold their prices better over time than those with lower premiums.
* *Unless the premium is very high, options do not move as fast as the underlying instruments.* The percentage of the underlying instrument's move that an option moves is called the *delta,* or *hedge ratio.* The delta of an at-the-money option is usually about .5 and it rises or falls as the intrinsic value rises or falls.
* *An option's premium does not increase as much as the term increases.* For an at-the-money option, the premium will increase by the square root of the increase of the term. Thus if a three-month option has a premium of one point, you would expect the six-month option to have a premium of 1.414.

With this information and several uninterrupted days, you could work out many options strategies, but we need to get on with the tour; let's see how a typical Primary Dealer conducts its business.

Chapter 6

Inside
a Primary Dealer

If a market, or marketplace, is defined as the location where buyers and sellers of a commodity meet, then there is no government securities marketplace at all. Unlike a stock exchange, the government securities market has no central location at which all trades take place. Instead, the market is made up of a *network* of participants, located all over the United States and in several foreign countries, who buy and sell a variety of securities issued by, or related to, the U.S. Treasury. Instead of sharing a common meeting place, they share access not only to the information necessary to transact business, but also to each other.

Just like a stock exchange, where participants are acting in specific and widely recognized capacities, the participants in the government securities market play specific and generally accepted roles. Certain firms have undertaken the responsibility of making markets to the public in all government and agency securities, bidding on all Treasury and agency offerings and dealing directly with the Federal Reserve Bank of New York's Open Market Trading Desk. These firms make up the list of *Primary Dealers*, and are members of the Primary Dealer Association.

Other firms act as intermediaries between the Primary Dealers, providing them with information about the best bids and offerings in any security, and executing their trades with other primary dealers. These firms, called *brokers*, maintain an electronic network of CRT terminals, called *screens*, which show the highest bid and lowest offering currently available on every security they trade. These screens — which, in effect, create the ability to trade with the brokers — are currently available only to the Primary Dealers, although attempts have been made through the courts to give access to the screens (and hence to the brokers) to anyone with a trade to do.

As of now, however, anyone who is not a Primary Dealer or a broker is a *customer*. Customers occupy a very different role from a dealer, even if the business they do looks very much like the business a Primary Dealer does. In many ways they are on the outside looking in, even if they have larger capital than a primary dealer, maintain larger trading positions, and routinely do more business on a daily basis. Some of the differences between a Primary Dealer and a customer relate solely to access to market information, but other differences relate to such esoteric questions as how late in the day one party can deliver securities to another. For all these reasons, the line dividing Primary Dealers from the rest of the trading community has taken on a very great significance.

Another participant in the market is the Federal Reserve System, along with its agent, the Federal Reserve Bank of New York. As implementor of monetary policy, the New York Bank's Open Market desk enters the market on a daily basis to add or drain reserves within the banking system, through the mechanism of the government securities market. Since the Fed never comments on the reasons for its actions, and since the minutes of its Open Market Committee meetings are not released for some time after the meetings themselves, there has grown up a whole army of "Fed watchers" who try to divine the monetary policy of the country by observing every little action of the central bank.

THE PLAYERS

Primary Dealers

The Primary Dealers make up the most visible part of the government securities market. A firm becomes a primary dealer by being so designated by the Federal Reserve Bank of New York. The Fed signifies that event by allowing the firm to install a direct line, called a *Fed wire*, between the firm's trading desk and the one at the Fed. Then the firm becomes one of a select group of dealers who can deal directly with the Fed and with the brokers.

The process of becoming a Primary Dealer is a relatively long one, in which the dealer gradually builds up its daily volume of business in the market. After it has been running a respectable volume of business, it approaches the Fed to ask for recognition. Usually, the firm must go through a period of making regular reports to the Fed on all aspects of its market activity, until the Fed finally decides that it is a significant enough factor in the market to be awarded Primary Dealer status.

The number of Primary Dealers varies, with some dropping off the list due to merger or other reasons and others being added.

The list of primary dealers can be broken down into three general groups:

* Full-service securities firms, such as Drexel Burnham Lambert Government Securities, Inc., or Bear Stearns & Co.
* Commercial banks, like Chase Manhattan Bank, N.A., or Chemical Bank.
* Specialist government securities firms, such as Kleinwort Benson Government Securities, Inc. or Briggs Schaedle & Co., Inc.

Each of these groups, compared with the others, has some advantages and some disadvantages in the areas of available capital, concentration of effort, and breadth of scope.

A *full service securities firm* has the widest range of services to offer to a customer, since they generally deal in a wide variety of fixed income securities. This means, however, that their salespeople cannot concentrate their efforts on the government securities market. Also, they tend to have limited capital available to trade the market, so they are dependent on the availability of financing.

A *commercial bank*, on the other hand, has a large reservoir of trading capital through its access to the Fed Funds market. Its status as a commercial bank, however, precludes it from dealing in debt securities issued by corporations. So the range of services it can offer to a customer is necessarily limited to government and agency securities, as well as the normal commercial banking services.

The *specialist government dealer* is the oldest type of firm, dating from a time when the government market was a world unto itself. Their number has been falling as a fraction of the total market, but several still survive. Their limited capital positions and lack of a wide product mix are offset by a strong tradition and their ability to concentrate all their resources on one market.

Government Securities Brokers

If buyers and sellers of government securities do not have a central meeting place, they do have the government securities brokers. These firms, virtually unknown outside the government securities market, serve as a conduit between the Primary Dealers and do business only with the dealers. They have names that very few people have heard, like FBI, RMJ, Garban, or Chapdelaine. At least one broker, though has a name that many customers have heard of, and perhaps done business with — Telerate.

All the brokers maintain a network of CRT terminals on the trading and sales desks of the Primary Dealers. Those screens show the best bids and offers the brokers are in touch with for all the issues they broker. Since that list covers many times the number of issues that can be shown on one screen, the issues are arranged on "pages" with all the bills on one page, short coupon securities on another, and so on. Not only do the screens shown the best bids and offers, with the size of each, but they also show any trades that the broker executes in these securities. Thus, by looking at all the screens provided by all the brokers, a dealer can determine quite accurately where the market is and what his bid or offer should be.

With the exception of Telerate, however, these screens are not available to anyone who is not a Primary Dealer. By the same token, only Primary Dealers can have direct lines to brokers. This obviously anticompetitive arrangement has been challenged in court by the Department of Justice, as well as by firms outside the Primary Dealer community. Yet it continues as it has for many years. One reason is that the Fed is very satisfied with the Primary Dealer arrangement, since it keeps the market manageable enough for them to control, and gives them an arena in which to execute monetary policy. Should access to the brokers and their screens be opened to firms who are not Primary Dealers, the advantages of being a Primary Dealer would disappear, and most of them would not be able to justify the higher costs and risks of the role.

Government Securities Customers

Basically, anyone who does business in government securities, and who is not either a Primary Dealer or a broker, is considered a customer. This category covers a wide range of firms or parts of firms. Some fall under the traditional heading of a customer, like a commercial bank, savings bank, savings and loan association, insurance company, or pension plan. These all tend to have the same needs in the market: They have money that needs to be invested, some of it in government securities. With the large Federal deficits of the last ten years, and the consequent large issues of government securities, the yield spreads between governments and other securities have narrowed. This phenomenon has brought many customers who had never utilized governments into the market, as they sought the additional safety of governments at an historically small sacrifice in yield.

Other, less traditional, players in the market are also thought of as customers. Some of these are dealers in securities, including governments, who may do a large daily volume of business, but who are not Primary Dealers. Some of the transactions they execute may be for their own customers, and some may be for their own trading accounts. Many stock and commodity brokerage houses fall into this category.

There are also many firms whose sole purpose is to trade for their own account, using the high degree of leverage available in governments. Often these firms are manned by successful traders from Primary Dealers who, feeling the entrepreneurial spirit, raised seed money and went into business for themselves. Although these "speculators" are often thinly capitalized, they represent an important source of liquidity for the market because they trade actively and are often willing to assume large positions.

Perhaps it is best to think of the government securities market as a giant wheel. At the center are the brokers, who maintain a network of both screens and telephones to all the Primary Dealers, but to no one else. Around that hub are clustered the Primary Dealers, doing business with each other, the brokers, the Fed, and customers. Around the outside are all the customers, whether traditional institutional investors, non-Primary Dealers, or speculators. Transactions tend to flow toward the center of the wheel or away from it (that is, from customer to Primary Dealer to broker and vice versa) more often than around it (from customer to customer or from one Primary Dealer to another). How each trade takes place, though, is largely a function of the nature of the individual securities.

WHO DOES WHAT INSIDE A PRIMARY DEALER?

If you were to walk into the trading room of a Primary Dealer, you could be forgiven for feeling a little disoriented. The internal structure of a government bond dealer has evolved, over many years, in response to the demands of a very specialized marketplace. In recent years, the marketplace itself has changed with alarming speed, and not every dealer has been able to adjust at the same rate. As a result, there are about as many kinds of structures — physical as well as managerial — as there are dealers.

In laying out a trading room, the biggest problem facing a dealer is the need for good lines of sight for visual communication: Too many people have to be packed into too little space. Primary Dealers solve this problem in different ways. For example, one made a trading room out of an abandoned dinner theater. One had the details of all the trading room furniture custom-designed from the beginning. Whatever the solution, trading rooms always give outsiders a feeling of claustrophobia.

When you first enter a trading room, you may find it hard to determine who is doing what. All the desks are occupied by people talking on the telephone, writing on pads of paper. Those who are not on the phone are staring at monitors on their desks, the screens overflowing with numbers. Every so often one of the numbers flashes, or someone stands up and yells to someone else. Often, a loudspeaker fills the room with a constant drone of conversations between the main office and the branch offices.

In addition to feeling closed in, a visitor might also suspect that the traders are speaking a foreign language. In fact, government bond trading has a language all its own: "Bid a million old ten years," and "Can we do the reverse roll give three and a half ?"

Surely this is the ultimate form of confusion. Not really. This firm is merely dealing with and reacting to the immediate matters of the market, not with issues stretching into the future. As we will see, it is really very organized.

Most Primary Dealers are divided into three parts: trading, sales, and research, each with its own manager.

THE TRADING DESK

The central part of every Primary Dealer is known as the *trading desk*, although obviously the phrase refers not to the funiture, but to the traders occupying the desks and dealing in all the different securities and instruments in which the dealer does business. Commensurate with the importance of trading, these desks are usually located in the center of the trading area. Each trader's desktop is at least partly taken up with a series of monitors, provided by the government securities brokers who are at the real center of the marketplace. Each monitor shows the best market that the corresponding broker is in touch with at the moment. So from all the screens, traders can construct the best bid and offer in any security that they trade. Figure 6.1 shows what a screen might look like for, say, coupon securities maturing under two years, or *short coupons*.

Figure 6-1. A Short Coupon Trading Screen.

12 5/8	5/86	100.30-101.02	2X1	9 7/8	12/86	101.20-24	5X1
13 3/4	5/86	104.08-	3X	10	12/86	-101.30	X3
13	6/86	104.08-12	10X5	9 3/4	1/87	101.10-14	6X8
14 7/8	6/86			9	2/87	100.10-14	1X7
12 5/8	7/86	104.05 HIT	8	10	2/87	*101.21-25	2X5
8	8/86	99.29-01	3X5	10 7/8	2/87	102.29-C1	12X8
11 3/8	8/86	103.00-04*	5X5	12 3/4	2/87	TAK 102.07	7
12 3/8	8/86	104.00-04	3X8	10 1/4	3/87	102.03-07	7X15
11 7/8	9/86	-103.28+	X8	10 3/4	3/87	102.27-31	1X5
12 3/4	9/86	104.05-09+	10X6	9 3/4	4/87	101.09-11	20X25
11 5/8	10/86	103.19-19+	30X50	9 1/8	5/87	100.06-08	9X5
6 1/8	11/86	97.20-98.20	1X1	12	5/87	105.00-04	2X5
10 3/8	11/86	102.06-10+*	15X10	12 1/2	5/87	105.20 HIT	10
11	11/86	102.29-01	1X1	14	5/87	-108.05	X6
13 7/8	11/86	106.12+-16	7X10	8 1/2	6/87		
16 1/8	11/86	-109.21	X10	10 1/2	6/87	102.19-23	2X3

Although this may look like a meaningless collection of numbers, it is in fact a great deal of information presented in a small space. Each issue is identified by its coupon rate (such as 12⅝% in the first issue listed) and its maturity date (May of 1986 in the same issue). The next bit of information is the best bid and offer the broker is in touch with at the moment. In this case, the best bid is 100 ^{30}⁄₃₂ for 2 million, and the best offer is 101²⁄₃₂, with 1 million offered. Each issue has that information displayed, with a few exceptions. Where only a bid or offer is available, only that side is shown, with the size of the bid or offer shown. When a bid has been hit, the word "HIT" appears on the screen, along with the amount traded. When an offering has been taken, it shows as "TAK", again with the amount. In each case the "HIT" or "TAK" flashes, to draw the viewer's attention to the trade.

The asterisks you see are a result of a special rule of the brokers' markets. Whoever makes a bid or offering on the screen is entitled to see a response to it before the rest of the market can act on it. Thus, in the case of 11⅜ of ⅚₆, about one third of the way down the left column, the 103¹⁵⁄₃₂ offering came in as a response to the 103 bid. It must be shown to the bidder before anyone else can take the offering. The asterisk disappears as soon as the bidder has seen the offering and declined to take it. Then the offering becomes available to everyone. Such screens are kept up-to-date in every sector of the Treasury market, agency securities, mortgage-backed securities, money market instruments, financing markets, and futures markets. With all of the brokers' screens set up on a desk, a trader has as complete a flow of information as any trader on any exchange in the world.

A *trader's* job is to buy and sell the specified securities for the firm's account and risk. By virtue of their Primary Dealer status, traders must make markets to the general public in all the securities they trade, but that role is not a good measure of their responsibilities. Since the Primary Dealers are the prime source of liquidity in the government market, and since the government market is still dominated by large customers — such as big banks and other institutions — the trader can be expected to bid for and offer large blocks of securities to a relatively small universe of customers. Because competition is fierce among the Primary Dealers, the trader can expect that a difference of one or two 32nds can spell success or failure.

In such a tight and competitive market, pressures can be intense. Information about which blocks of securities are around to be bid on, which issues are in short supply, which large blocks just traded, and which customers own which issues often can mean the difference between large profits and large losses. Traders can therefore be forgiven if they become protective of what they know. When customers expect to be given such information without the return flow of orders or information about what they are planning to do, they are often treated as adversaries. That's the trader's point of view. Of course, dealers themselves have varying levels of competence and knowledge, and from the customer's point of view, trading information and securities with one may be much more rewarding than with another. Astute customers will cultivate relationships with the dealers they need.

Traders are therefore required to perform a unique function; they endeavor to make profits in a highly sensitive, high-risk, fast-moving market environment through sheer hunch, intuition, and their "feel" of market trends. The ability to do so depends on a highly developed sense of professional and intuitive judgment. Traders must assess a multitude of influences seen or felt in the market during every minute of the trading day. The judgment of account managers and that of their traders cannot be "second-guessed," for this would destroy their unique function. They must play out their act to the end. There is not time for committee decisions. Price quotations are not subject to question; traders' quotes indicate exactly where they are willing to do business, whether others agree with them or not.

Traders are subject to great pressure, and trading is for the most part a young person's game. The pace and intensity of trading, combined with the emotional impact of dealing in unit trades in the millions, can take its toll on physical health. Traders can become ineffective because of loss-trading, which may result in an inability to trade with strong conviction. Traders play a numbers game, and their world is one of sheer arithmetic and emotional "feel" for the market. They have a hair-trigger reaction pattern to the trading pictures which they constantly see in the market. They may become myopic. From where traders view the world, everyone is out to take them apart. Customer profit, as they see it, must come out of their hide.

Treasury Bill Traders

Generally, there are two or more traders in the T-bill area. Each handles a specific type of bill or group of bills: short end, long end, inactive bills, active bills, 90-days, and so on. Treasury bill traders are also responsible for preparing the dealer's weekly bids in the bill auctions and the monthly year bill auctions.

Most of their time, however, is spent in making very large bids and offers, often well into the hundreds of millions of dollars, arbitraging between the bill market and the bill futures market, or executing a customer's swap orders in bills. Because bills are very liquid, have very low price volatility, and represent a very large percentage of all Treasury securities outstanding, these traders may represent half or more of the dealer's total daily trading volume in securities. Competition among the traders is fierce, and profit margins are razor thin. It is not unusual for $100 million bills to trade for a profit of $2,500 dollars or less. Since the lost interest on that amount of money for one night is over $27,000 at 10%, accuracy is paramount in the bill market. Here, more than anywhere else, knowing with whom you are dealing is the key to success.

Treasury Coupon Traders

Sitting somewhere near the bill traders, and at the center of the trading desk, are the people who trade Treasury notes and bonds. Because these securities pay interest seminannually, as if they had coupons attached, these people are traditionally called *coupon traders*. Usually, there are three of them or three groups of them. One group trades securities that mature in two years or less; they are called *short coupon traders*. Another group trades securities that mature from just over two years to ten years; they are called *intermediate coupon traders*. The last group, called *long coupon traders*, trades securities that mature beyond ten years. Although these divisions may appear arbitrary, they correspond to natural divisions within the securities market, as well as to divisions among customers, and they have evolved over many years.

1. *Short coupons* have traditionally been regarded as commercial bank securities, because commercial bank portfolios have historically stressed the liquidity inherent in shorter-term securities. Whatever logic may dictate, the short coupon market is still the preserve of the commercial banking sector. For this reason, and because the two-year note is issued on a monthly cycle, the short coupon market has become highly ritualized. Issues shorter than a year are usually traded against the yield equivalent of the closest bill, and issues between one and two years are traded based upon the market's perception of the month-to-month yield curve. It is not unusual to have a customer give a dealer a standing order to swap out one month on the curve for a yield pickup of 8 basis points and back one month for a giveup of 2 basis points. Such ritualized trading makes for small spreads, small profit margins, and a lot of spread trading. The large volume of securities available, along with the occasional large arbitrage opportunity, is all that relieves the boredom of continuously following the spreads.

2. The *intermediate coupons* are a different kind of security altogether. Here the customer base is much more varied than in the commercial banking sector. In fact, the intermediate sector is the meeting ground of all the market participants. Ranging all the way from money market funds taking the occasional foray into the three-year note to the pension fund shortening maturities by buying ten-year notes, the intermediate sector is like a street market. Everywhere you look is another kind of buyer or seller, with something different to accomplish.

This varied market makeup both comforts and challenges the intermediate coupon trader. With all these players, someone is always around to take the other side of traders' positions, but such a varied customer base taxes their ability to keep a finger on the market's pulse. The tremendous range of customers, coupled with the inability of most Primary Dealers to cover all sectors of this market, leads many intermediate coupon traders to rely much more on the brokers to provide them with the necessary liquidity, and much less on their sales network. The uncertainty of each issue's size and the shifting nature of the customer base make the intermediate sector the most fluid part of the market, if not the most liquid.

3. Liquidity is definitely not the hallmark of the long sector of the market, but *long coupon traders* have some powerful allies on their side. First, the customer base is well defined as the pension funds and arbitrageurs. Second, the futures market has grown to a large enough size that it can provide a significant source of liquidity. Third, the Treasury traditionally issues fewer bonds than any other kind of security. For long coupon traders, success depends on keeping track of a much smaller customer base, tracking their securities against a universe of corporate issues, and keeping a sharp eye on the futures market. In this way, the long coupon market has much more in common with the short coupon market than it does with the hodgepodge in the middle. Whatever their differences, though, the coupon traders on a good trading desk work like a well oiled machine, sharing market information, customer inquiries, and cross-market orders.

Other Trading Desks

While the coupon and bill traders are at the center of the trading universe, other traders play an important role. Three trading desks contribute a great deal to the Primary Dealer's arsenal:

1. The *agency trader* must oversee an array of securities that is mindboggling in its complexity. There are three major issuers of securities: the Federal Farm Credit

Bank System, the Federal Home Loan Bank System, and the Federal National Mortgage Association (FNMA). The credit quality of each of these issuers fluctuates, and the sizes of their issues vary. The agency trader's primary task is therefore to provide liquidity in a very fragmented market. Being asked to bid on an issue once every two months requires good records on the spreads between various issues, as well as a good network of customers.

2. The *mortgage-based securities desk* covers the various mortgage-backed securities. Here the trader must deal with a market that, in the recent past, has grown faster than any other debt market. Over the last few years, FNMA and FHLMC have joined GNMA as sponsors of mortgage-backed securities, so some variety is beginning to enter the market. The MBS trader's biggest problem, however, is the fragmented, unregulated, and secret method of issuance. Instead of regular auctions or public issues, new mortgage-backed securities are sold by thousands of mortgage bankers all over the country, for delivery months in the future, in amounts that may not correspond to the amount actually created. For these reasons, MBS traders must have a good flow of information from the marketplace and from the issuers in particular. Although trades are done in the brokers' market, a trader who depends too much on the brokers will have a hard time making money.

3. The *repo (financing or collateral) desk*, often the least known, can draw all the other desks together into a profitable team. Whether it is called the repo, financing, or collateral desk, it consists of the group of traders who control the availability and financing cost of securities. Their job is more complex than any other trader's, and the time pressures on them can get terribly intense. Yet their job is often overlooked and the desk is often not even part of the Primary Dealer department. Every day these traders match off available short-term money with securities to be financed, find securities to make deliveries for short sales,

and assist the clearance department to cover deliveries in which the other side has failed. Because of the huge cost of fails, and because the current high coupons have placed a potentially high cost on short sales, a good collateral desk can contribute as much to profitability as any other desk in the room.

The Trading Manager

The trading manager's job is to set the overall trading stance, or risk position, of the organization. The traders will perform according to the manager's specific objectives, but may be given latitude to trade within these objectives. For example, the trading manager may fear a market decline and instruct a bill trader to "short" the bill market in an amount of X dollars. At the same time, the long coupon trader may be instructed to "stay-even" and out of trouble. This means the long bond trader is not to short the market or run a "long" position. If required to offer a longer maturity bond, the trader should be reasonably certain of being able to cover the sale quickly, without losing money. If asked to bid a long bond issue, the trader should have a good idea at what price, and to whom, the issue can be sold quickly.

The trading manager then instructs the intermediate bond trader to "short the market" by a small amount (that is, to sell short a little), to test the downside vulnerability of this maturity range. In the event of resistance (that is, if prices do not decline below a certain point), the trader may quickly decide to purchase a few bonds to test the market's upside potential. The short bond trader may be instructed to "stay-even" because bills in the same maturity range as short bonds are already being shorted. The agency trader will probably perform a more usual role, which is to stay-even with the market. Market conditions can change quickly, however, and the trading manager must be prepared to reverse the game plan instantly. A successful manager does not have to be told twice upon seeing a change in market direction. He reacts immediately, passing down new instructions to the traders. *Flexibility* and *speed* are the hallmarks of all good traders.

As stated, traders may have great latitude to trade within the limitations imposed by the trading manager. In the preceding example, the bill trader could very well have purchased particular bill offerings while establishing a short, judging those bills to be a bargain at that moment. Or the trader could be making a routine bill "run" to another dealer (quoting the active bills, three-month, six-month, one-year, and "tabs," or tax anticipation bills, if any) and be "hit." Being "hit" means that the trader's bid price is accepted by another trader, who sells the securities based on his or her quoted price. This is the result of agreements among dealers that specify standard amounts to be transacted by a trader on his quoted market. Therefore, two explanations are possible for the situation in the preceding example where the trader was "hit" while trying to establish a short. Either the trader erred in quoting too aggressive a market, or another trader got in front of the first one in trying to establish his or her own short. A trader is usually simultaneously bidding and offering bills in the retail market, which can cause additional complications. In the last analysis, a trader who is having difficulty establishing a short can always use the "meat-ax" approach and slam bills into the market. But this reveals the plan to competitors, and they will be around later to move prices up gleefully when the trader returns to cover the short.

THE SALES FORCE

One of the most important functions a dealer can perform is to keep customers well informed concerning market conditions, thus insuring that customers' trading decisions will be as timely and as well executed as possible. Good coverage of reliable market information from the salesperson is a most essential ingredient in a portfolio manager's trading performance.

The function of the *salesperson*, or *contract person*, is to keep close tabs on trading activity in both the "retail" or nondealer market and the dealer market. On the one hand, salespersons earn their way with customers by giving them good "coverage" — by passing along important information and swapping ideas. In giving feedback to the traders, they also help them maintain a constant awareness of the trading pattern and mood of the retail market, which is essential to the traders' overall "feel" of the market.

The salesperson keeps in touch with major retail trading accounts hour by hour, or even minute by minute, in fast moving markets. Other less active accounts may receive calls once each day, once a week, or even once a month.

Some dealers like to maintain a large network of customer contacts, enabling them to "work out" transactions between buyers and sellers in the retail market without exposing trades to "the street." There are clear advantages to the customer in this situation.

Spread out around the traders, figuratively if not literally, are the members of the salesforce, acting as the contact points between the trading desk and the customer. This job requires a special ability to walk an emotional tightrope. While the trader has a clear mission to make as much money as possible for the dealer, customers are clearly, and naturally, looking after their own interests. The salesperson must defuse potentially adversarial relationships and redo the job day after day.

Good salespeople accomplish this by become the focal point and conduit for *information*. Contrary to the beliefs of many people both within and outside the market, the commodity traded is not securities or money, but information. Those who have good-quality information will make money more often than not. Those with bad, out-of-date, or too little information have a hard time showing a profit on a regular basis. This is true of customers, as well as of dealers.

What kinds of information make up this commodity? Some of it is quite simple. Who owns which securities? Who is short which ones? Along those who own an issue, who would sell it? At what price? When the Treasury is auctioning securities, who is willing to buy them? Again, at what price?

Some information is more complicated. Who has a futures position that hedges a particular position in securities? What large blocks of securities have recently traded between dealers, and between customers and dealers? At what prices? What do people think the market is going to do?

What people think the market is going to do serves to illustrate how information is the real commodity in the marketplace. A customer who has a block of securities to sell may simply ask the salesperson how the firm's traders feel about the market. If the salesperson responds that the traders are bearish, the customer may let the subject drop, feeling that bearish traders will not be good bidders. Somewhere along the line of many conversations, the customer will discover a firm whose traders are bullish, and may then reveal to the firm's salesperson that he or she has a block of securities for sale. Obviously, the customer wants to get more than the bid side of the market for the securities. With this dealer, the customer has a chance to get a better price, especially if the securities are offered to the dealer at the customer's price instead of asking for a bid. Had the customer told the bearish firm about the securities for sale, those traders, while not bidding aggressively for the securities, might move to sell the issue short, hoping to cover their short position at a cheaper price when the market falls.

If the marketplace may be thought of as a huge game of chess, the salespersons are the pawns. Unable to buy or sell on their own, as the trader or customer can, they are nonetheless vital to the game. They spend their day constantly on the phone, gathering and dispensing information, looking for potential buyers and sellers, convincing traders and customers to do business. Theirs is a vicarious or indirect participation in the market. Being a good salesperson requires enormous self-confidence, persistence, and a willingness to participate through someone else. The rewards are, in large part, monetary, but they also include the loyalty and affection of both customers and traders, along with the opportunity to assume a management role.

THE ECONOMICS DEPARTMENT

The *research group*, usually headed by the chief economist, is where the "Fed watchers" hang their hats. Generally, the research group is responsible for projections of Fed activity of significant economic announcements and analysis of their impact on market movement. The output of the research group is utilized by the trading desk in managing its position, but it is also made available to the firm's customers. Often, the output of the chief economist is published weekly as a form of public relations for the dealer. For larger customers, the economist may also be available for private consultations.

Either in one corner of the trading floor or in offices off the trading floor, the department's money market economist and staff ply their trade. In many firms these people are called the *Fed watchers* since a large part of their job is to interpret the actions of the Federal Reserve. But their job is really larger and more complicated than that. They must make sense out of all the economic data and political factors that come to bear on the market.

Part of the audience is the firm's customer base. In fact, a good money market economist is an important marketing tool. Firms whose economist commands a large following can turn that following into increased business. Since the economist appears to give advice and publications away without charge, the salesperson's task is to extract enough business from the customer to compensate the dealer.

As ultimate holders of negotiable contracts, customers require dealer organizations to clear their purchase and sale transactions. This would not be so if the *ideal* of a willing buyer for every willing seller, at a mutually acceptable price, at the same moment in time, were present in every transaction. The market being what it is, dealers fill the gap and equalize (or "clear") imbalances in bids and offers at any moment in time in the market through buying and selling out of their own accounts and at their risk.

Sometimes retail traders take a cavalier attitude toward dealers. Trading against the street without benefit of friends, however, can be very costly when the other fellow holds most of the chips.

Another part of the research department's audience is their own firm's traders and sales staff. Although not all the traders may agree with the economist's projections for the market, the expert's input is important both in the traders' attitudes and in the way salespersons talk to customers.

Although each economist interprets the job a little differently, they are all concerned with the same thing: determining the future course of interest rates by analyzing economic information. Since the Federal Reserve plays a major role in determining rates, and since the Fed is quite secretive about its motives and plans for rates, much of the economist's job lies in keeping track of everything the Fed does and fitting it into the larger scenario of interest rates and the market. Some economists begin with the Treasury's spending and tax collecting plans, deriving from them the demands on the banking system. Then they predict whether the Fed will need to add funds to or drain them from the banking system, interpreting the Fed's actions from that perspective. Others begin with the relative strength or weakness of the economy, add in the current and expected inflation rate, and thereby predict future Fed actions.

Whatever its method, the economics department puts out its conclusions in two ways. First, it publishes a pamphlet or letter, usually weekly, covering the salient points of its conclusions for the week. That pamphlet is sent to a mailing list of customers, potential customers, the press, and certain political figures. Second, the economist and/or staff members speak on a regular basis to the firm's traders and sales staff, as well as to customers. Between the written word and the spoken word, the economics department is a major part of what the world sees of a Primary Dealer.

Obviously, the dealer is made up of all three parts — traders, salespersons, economists — working together. The economist's feelings about the market, when communicated to a customer by a sales representative, may result in an order, which is handled by the trader of that security. One order may result in another transaction with another customer, and so on throughout the day.

FINANCING GOVERNMENT SECURITIES

With the large volume of government securities issued and traded every day in the marketplace, and with the limited capital available to the Primary Dealers, the ability to finance a large portion of the purchase price of any government security is essential to the operation of the market. The financing market has become so large that on many days the volume of securities financed exceeds the volume of securities traded. Since the financing market has the same degree of regulation as the securities market, and since very high leverage is available, it should not surprise us that most of the collapses of government securities dealers in the mid-eighties occurred in the financing market, not in the trading market.

Repos and Reverse Repos

The simplest method of financing securities is borrowing against them at the bank. This method, however, is almost never used in governments, because the lender views the resulting obligations as a collateralized loan. Such an arrangement means that the collateral could be frozen by a bankruptcy trustee for an extended time. Instead, financing of governments is usually done by a sale/purchase transaction called a *repurchase agreement*, or *repo*. In this case the owner of the securities sells them to the financer for immediate settlement and agrees to buy them back (or repurchase them) at a later date, paying interest on the money received during the interim. Under a repo, title passes to the financer for the period of the financing, thus removing the securities from any bankruptcy trustee's control.

If a sale and repurchase agreement is called a repo, a purchase and resale agreement is called a *reverse repo*. If holders of securities view repos as a method of financing securities owned, reverse repos are viewed as a method of putting short-term funds to work or of borrowing securities needed for delivery. Repo and reverse repo are opposite sides of the same transaction, so confusion often results. For example, the quarterly reports that savings and loans file with the Federal Home Loan Bank list securities financed by this method as "Reverse Repos," even though they are obviously repos from the S&L's point of view. Thus it behooves anyone doing business in the financing market to be absolutely sure what is being agreed to.

Inside a Financing Transaction

The financing can be accomplished in many ways, and not understanding the ins and outs of the business has been very expensive for many market participants. In the mid-eighties, there were several failures just because someone did not understand the complete transaction.

Although the concept of a repo transaction is simple in itself, the actual execution is not. Essentially, a repo is the exchanging of securities for cash today, with an agreement to reverse the transaction at some time in the future. That being said, the complications begin.   The parties must agree on:

* How much cash for each security?
* How long will the repo be in place?
* What will be the interest rate, and will it be fixed or floating?
* Who will hold the securities during the repo?
* How often will the transaction be marked to the market and accrued interest paid?
* Will the seller and repurchaser have the right to substitute other securities if the original ones are needed back?

Obviously, with all this to be agreed to, establishing a repo takes some care. In entering into the transaction, one needs to clarify the following points:

Rate. The interest rate charged on the money for the life of the repo. The longer the term of the repo, and the lower the quality of the collateral, the higher the rate usually is.   Certain securities in short supply and needed for deliveries may command a lower financing rate.

Term. The period over which the repo will last. It can run from overnight to years, and it can be left open when the repo is established. In an open repo, the rate is reset every day.

Collateral. The securities being sold and repurchased. Specific securities needed for delivery, called *specials*, can be financed at a lower rate than *general collateral.* The parties need to establish whether the seller/repurchaser has the *right of substitution*, should the original securities be needed back.

Proceeds. The cash being exchanged for the securities. It usually is made up of the current bid for the securities, less an amount called the *haircut*, plus accrued coupon interest from the last coupon date to the settlement date.

Delivery. Where the securities will be delivered to receive the money. This usually consists of wiring instructions for Treasuries and most agencies, as well as physical delivery instructions for most pass-through securities.

Repricing. How often the securities will be marked to the market, with accrued interest on both the securities and the repo brought up-to-date. This arrangement applies only to repos done for a fixed term with the termination date left open.

Kinds of Financing Transactions

To understand the many kinds of repos, simply divide them into those originated by the party with the money and those originated by the party with the collateral. Transactions originated by those with the collateral are for the most part homogeneous. Two kinds of repos, however, are originated by the parties with the money. When these parties need specific securities for deliveries, most often because of a short sale, the repo is called a *special repo.* When the party simply has cash to invest, the repo is called a *general repo.*

Customer's Money

When someone with money contacts a dealer to initiate a repo transaction, he or she indicates the conditions for the repo and asks what rate the dealer is offering. The conditions specified are: the term of the repo, the kind of collateral acceptable, the amount available to put to work, and the number of different securities that will be accepted as collateral. The dealer responds with the rate at which he or she is willing to do the repo. If the customer accepts the rate, delivery arrangements are made and the trade is settled that day. The exchange between the customer and dealer might go like this:

Customer: What can you do on $50 million for a week, Treasuries under five years, five pieces?

Dealer: I can do 7⅝.

Customer: That's done.

Dealer: Okay, the collateral is $30 million three-year notes and $20 million year bills.

Customer: Fine, wire to Harris Bank for my account.

The dealer would then establish a price for the collateral and calculate the proceeds of the repo. This amount would be told to the customer and relayed to Harris, so they would be ready to settle the transaction. Sometimes collateral is held in safekeeping instead of delivered out. This kind of repo is particularly dangerous if the customer does not verify that the collateral is indeed being held for his or her account. Although safekeeping repos are more convenient than ones where the collateral is delivered, many regulators frown on them because they contain the potential for abuses, sometimes resulting in the "collateral-less repo," which is an unsecured loan to a dealer.

Customer's Collateral

The customer who has collateral asks the dealer where he or she can finance it for a specified period. The only other condition is possibly the right to substitute other collateral, in case the specific security is needed back. The dealer responds with a rate quote and, if that is acceptable, the delivery instructions are given. For example:

Customer: Where can I put out $10 million two-year notes until the fifteenth, no right of substitution?

Dealer: 8%.

Customer: I need to do it at 7 ⅞.

Dealer: Okay, done. Wire to Harris Bank for our account.

Again, the proceeds will be calculated, communicated to the customer, and relayed to Harris for settlement.

Special Repo

Special repos are most often initiated by a dealer who is looking for a specific security. Since the dealer doesn't know how long he or she will need that issue, all specials are done on open, or with no specified term. Open repos can be terminated by either party's notifying the other side before 10:30 a.m. New York time. Often, customers want an investment to replace the security going into the repo, giving them an interest rate arbitrage for the time the repo is on. Again, for example:

Dealer: We are looking for $60 million old three-year notes on open at 6%.
Customer: I have them, but I need a replacement.
Dealer: I can show you $60 million six-month bills at 7% on open.
Customer: Fine. Wire to Harris for my account.

In this case the customer will be financing the notes at 6% and using the money to finance the dealer's bills at 7%, netting a 1% interest spread, or $1,643.83 on the $60 million per day.

A TYPICAL DAY

An over-the-counter market does not have an opening or closing bell, as an exchange does, and what goes on in a Primary Dealer's trading room looks disorganized. Nevertheless, there is actually a great deal of logic to what is happening. In the last chapter, we saw how the personnel were organized. In this chapter, we will see how a dealer's day is organized.

To do this, we will "spend" a typical day in the trading room, observing the ebb and flow of action. At times, the noise level suddenly rises. At other times, it seems so quiet that one wonders if anything is happening. The focus of attention shifts from one trading desk to another, and behind all the action looms the Federal Reserve.

Once again, we have entered the offices of our representative Primary Dealer. It is the Tuesday of the first week of November, a week in which the Treasury is auctioning its refunding package. So the day promises to be a busy one. Let's go into the trading room and look around.

8:00 A.M.:
New York, Eastern Daylight Time

Trading government securities is definitely not a nine-to-five job. When we enter the trading room at 8:00 a.m., about half the desks are occupied. Although the noise level is very low, a lot is going on.

Many of the traders are busy at their desks at this hour, but most are not trading. Instead, they are updating records — of trades, of spreads between issues, of price charts, or of the previous day's trades.

Records are the tools of the trade. In making bids or offers on an issue, traders want to know where the issue is trading in relation to other securities issued by the same entity, as well as securities issued by other entities. In predicting where the market will go, traders depend both on charts and on historical price spreads. Finally, yesterday's trades are today's settlements, so the last chance to correct any errors before they become failed settlements is now.

Although they may be having coffee with a doughnut and chatting about last night's ball game, the traders are performing other tasks essential to their job. The bill traders have a special job this morning. Because they bid in the three- and six-month bill auctions yesterday, they are matching up the securities bought against customer orders and short positions.

One trading desk, the financing or repo desk, is already transacting business. Since dealers already know which securities they will need to finance or borrow for the day, financing transactions begin long before securities start to trade. The repo traders are giving out rate quotes to customers (who have money or securities to place for a few days) and to securities traders (who need to know the availability of securities and money to assess the profitability of trades). As the volume of financing transactions builds, the pile of tickets on the repo trader's desk grows. There is no time for idle talk now. By 10:00 a.m. a large amount of business must be done; the afternoons are the less busy part of the repo trading day.

Many of the salespersons are already at their desks, updating their own records, talking to their early-bird customers, or scanning the daily press for items of interest to use later in the day. Every salesperson has an individualized ritual, developed over years in the business, to which he or she adheres closely. Every so often a salesperson gets up and goes to a trading desk to talk about one of yesterday's trades, get a rate quote from the repo desk, or discuss a customer's desires with a trader.

The economics department is also busy at this hour. Yesterday's economic releases from Washington are being pored over, the computer databases are spewing out charts and figures, and various theories are being dissected.

8:30 A.M.

The trading room intercom comes to life as the firm's money market economist begins the ritual morning meeting. Every meeting follows a slightly different pattern, but they all cover most of the same information. Throughout the trading room, phones are hung up, charts are set aside, and pads of paper are brought out for notes.

The economist begins by covering any economic releases from the previous day, pointing out things in the release that others might have missed, assessing the information in light of market expectations, and fitting the results into a macroeconomic picture. Then he covers the reserve position of the banking system for the day and the

Fed's expected action. Finally, he updates his projections for interest rates in general and makes several predictions — for today's economic releases and for Thursday's money supply number.

Next the traders cover any salient items in their market areas. The bill traders discuss the auction results from yesterday, the short coupon traders cover today's auction of three-year notes, the long coupon traders talk about the relationship of the bond to the futures contract, and the agency traders draw attention to some expected financing announcements. The sales manager finishes the meeting by making some general announcements.

9:00 A.M.

With the opening of the futures markets, the trading day begins for real. Quickly the brokers' screens fill up with numbers, and the noise level in the room rises substantially. Quotes and orders are shouted back and forth between traders and salespersons. Nearly everyone is on the telephone, staring intently at the screens as the day's market action unfolds. The first hour or so of the trading day is one of the busiest as the pent-up trading demand from the night before is let loose.

Nowadays, government securities are traded all over the world, with trading centers developing in London and Tokyo, so there is what amounts to round-the-clock trading. Yet the real center of the market is New York, and the real trading day starts at 9:00 a.m. Eastern Time.

Most firms have an intercom or open microphone system between the trading room and the branch offices. At this time of day, the intercom is a constant buzz of requests for bids and offers, of orders, and of reports of trades completed.

11:30 A.M.

After a mid-morning slowdown, tension in the trading room suddenly begins to build. Traders and sales staffers who had been out getting coffee or using the restroom are back at their desks. Everyone is ready for action.

It is "Fed Time," one of the most important parts of the trading day. The Federal Reserve conducts all of its open market activity through the trading desk at the Federal Reserve Bank of New York. Any open market action by the Fed takes place between 11:30 and noon, and most likely between 11:40 and 11:50. All morning, salespersons, traders, and economists have been discussing the possibility of Fed action, and what that action might mean. Now the moment of truth has come. For the next ten minutes or so, not much trading will be done, but everyone is primed for action.

All the traders are watching the firm's direct line to the Federal Reserve Bank of New York. Suddenly, at 11:42, the line flashes. A trader picks it up, listens intently for a few seconds, and shouts out, "System repos! System repos!"

He is indicating that the Fed is doing repos for the Open Market System account, as opposed to repos for the account of a customer. Since this adds reserves to the banking system, it is a bullish sign. But the important question is: What did the market expect the Fed to do? If system repos were expected, the market may not do anything in response, but if the action was unexpected prices could rise sharply.

In this case, the market was expecting repos for the account of a customer, but not for the System, so action erupts in the trading room. All the trading screens display the legend "MARKETS SUBJECT," which indicates that a recent development may have invalidated the bids and offers currently showing on the screen. One by one, the markets are erased and replaced with new ones. The traders immediately reassess their positions, in light of the Fed's actions, and move to cover any short positions.

Salespersons contact their customers, determine if they need to effect a trade, and attempt to accommodate those needs. Throughout all this activity, the repo desk is assembling the collateral needed to offer to the Fed.

The net result is a great deal of activity. Traders and salespersons are repeatedly calling each other, speaking on the telephone, and writing furiously on pads of paper and trading tickets.   As the market moves, the exchanges among traders and salespersons become clipped, as each is absorbed in the urgencies of the market. Seconds count! Compared to the scene of a quarter-hour ago, this is pandemonium.

12:30 P.M.

The market has stabilized after Fed time, and the atmosphere in the trading room is much calmer. Traders and salespersons are eating lunch at their desks or entertaining customers at a nearby restaurant. In a quieter environment, the economists and some of the traders are assessing the meaning of today's Fed action, with a few sales staffers listening in or commenting from time to time. The repo desk, having offered the Fed some collateral, is relaxing and waiting to hear back. The response from the Fed, and the rates at which they are willing to take collateral, will have a significant impact, but in a calmer time.

One trader is busy at this hour. At one o'clock, the Treasury's auction of three-year notes will close, so the short coupon trader is busy preparing bids. On this trader's desk is a pile of tender forms, which are the official bidding documents in Treasury auctions. Already they have the firm's name and clearing agent filled in, and they are signed by the appropriate officer. Now the reader is filling the amount of securities bid for and the bid yield. At this early point, a half-hour before the bidding closes, the trader is filling out the tenders for customers' bids. As the time draws closer to 1:00, he or she spends more time on the phone to other dealers, discussing the projected yields for the average accepted bid (called the *average*) and the highest yield (and lowest price) accepted (called the *stop*).

Everyone's objective is to buy at the stop. So, as auction time approaches, salespersons ask the trader what the "stop talk," or projected high yield winning bid, is. As late customer bids come in, the trader fills out more and more tenders, both for customers and the firm. The tenders then have to be relayed to the appropriate Federal Reserve Bank where they are to be presented. Tenders may be conveyed by electronic transmission, telephone, or even by runner.

2:00 P.M.

After the excitement of the Fed's intervention and the submission of bids in the auction, the activity level in the trading room settles down. The repo desk has effectively finished its work for the day, except for arranging the settlement of all the transactions. As we approach the point in time when the wire transfer of securities and money ends for the day, those trades left unsettled assume a larger importance. As we saw in an earlier chapter, the cost of failing to deliver $10,000,000 of a 10% security for one day is $2,740. So the repo desk is shepherding their settlement along.

Elsewhere salespersons are working on trades that their customers need to effect, and traders are keeping an eye on the market as they watch over their long and short positions. Every so often a salesperson asks for a bid or offer, or the intercom squawks to life, but this is one of the lulls in the trading day.

The lull, however, doesn't mean that nothing is happening. Trades still flash on the screen with regularity, the traders' phone lines to the brokers still ring often to report trades and other information, and the market is still active. At times like these the market can suddenly move a quarter of a point or more, generating substantial profits or losses in a few moments. The giant may be resting, but he is not asleep.

2:55 P.M.

The activity of the long coupon trader and the repo desk picks up temporarily as we close in on two events of 3:00 p.m.

At that point, the futures markets close, and the long bond traders, who keep offsetting positions in bonds and bond futures (or options), need to balance their positions. As they have done all day, they are on the phone to the firm's staff on the floor of the Chicago Board of Trade, but now there is more urgency in their voices. "Buy 10 at 16! Where are they now? Pay 17! Pay 17! How many?" As they talk, they watch the screens intently and scribble on pads of paper.

Also at 3:00 p.m., the repo traders are on the phone. They are speaking with the clearance department to determine which securities will be coming in over the Fed Wire at the last moment and where they have to go. There are specific rules about when Primary Dealers must accept deliveries from other dealers or from customers, as well as how late they can deliver securities. As the time draws close to 3:00 p.m., the firm's ability to turn securities around from one party to another becomes strained, and the possibility of having to carry a security overnight looms large. The events of these last few minutes can turn a profitable day of trading into a loss. So everyone is on their toes.

4:00 P.M.

The activity in the trading room has again slowed. Yet, as 4:00 p.m. approaches, the bill traders and many of the salespersons start to watch the Dow Jones Broad Tape, even as they talk on the phone. Precisely at the hour, the headline flashes across the screen "Treasury to auction 3-month and 6-month bills." This official announcement of next Monday's bill auction is the signal to begin trading those bills on a "when-issued" basis.

Activity in the trading room once again erupts, this time concentrated around the bill desk. Most of this activity is in transactions between the issues auctioned yesterday, now known as the *regular way bills,* and the *when-issued,* or WI bills. Customers who sell the regular way and buy the WI bills are said to be doing a *forward roll,* while those who sell WI and buy regular way are said to be doing a *reverse roll.* For as long as half an hour, the bill traders are busy quoting forward and reverse rolls for customers, keeping track of their positions, and writing tickets. When their activity finally dies down, they join the growing number of people headed for the elevators.

5:30 P.M.

At this hour the trading room is almost deserted, but the short coupon trader and a few salespersons are still around, along with the department manager. As they make small talk, they keep an eye on the Broad Tape. Suddenly, the ticker prints out the results of the three-year note auction. Along with the high price, low price, and average price, the story includes the total amount bid for, the percentage awarded at the low price, the size of the noncompetitive bids, and the amount awarded in each of the Federal Reserve Districts. All this information paints a picture of how well or how poorly the auction went, and the trader discusses it with the manager in a few cryptic sentences.

As the remaining salespersons call their customers with the auction results, the trader checks the bids he or she submitted, both for the firm and its customers, and prepares for a busy day tomorrow. The room clears quickly now, and by 6:00 P.M. the only people left are the cleaning people.

With the close of the trading day in the U.S. government securities market, we turn to another large market in the next chapter — the municipal bond market.

Chapter 7

Municipal Debt

In 1975, New York City seemed to be going broke. After rapidly increasing its outstanding debt for more than ten years, the City defaulted on a note issue. Suddenly the market prices of its other debt obligations — rated A by the agencies till the — declined dramatically. The City was in trouble: Not only was its existing debt issues losing value in the fixed income market, but its looming bankruptcy cast a shadow over the entire municipal bond market. After ten years of — at times painful — austerity, the City regained its former high ratings and became a "going concern" once again. Yet its troubled times made it impossible to regard the quality of local debt as unimpeachable.

New York City, however, was not the first municipal issuer to encounter rocky times. Ancient historical documents tell of occasional defaults as long as 2000 years ago.

WHAT ARE MUNICIPAL BONDS?

Municipal bonds are debt securities issued by states, cities, townships, counties, political subdivisions, and U.S. territories. The capital raised by these securities is used to build a new high school, to construct a water purification plant, to extend a state highway spur through a rural area, to erect a multisport center, and sometimes just to refund old debt. "Munis" provide the finances that fuel growth and that generate income for local government.

In the United States, municipal debt has a history almost as long as that of the country itself. In the 1820s, booming cities needed money to grow, and they raised the needed funds by issuing bonds. By 1843, when the first records were kept, outstanding municipal debt was at $25 million. Spurred by the needs of a (sometimes violently) growing nation — particularly by the building of the railroads and the development of the West — state and local governments issued more and more debt. Only the Panic of 1873 took the momentum away for a few years, and by 1900 the outstanding municipal debt level had reached the $2 billion mark.

In 1913, the introduction of the federal income tax was to have profound effects on just about all aspects of living in America. With respect to municipal bonds, it raised a state's rights question: May the federal government tax income from state and local debt? Two landmark cases of the 1800s had laid the groundwork for a decision in this area: The Supreme Court cases of *McCullock vs. Maryland* (1819) and *Pollock vs. Farmer's Loan and Trust Co.* (1895) made states all but immune to interference by the federal government. As a result of these cases, municipal bond debt was completely exempt from federal taxation until the Tax Reform Act of 1986 was passed.

This act distinguishes between municipal bonds issued before August 15, 1986 and those issued after that date (with exceptions, of course). Munis issued prior to this date retain the tax-exempt features that they offered before it. Any municipal issued after this date falls into one of three categories, depending on its purpose:

* *Public purpose bonds*, issued directly by the state or local authority, are used for traditional "municipal" projects such as a new school building or highway improvement program (projects that are clearly the responsibility of government). These munis are tax-exempt.

* *Private activity bonds*, although issued by the state or local government, supply funds for "private" projects, like a sports arena, shopping mall, or civic center. These bonds are subject to federal taxation, but they may be exempt from state/local taxation in the states in which they are issued.

* *Nongovernmental purpose bonds* raise funds for "nongovernmental" (but not "private") uses, such as housing or student loans. These are tax-exempt, but the TRA puts a cap on the amount that a municipality may issue of such bonds *and* the interest is treated as a preference item for purposes of the alternative minimum tax.

As a result, the phrase "municipal bonds" is no longer synonymous with the term "tax-exempts." Although a tax-exempt municipal bond's interest payments (usually on a semi-annual basis) are exempted from federal taxation, any profit from its purchase or sale is *not* exempt.

Because of the tax-free feature, municipal issues generally carry lower interest rates than corporate or U.S. government bonds. Investors in higher tax brackets may actually achieve higher dollar returns with the lower yields. Suitability is partly determined by asking: What pretax corporate bond yield would the investor need to equal the tax-exempt return of the muni being considered? To answer this question, you must convert the tax-free yield into the equivalent taxable yield. The formula is:

$$\text{Taxable equivalent} = \frac{\text{Tax-free yield (\%)}}{100\% - \text{Tax bracket (\%)}}$$

For example, an investor is in the 28% tax bracket. She purchases a municipal bond paying a tax-free 7% rate. She is also considering a corporate bond with a yield of 8.93%. Which bond — the muni or the corporate — offers her the greater yield?

$$\text{Taxable equivalent} = \frac{\text{Tax-free yield (\%)}}{100\% - \text{Tax bracket (\%)}}$$

$$= \frac{7\%}{100\% - 28\%}$$

$$= 9.72\%$$

To get the same yield as the muni, the corporate bond would have to offer a 9.72% return. The investor buys the muni.

In some instances, the interest payments are also free of state and local taxation, usually on the condition that the bondholder live in the same state as the issuer. This *triple exemption* is always a feature of some issues, such as those of Puerto Rico, the Virgin Islands, the Trust Territory, and Washington, DC.

If anything, the introduction of the income tax into the American way of life had the effect of fostering interest in municipal bonds. Although the Great Depression of the thirties certainly set the market back, defaults were not as severe as after 1873. During World War II, outstanding municipal debt levels actually dropped because the country's resources were being used to win the war. After the war, however, new issues proliferated: From a $14 bil-

lion outstanding debt level in 1945, the 1980s saw levels
first over $300 billion, and ultimately, over $400 billion.

THE PRIMARY MARKET

When a municipality needs more money than it is
receiving in the form of tax revenues, it has the option of
"borrowing" against future tax revenues. That loan takes
the form of a municipal bond issue. In effect, the state or
local government is promising to pay lenders the face value
of the bond (the principal amount of the loan) at maturity,
out of future tax dollars. Given that a municipality chooses
to take such a loan, how is it arranged?

The Federal Reserve System brings U.S. government
(Treasury) bond issues to the market through the primary
dealers. Is there such an agency that does the same for
state and local issuers? There is no agency, but there are
brokerage firms that specialize in "underwriting" municipal
bond issues — that is, bringing them to market.

The Municipal Bond Dealers

The many new municipal issues — or "primary offerings" — have fostered a vast underwriting industry. Of the
couple of thousand securities dealers and commercial
dealer banks registered with the SEC, only about a third
are active underwriters. Many of them are regional underwriters that handle their communities' business and even
some major state issues. Still, over half of the total volume
in municipal underwriting is conducted by fewer than thirty firms in New York, in Chicago, and on the West Coast.

The community of municipal bond dealers is varied.
Most major brokerage houses have departments devoted to
underwriting and trading municipal securities. Other,
smaller firms specialize in municipals, sometimes even in
particular types of munis such as housing bonds. Some
"retail" dealers trade munis largely or soley with individual
investors. Commercial banks, also members of the dealer

community, must limit themselves to underwriting general obligation bonds, which is all the Glass-Steagall Act permits them to do.

These dealers and dealer banks take care of the distribution of the new bonds, through their salesforces, to traditional muni bond investors. Accounting for 90% of all bond purchases are commercial banks, property and casualty insurance companies, and households. (Pension funds don't buy municipal bonds because, being already tax-exempt, they can buy higher-yielding corporate or Treasury bonds.)

The Financial Advisor

The first step for the issuer is to seek the services of a financial advisor. (Most state and local governments are not adequately staffed or experienced to offer a bond issue without such "outside" advice.) This financial advisor's role is more often assumed by the relatively small regional underwriter than by the major dealer, where financial advisor specialists may undertake service in this capacity on a fee basis.

One of the first decisions that the advisor helps the issuer make is the type of bond to be offered. Municipals can be divided into two broad categories:
*   General obligation (GO) bonds, which include limited tax bonds and special assessment bonds.
*   Revenue bonds, which include industrial development bonds, special tax bonds, and public housing authority bonds.

Any of these types may or may not be tax-exempt, depending on their date of issuance and purpose.

General Obligations may be issued by states, cities, towns or counties. All GO bonds are, in one way or another, backed by the taxing power of the issuer. Hence these bonds are also referred to as *full faith and credit bonds*. Defaults are rare, and principal and interest are paid regularly.

Generally, states have greater taxing powers than their political ("local") subdivisions — cities, towns, countries — and they usually rely on personal and corporate income taxes, as well as on sales, gasoline, or highway use taxes as security. Since local issuers don't have the taxing powers of states, they usually rely on *ad valorem* (assessed valuation) taxes to back their GOs. Such taxes, the most common source of security revenue, are often levied in mills per dollar of assessed valuation (a mill equals one-tenth of one cent). For example, if a property is assessed at $100,000 and the tax rate is 8 mills, the tax due is $800 ($100.000 x 0.008).

When a legal limit is imposed on the taxing power of the issuer, general obligation bonds are then called *limited tax* bonds; in other words, taxes may not be raised indefinitely to cover the debt. Bonds *not* restricted in this way are called *unlimited* tax bonds.

Special assessment bonds are secured by an assessment on those who benefit directly from the project. For example, if sidewalks are put in with the proceeds of the issue, the residents of the area in which sidewalks were put in are assessed.

Revenue bonds may be issued by an agency, commission, or authority created by legislation in order to construct a "facility," such as a toll bridge, turnpike, hospital, university dormitory, water, sewer and electric districts, or ports. The fees, taxes, or tolls charged for use of the facility ultimately pay off the debt.

Since the municipality itself doesn't back such bonds, they are usually riskier than general obligation bonds and generally pay a correspondingly higher coupon rate. Defaults, while not frequent, can occur.

In some cases, especially with respect to sewer and electric system special assessment bonds, the underlying municipality or state assumes liability for the debt service if the income from the project is insufficient. Such issues are thus more like GOs than revenue bonds and they are referred to as *double-barrelled issues.*

Industrial development (or industrial revenue) bonds enjoyed a vogue in the sixties, but they have since been curtailed by legislation. With this type of issue, an authority created by a municipality would float a "tax-exempt" bond, construct a factory with the proceeds of the bond issue, and then enter into a long-term net lease agreement with an industrial corporation. The "rent" would pass through the authority to the bondholders as tax-exempt income. In effect, the corporation constructed a new plant at municipal borrowing rates, which are lower than corporate borrowing rates due to the tax-free nature of the interest income. Smaller issues (below $10 million) may still be offered, and issues already outstanding in the secondary market are not affected. However, new issues are essentially restricted to those that improve civic services, such as airports, harbors, mass transit, or pollution control facilities. The security behind any industrial revenue or development bond is the lease entered into by the corporation and the issuer.

Special tax bonds are frequently paid for by an excise tax on items such as liquor or tobacco.

Public Housing Authority (PHA) bonds offer government backing to locally issued project bonds to assist in constructing low-income housing. The revenues (rents) are expected to pay the debt service, but if they do not, the full faith and credit of the U.S. government provides the ultimate security through the Housing and Urban Development Department (HUD). Investors get tax-exempt income, plus a government guarantee (municipal notes — or *project notes* [PNs] — like these mature in one year or less and are issued under this arrangement for financing short-term projects).

In addition to determining the type of bond to be offered, the advisor also helps the issuing municipality to set up a repayment schedule. Issuers have three options: serial bonds, term bonds, or a split offering.

Usually, general obligation bonds are issued in *serial* form, that is, they mature in stages. The issuer's purpose is often to maintain level debt service.

When a serial municipal bond issue comes to market, the managing underwriter writes a *scale* that lists (1) the dollar amount maturing in each year and (2) the appropriate offering price (stated as a percentage of par or as a basis price, as the case may be). If the yields are lower in the shorter-term than in the longer-term maturities, it is known as a *normal scale*. If the shorter-term yields are higher than longer-term yields, the scale is said to be *inverted*.

Generally used for revenue offerings, all *term* bonds mature on a single date, and they are frequently paid out of a sinking fund. Term bonds may be quoted in dollar amounts and in this case are referred to as "dollar bonds."

A *split offering* combines serial and term bonds in a single offering.

Regardless of type, municipal bonds are almost always callable prior to maturity, often with a 10-year call protection and a sinking fund schedule. If bonds are called, they will be called by inverse order of maturity, that is, the longest maturity will be called first. Within a given maturity, the bond numbers selected for redemption are chosen by a lottery.

Besides the financial advisor, the issuer often calls in other specialists for expert help on engineering, architectural, ecological, and other aspects of the undertaking.

The Bond Counsel

The legal "specialist" is the bond counsel, who is responsible for the legal opinion that accompanies almost every municipal issue. (See Figure 7-1.) In preparing the opinion, the bond counsel addresses two key legal needs: one is that the requirements of local laws, the state constitution, judicial opinions, and enabling legislation or procedures are all met. The second is that the interest is exempt according to federal laws and regulations.

The bond counsel collects all the documents that ensure the legality of the issue into what lawyers call a "transcript of proceedings." The transcript is given to the underwriter before the bond issue is distributed to investors. The counsel also makes sure that the bonds are issued properly, and usually examines one final bond to check signatures and terms.

Nationally, the lion's share of the bond counsel work is done by fewer than ten major law firms. Another dozen or so conduct most of the regional business. Some hundreds of local law firms also do most of the bond counsel work in their own locales.

The Syndicate

Neither the financial advisor nor the bond counsel, however, actually bring the issue to the market. That is the work of the underwriter, or more specifically the syndicate, which is a temporary group of dealers under the direction of a senior manager. Normally the syndicate has a lifetime of 30 days, although it may be disbanded if it sells the bonds sooner.

The makeup of syndicates varies. For example, one co-manager might be a major dealer with branches from coast to coast, and the other co-manager could be a regional firm with extensive distribution channels in the issuer's locale. Another dealer/member of the syndicate might specialize in sales to institutional clients, and still another in sales to individual investors.

The dealers involved in syndicates may bid on ten or a dozen underwritings a day and actually participate in that many per week. The staff involved are used to keeping up a fast pace and making spur-of-the-moment decisions.

Syndicates can have as few as two members or as many as a hundred. They can have more than one manager (that is, co-managers) but only one — the "senior" or "lead" manager — "runs the books of the account."

Syndicates are held together by the "syndicate letter" or contract, which lays out the conditions and obligations of membership and specifies the details of the underwrit-

Figure 7-1. Sample Bond Counsel Opinion.

Dear Sirs:

We have examined the transcript of proceedings relating to the issuance of $6,000,000 of Sewer System Improvement Bonds (Seventh Series) (the "Bonds") of the City of Windsor (the "City"), in the County of Orange, and State of New York, being a series of bonds numbered from 961151 to 970150, inclusive, dated............bearing interest at the rate of ....% per annum, payable June 1, 1989 and semiannually thereafter, maturing serially on June 1 from 1990 to 2014, inclusive, and issued for the purpose of paying costs of improving designated expressways and streets in the manner described in the ordinance authorizing the Bonds.

We have also examined the law under authority of which the Bonds are issued and executed Bond No. 961151, and from this examination we are of the opinion that the Bonds constitute valid and legal general obligations of the City and that the principal of and interest on the Bonds, unless paid from other sources and subject to the provisions of the federal Bankruptcy law and other laws affecting creditors' rights, are to be paid from the proceeds of the levy of ad valorem taxes on all property in the City subject to ad valorem taxes levied by the City, which taxes are unlimited as to amount or rate.

We are further of the opinion that, under the law existing on the date of this opinion, the interest on the bonds is exempt from federal income tax, New York corporate franchise tax, New York personal income tax and municipal income taxes in New York.

Respectfully submitted,

---

ing: the amount of bonds, bid and offering terms, name of the manager, priority of orders, and the like.

Syndicates fall into two general categories: Eastern (undivided) account, or Western (divided) account.

The *Eastern (undivided) account* is the most popular type of syndicate. In this type, each member is responsible for selling at least an agreed percentage of the issue. But in the event that a member cannot, for any reason, distribute its participation, the other members become responsible for a percentage of that unsold portion. If a member was originally responsible for, say, 10% of the issue, it would be responsible for 10% of the unsold portion. Hence the account is "undivided" as to selling and liability. By definition, an Eastern account obliges members to "pull together" to complete the distribution.

In the less common *Western (divided) account,* each member is responsible only for its own participation, with no liability for other members' unsold bonds. Western accounts are sometimes seen in an offering of municipal *term* bonds, all of which have the same coupon rate and maturity date.

Syndicates may be involved in two types of underwriting mechanisms: *competitive bids* for most larger GOs or *negotiated* offerings for almost all revenue bonds. (See Figures 7-2 and 7-3.)

In either type of underwriting, the essential business structure is the same: The syndicate buys the bonds from the issuer at one price and resells them at a slightly higher price for a profit. The firms charge no commissions on the sales of the bonds because they are acting as "dealers" or as "principals." Either term means that they buy and sell for their own accounts. They may charge a commission only when they execute trades in behalf of clients, that is, when they act as "brokers" or "as agents."

The difference between the price at which the syndicate buys the bonds and the price at which the bonds are sold is called the *spread* or the maximum gross profit in the municipal underwriting. The manager allocates the bonds

Figure 7-2. The Competitive Bidding Process

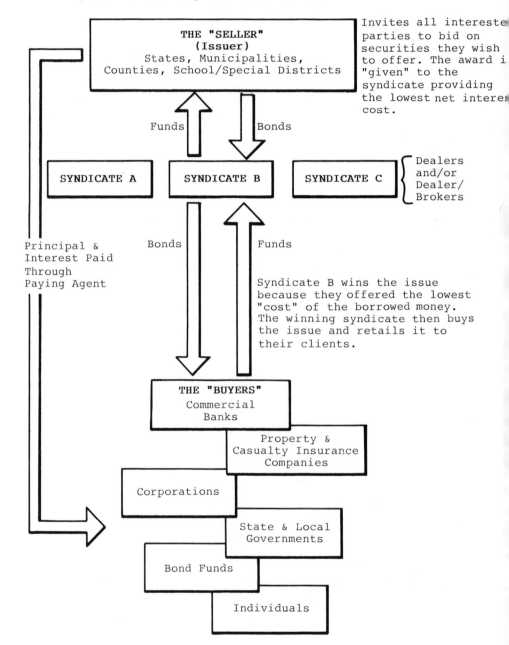

Figure 7-3. The Negotiated Sale Procedure

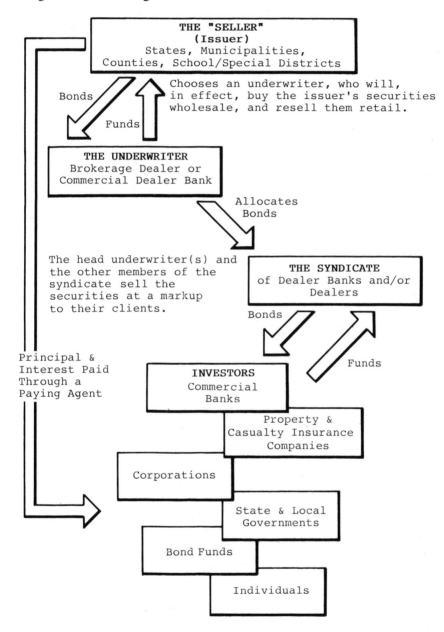

to syndicate members at the *takedown* price. The takedown is typically 1 to 2 points ($10 to $20 per $1,000 principal amount). These bonds are then sold to the public.

As an example, the syndicate purchases each bond in an offering at a 1½ point discount. For each $1,000 bond, it pays $985 to the issuer. The spread is therefore 1½ points, or $15. If the takedown is 1¼ points, each syndicate member purchases its bonds at $987.50 each ($1,000–$12.50), and then offers them to the public at par. Thus the managing underwriter keeps ¼ point per bond, and each member keeps 1¼ points. (See Figure 7-4.)

Sometimes a nonmember of the syndicate has a client order to fill and buys from syndicate members to fill it. The nonmember's compensation is the *selling concession*. It is included in the takedown. For example, if the takedown is 1 point, and the selling concession is ⅝ of a point, the nonmember makes $6.25 (⅝) on the sale, and the member makes the other $3.75 (⅜). This is typical, and reflects the fact that "selling" is usually more difficult than risk taking.

Whereas in a negotiated offering the issuer approaches the underwriter directly, a competitive underwriting involves many more steps, the first of which is for the issuer to make its intentions known to prospective underwriters.

By law, *competitive bidding* must be used for the underwriting of general obligation bonds. To solicit bids, the issuer publishes an "official notice of sale" in the financial news and in legal publications. Active issuers also generally send copies of the notice to dealers they have worked with in the past.

An ad in the municipal bond's trade paper, *The Daily Bond Buyer*, is a must. Anyone who is involved in munis reads this paper — especially people in the syndicate departments of dealer firms. This paper itemizes most negotiated and competitive issues in one of three sections: "Proposed New Issues," "Invitations for Bids," and "Official Municipal Bond Notices." It also offers a yield worksheet service, "New Issue Worksheet and Record Service," that has become accepted industry-wide.

Figure 7-4. A Typical Spread, Takedown and Selling Concession

```
Face Value:     $1,000.00
Spread:         $   10.00   (1 point)
Concession:     $    2.50   (¼ point)
Takedown:       $    5.00   (½ point)
```

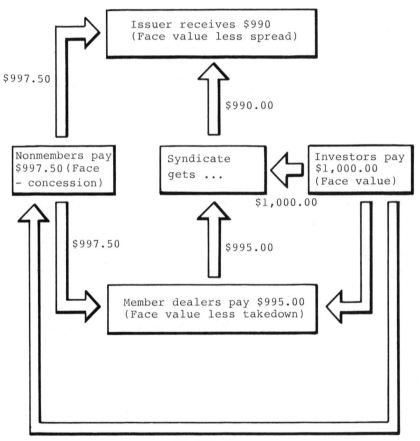

With the word out about an upcoming competitive offering, the initiative rests with the dealers. To understand how dealers conduct a competitive bid, however, you need to know who does what inside the firm's municipal bond department.

WHO DOES WHAT INSIDE THE MUNICIPAL SECURITIES DEALER?

Within the dealers, the municipal department is normally composed of six areas:

1. The *underwriting*, or *syndicate*, area consists of one or more people who decide on and conduct underwritings. They set prices and yields on new issues, sit in on price meetings, coordinate with other dealers, and keep the firm's traders and sales staff current on upcoming offerings.

2. The *traders* do not actively participate in selling a new issue. Instead, they buy and sell the bonds in the "secondary" market, after the primary offering is complete. Nevertheless, they need to be informed of pending issues in order to prepare for maintaining an inventory of the bonds later on. Larger trading sections have traders who specialize in types of municipal bonds.

3. The *sales* personnel become very involved in primary offerings. While the syndicate staff may evaluate the salability of a new issue and price it approximately, the salespeople are the ones who actually make the calls and make the sales.

The large brokerage houses with a retail (or individual investor) orientation may even locate a portion of the sales staff near the trading desk at the main office. As the branch salespeople call in orders to the sales group at the main office, the orders are passed on to the traders for execution. In other firms, instead of installing a "liaison" sales group with the main office traders, traders are located at each of the branch offices.

In an underwriting, the syndicate, sales, and trading people all sit in a large room that is equipped for trading. Before them are quotation consoles and phone systems that link them with customers and other members of the dealer community. The offering itself, if priced properly and sold aggressively, is often sold out within the day.

4. The *public finance* group has the task of drumming up new negotiated underwritings and may offer their services as financial advisory for a fee.

Commercial banks, forbidden by law to become involved in GO bond offerings (which are usually offered in negotiated underwritings) have a financial advisory group, not a public finance group. They can still, however, have a "new business" staff, whose aim is to generate new housing and education revenue bonds.

5. *Municipal research* has assumed greater importance in the eighties, when it became apparent that municipal issuers could default — New York City being the premier example. While at one time the rating agencies were the sole source of credit information on state and local issues, municipal research sections have come to be increasingly vital to successful underwritings. Generally this department prepares a concise opinion before the dealer makes a commitment in a negotiated offering or a bid in a competitive deal. Like the research of the economics section in a primary deal, this opinion may be made available to the institutional and individual clients of the firm.

6. *Operations* processes orders, issues payment checks, takes and makes deliveries of securities, and performs other required recordkeeping functions. This area,

also known as the "back office," is responsible for "clearing" the trades that the firm makes either with or on behalf of its customers and other dealers.

With the exception of the traders, each of these six areas has an important role to play in a competitive underwriting.

HOW A COMPETITIVE UNDERWRITING WORKS

As the firm bids on upcoming bond issues, the syndicate people keep the salespeople up-to-date, usually in a Monday morning meeting. As these meetings, each issue is received and a sales strategy devised. (As a rule, the salespeople work a little harder on upcoming negotiated offerings because they are certain the firm will be working on them.)

The actual competitive bidding process on a particular issue begins with an opinion from the research staff. While municipal issuers call on rating agencies to rate their offerings, the syndicate staff in the brokerage firm generally wants an independent evaluation. The second opinion, if strong enough, may enable the firm to put in an aggressive bid, on the assumption that, given an assurance of selling out the issue, they can offer a lower net interest cost to the issuer. Of course, if the research department's analysis is weak, the dealer may not even submit a bid.

To come up with a competitive bid, syndicate members hold several "price meetings," usually in the manager's office. If the underwriters are widely dispersed, meetings can be held by teleconferencing. For very large syndicates, the manager may communicate with members by means of the Munifacts wire, a news wire for the municipal industry that may be used to communicate information only to specified clients of the service.

Preliminary price meetings, held one or two days before the bid must be submitted, are low-keyed. Representing each syndicate member, one or more members of the syndicate groups discuss the salability of the impending offering and other similar issues — spread, prices, yields, and so on. One of the key topics is the "reoffering scale," which is the array of prices and yields for each maturity in the issue. (See the official statement in Figure 7-5.) These prices and yields are entered onto the Bond Buyer worksheets.

The overall goal is to reach agreement on a set of yields for the new bonds that balances two objectives. One is to keep yields high enough to attract investors and to make the issue salable. As input on this score, the syndicate group gets the feedback of their sales and trading people, who advise the group on what yields investors are looking for. The second objective is to be low enough to win the bid. To issuers, interest represents cost, so the lower the interest the better. That is why competitive bids are awarded on the basis of "net interest cost," that is, whichever syndicate offers to buy the issue at the lowest yield.

At the end of the preliminary meeting, the syndicate turns its proposed scale over to the salespeople, who proceed to solicit orders from the firm's clients. The number of orders taken at this time is a reliable indicator of whether the issue can be sold out at the proposed scale.

About an hour before the bid is due, the manager convenes the final price meeting, which is usually more tense than the first meeting. The meeting begins with the manager presenting the proposed scale, perhaps suggesting the spread, and reporting on orders and on the latest developments in the municipal bond market. Then the floor is open for discussion. Members suggest other scales, often disagree, and even occasionally drop out of the syndicate. While orders continue to come in, with some issues sold out before the meeting is concluded, members argue for perhaps a wider spread or a lower scale. The last order of business is the order period — the time during which orders will be taken, which is usually one or two hours.

Only minutes before the deadline, the final scale is calculated by the firm's computer and the bid phoned to the person who is to deliver it to the issuing municipality. The manager is responsible for ensuring that the sealed bid is delivered, usually by hand, to the muncipality. With the bid goes a good faith check for about 2% of the total value of the issue, which the municipality may use if the dealer should fail to deliver the proceeds of the sale.

With all the bids in hand, the municipality computes the net interest cost of each and awards the issue to the dealer with the lowest one.

The winner is known within minutes of the deadline, at which time the competing syndicates generally reveal their bids to one another.

If their syndicate is the winner, the salespeople start selling immediately. From this point on, competitive and negotiated underwritings are the same. In both types of offerings, the senior manager has, by the time selling commences, issued a release letter, sometimes called a syndicate account letter or agreement among underwriters, to the syndicate members. The letter describes the purchase of the bonds, and it names the account manager who will keep the records.

It also describes the priority of orders; that is, which types of orders are to be filled first. This priority is usually as follows.

* *Presale orders* — Orders received by the syndicate prior to the actual award of the issue are filled first.
* *Group account orders* — Next filled are orders that are credited to the whole account. These orders are credited according to each member's participation in the offering.
* *Designated orders* — Next filled are orders from customers who specify which syndicate member is to fill it.

Figure 7-5. Illustrative Official Statement

---

① $92,820,00
②   STATE OF WASHINGTON
③   General Obligation Bond

State and Local Facilities Loan of 1989 — First Series

④ Interest will accrue from April 1, 1989 and will be payable October 1, 1990 and semiannually thereafter on April 1 and October 1. The Bonds will be
⑤ issued as coupon Bonds in the denomination of $5,000 each, and such coupon Bonds may be registered as to principal only, at the option and ex-
⑥ pense of the holder. Bonds which have been registered may be registered to bearer and thereafter transferred by delivery. The Bonds will be payable
⑦ as to both principal and interest at the office of the State Fiscal Agent, Merchants Deposit & Trust Company, Seattle, Washingon.

⑧ The Bonds are not subject to redemption prior to their stated maturity.

The Bonds have been rated by Moody's Investors Service, Inc. as Aaa and by Standard & Poor's Corporation as AAA. See "Ratings" as to the bases, significance and possible effects of any changes, of the ratings.

In the opinion of Samuel R. Benson, Attorney General of the State of Washington, and of Messrs. Kenny & Kearney, Bond Counsel, (i) the Bonds will be valid and legally binding general obligations of the State of Washington to the payment of which the full faith and credit of the State are pledged; (ii) the Bonds, as property, and the interest thereon, will be
⑨ exempt from taxation by the State of Washington and all its political subdivisions (however, interest on the Bonds will be includable in income of certain financial institutions in determining the amount of State franchise tax payable by them); and (iii) interest on the Bonds will be exempt from Federal income taxation under existing laws as now construed. See "Structure of State Debt" and "Tax Exemption."

Figure 7-5. Illustrative Official Statement (cont.).

---

⑩   Amounts, Maturities, Coupon Rates and Yields or Prices

Series	Amount	Maturing April 1	Coupon Rate	Yield or Price
A	5,640,000	1990	5.00	4.10%
B	5,890,000	1991	5.00	4.15
C	6,140,000	1992	5.00	4.25
D	6,380,000	1993	4.70	4.35
E	6,640,000	1994	4.50	4.45
F	6,890,000	1995	4.50	100
G	7,140,000	1996	4.50	4.60
H	7,390,000	1997	4.70	4.65
I	7,640,000	1998	4.70	100
J	7,890,000	1999	4.70	4.75
K	8,440,000	2000	4.70	4.80
L	8,390,000	2001	4.70	4.85
M	8,640,000	2002	5.00	4.85

(Accrued interest to be added)

The coupon rates shown above are the coupon rates payable by the State resulting from the successful bid for the Bonds on March 15, 1989 by a group of banks and investment banking firms. The yields or prices shown above were furnished by the successful bidders. Other information concerning the terms of the reoffering of the Bonds should be obtained from the successful bidders and not from the State of Washington. See "Sale at Competitive Bidding."

Delivery of the Bonds is subject to the receipt of the approving opinions of the Attorney General of the State of Washington and Bond Counsel, and other conditions specified in the Official Notice of Sale. It is expected that delivery of the Bonds in definitive form will be made in New York City on or about April 13, 1989.

March 15, 1989.

Footnotes:

① Total principal.
② Issuer's name.
③ Issue.
④ Relevant date.
⑤ Denomination at the issue.
⑥ Registration and transfer.
⑦ Trustee and paying agents.
⑧ Redemption features and/or sinking fund.
⑨ Tax status of interest.
⑩ Maturity dates and principal amount.

* *Member takedown orders* — Orders from the public where the member will take the bonds from the account at the takedown price — that is, the member will get the whole spread — are filled last.

All orders are contingent on the actual delivery of the bond certificates. Municipal bonds are arbitrarily "dated" as of the first or fifteenth of the month of issuance. The *offering date*, decided by the underwriters, is the date on which the bonds are sold to the public. Due to possible delays for printing the bonds and other legal procedures, the bonds are offered on a *when, as and if issued* basis. In other words, the firm will sell and deliver the bonds *when* they are issued, *as* they are issued, and *if* they are issued. Normally, the bonds are delivered about 3-4 weeks after the offering date. Interest accrues to the seller from the dated date, and it continues to accrue up to but not including the settlement date.

During the selling period, the manager performs a number of other duties. He:

* Keeps the books for the syndicate.
* Confirms orders over the phone when the order period is over.

Hot issues — that is, issues in great demand — can sell out in a couple of hours. Usually, however, bonds are left after the order period, and orders are taken on a first-come, first-served basis. The syndicate is disbanded when the issue is sold out. Most syndicates run for thirty days, but the members can renew if necessary. Few offerings run that long, however. When an issue does not sell in thirty days, the syndicate can change the terms of the offering, which usually requires the majority consent of the members.

If the issue still cannot be sold, the issue can be distributed among the members or given to a "bond broker."

A bond broker (or "broker's broker") trades only with other dealers. These firms do not deal directly with investors. Of approximately 20 or so such dealers in the country most, whether institutional or individual, are located in New York City.

Municipal bond dealers turn to these brokers when they want to sell bonds out of their inventories or buy bonds for inventory. When selling, bond brokers gather bids from other brokers; this is called the "bid-wanted" business. When buying, they circulate the fact that they are willing to buy a particular bond at a stated yield or price.

When an issue proves to be particularly difficult to sell, the remaining bonds can be given to one broker or to a group of them. The brokers then "put the bonds out for the bid." Syndicate members can, like any other dealer, bid for the bonds. Whoever has the best bid for the group of bonds gets them, although the manager has the right to reject all bids. Brokers usually get ⅛ of a point ($1.25 per bond) as a commission for the transaction.

Besides the obvious difference between the competitive and negotiated processes, there are other points of distinction. In a negotiated underwriting, the pace is a little slower. Preliminary pricing is done and possibly adjusted after some advance orders are taken, with the final prices not set until sale day. Also, the public finance department is more involved in a negotiated underwriting than it is in a competitive bid. Finally, manager's fees are a little different, usually 20% of the spread.

After the Offering

About one month elapses between the time that the issue is sold out and the bonds are actually delivered. During that time, the certificates are being printed, with the final legal opinion of the bond counsel printed on their backs.

At the same time, the manager has to wrap things up. The first order of business is a letter to syndicate members stating the "reoffering terms," that is, the terms by which the bonds are to be reoffered to investors and other buyers.

Such terms include the spread, takedown, and concession. The letter also explains how the issue will be advertised and how members will be represented in the ad. (Syndicate members are generally listed in accordance with the degree of their participation, with the greater contributors at the top of the ad.)

When the bonds are ready for delivery, all payments are made. To pay the issuer, the manager arranges a loan from a commercial bank. If the manager or any other member of the syndicate is a bank, it may extend the loan. The check to the issuer is for the amount agreed upon less the good-faith deposit. The bonds are then delivered and distributed to the members, who fill orders and channel payments for the orders back to the manager. With all payments in hand, the manager retires the loan, distributes the profits among members, and issues a final statement of participations, expenses, and profits.

All this takes a few days.

At about the same time, the issuer makes available a disclosure statement on the new issue. The Municipal Finance Officers Association (MFOA) encourages state and local governments to disclose primary offering information in what are known as "official statements." These disclosure documents, which are not required by law, include all the legal, financial, and other types of information that investors need to make intelligent decisions. The cover page of the official statement summarizes the terms and characteristics of the issue. Sometimes also found on the cover page is information on ratings, authority for issuance, delivery date and place, and security for the issue. The statement is usually sent to the Municipal Securities Information Document Central Repository, where it is microfilmed and stored.

As the syndicate disbands, the bonds become available for purchase and sale in what is known as the "secondary market," which is the subject of Chapter 9. In the next chapter, we will see how corporate bonds are created and marketed.

Chapter 8

Corporate Bonds

Corporations can raise capital in a number of ways. For short periods — that is, for less than five years — they can raise funds through commercial bank loans, promissory notes, or certificates, whether offered publicly or privately. Most banks, however, will not tie up funds in a loan for more than five years, because they are exposed to interest rate risk along with anyone else in the fixed income market. If, for example, a bank extends a loan at 8% for more than five years, what revenues would it lose if interest rates were to rise above 8% during the term of the loan? Its money should be earning greater returns.

To gain the use of capital for more than five years, corporations may turn to sources other than commercial banks. Borrowing from other financial institutions, such as pension funds or insurance companies, is one possibility. Another alternative is distributing stocks or bonds.

Of the two types of securities, bonds offer issuing corporations several advantages over stocks. Issuing stock, or shares of ownership, can weaken the control of the company's founders over decision making and policy setting. Bonds, on the other hand, do not dilute current shareholders' equity.

Bonds are also preferable to bank loans because they provide capital at rates of interest that are generally lower than bank rates. A commercial bank takes deposits from its customers, pays them one rate of interest, and lends the money to, among other clients, corporations in need of capital. When a company sells bonds directly to investors, it effectively cuts out the bank acting as a middleman — and a tier of interest rates. The borrowing process thus becomes more efficient and less expensive.

Bond issues are even more efficient in that the corporation is spared the burden of having to negotiate a separate loan agreement with every potential creditor. Large amounts of capital can be borrowed from hundreds or even thousands of investors through a single, uniform instrument.

HOW A NEGOTIATED UNDERWRITING WORKS

Once the corporation's board of directors decides to offer a bond issue, they employ the services of an "investment banker," that is, a securities dealer acting as an underwriter in a primary offering.

Corporate offerings are similar to municipal offerings in that an underwriter acts as the intermediary between issuer and investing public, but there are a couple of important differences. For one thing, corporations are not under a mandate, as municipalities are, to obtain competitive bids. So just about all corporate offerings are negotiated. Also, unlike municipal debt securities, corporate bonds are subject to the requirements of the Securities Act of 1933. So the underwriting process is different enough from the municipal offering to merit further description.

The Securities Act is simple: Unless the law classifies a security as "exempt," any security sold interstate must be registered with the SEC before it may be offered publicly. (Figures 8-1 and 8-2 list exempted securities and transactions.) Although "security" calls to mind stocks and bonds, the Act defines a security as *any* note, stock, bond, evidence of debt, interest or participation in a profit-sharing agreement, investment contract, voting trust certificate, fractional undivided interest in oil, gas, or other mineral rights, or any warrant to subscribe to, or to purchase, any of the foregoing. Thus the 1933 Act, sometimes referred to as the "Full Disclosure Act," protects investors in any public offering by threatening those who willfully violate the law with fines of up to $10,000 and jail sentences of up to 5 years.

The Cooling-Off Period

Unless either the security or the transaction is classified as exempt, all new issues of securities must be registered with the SEC. To do so, a *registration statement* must be filed with the SEC, and this statement must contain the information and documents relevant to the affairs of that company and to the offering in question. If the issuer omits or misrepresents any material fact, the purchasers of the offering may sue to recoup part or all of their investments from the issuer or the underwriter.

The date on which the public offering is to commence is usually set for 20 days after the statement is filed with the SEC. During this 20-day *cooling-off period,* as it is frequently called, the SEC examines the statement to determine whether it contains any obvious omissions or mis-

Figure 8-1. Securities Exempted from Registration Under the Securities Act of 1933

---

1. U.S. government, including ones it guarantees
2. State or municipality, including ones it guarantees
3. Domestic banks or trust companies (but not bankhold ing companies)
4. Commercial paper or bankers' acceptances maturing within 9 months
5. Building and loan associations
6. Farmers' cooperative association
7. Common or contract carriers, such as railroads
8. Court-approved receivers' or trustees' certificates
9. Small business investment companies (SBIC)
10. Intrastate (see SEC Rule 147 in "Private Placement" section)
11. Religious, educational, charitable, or nonprofit
12. Insurance policies or mixed annuity contracts (but not variable annuities and variable life insurance policies)
13. Offerings that qualify under Regulation A of the Securites Act of 1933. A less costly way to accomplish a distribution, Regulation A permits a qualified registration exemption for small yearly offerings of not over $1,500,000 by a corporation or for $100,000 by an affiliated person; however, it does require distribution of an informative offering circular.
14. Offerings that qualify under Regulation D of the Securities Act of 1933. SEC Rules 501-506, under Regulation D, set forth the terms and conditions under which issuers can offer unregistered securities for sale in limited dollar amounts to a limited number of investors and/or to defined "accredited persons." For the most part these unregistered offerings are called private placements.

Figure 8-2. Transactions Exempted from Registration Under the Securities Act of 1933

1. Those by anyone other than the issuer, a dealer, or an underwriter
2. Broker's transactions that are not solicited from the customer (in other words, the customer takes the initiative)
3. Private placements (as opposed to public offerings)
4. Transactions by securities dealers (*except* when the dealers are still handling an unsold allotment of a registered new issue, or handling trades within 90 days of an initial public offering or 40 days of subsequent public offerings of that registered new issue)

representations. If it finds any, it sends the issuer a *deficiency (or bedbug) letter*, and the effective date is postponed until the deficiency is corrected.

In some cases, the issuer may request an earlier effective date. If it has a record of compliance with previous issues, if it is up-to-date in its SEC reporting requirements, or if it promises to deliver a preliminary prospectus (covered later in this chapter) at least 48 hours prior to the effective date, the public offering may begin as soon as 48 hours after filing the registration statement with the SEC. After receiving either a regular registration statement or an application for an earlier effective date, the SEC notifies the issuer only if the date is not approved for any reason.

Whatever the effective date turns out to be, it must be strictly observed. In no case may a distribution take place before this date. Even an offer to sell before that date violates the law. On the other hand, if the issuer/underwriter does not make the offering within three days after the effective date, the SEC must be notified immediately.

Whether an all-or-none offering is going to be offered may be unclear for weeks or months. In such a case, the registration statement can remain effective for up to nine months, and in the case of bond or stock issues by large, publicly held corporations for up to two years, as long as no material changes occur in the affairs of the corporation.

Only the issuer — that is, a corporation, trust, or association that issues certificates in return for funds — may register the security with SEC.

When the statement becomes effective, it assures would-be investors *only* that the prospectus contains all the information required by law. By accepting the statement, the SEC neither guarantees the issue nor approves the security as an investment. It does not even state that the information is accurate.

Thus, investors have to make their own investment decisions based on what they see in the prospectus. The law does stipulate, however, that the prospectus is the only written offering for a new issue that may be used and that the prospectus must be delivered to purchasers with the confirmation of purchase — at the very latest. The prospectus, therefore, is the basis for any suit by investors against the issuers or underwriters whose names appear in the statement. Misrepresentation by a salesperson may also give rise to suits.

The Trust Indenture Act of 1939 picks up where the 1933 Act leaves off on bond issues. For SEC-registered debt securities, issuers are obliged to make the same relevant facts available to the SEC in a formal registration statement.

U.S. government and municipal securities are exempted from the Trust Indenture Act. However, corporate issuers of bonds with a principal amount of $1 million or more must give the SEC an *indenture qualification statement*. This statement specifies the obligations of the issuers and the duties of the trustee(s). The law also requires that one or more trustees be appointed to see to it that the terms of the indenture are carried out. Trustees, who must not have conflicting interests, qualify themselves with the SEC annually, and act as a fiduciary for the bond issue.

The indenture qualification statement registers only the indenture with the SEC. In general, the indenture qualification statement is part of the registration statement for a bond issue. If a bond is not required to be registered, the indenture qualification statement will be filed separately.

The corporate issuer may distribute securities without meeting the requirements of this Act, in what is known as a "private placement." Subject to numerous restrictions and requirements, a *private placement* is an offering of securities that has not been registered with the SEC. Since it does not require registration and a prospectus (because the investors do not intend to resell the securities in the immediate future), a private placement is less costly than a public offering. Such investors, however, must give the issuers "investment letters," which state the investors' intention not to resell the securities. (If they should resell the unregistered securities, they may be regarded as "statutory" underwriters under the terms of the Securities Act of 1933.) Each subsequent transfer of unregistered securities must be accompanied by an investment letter, which transfers title to the new private owner, who likewise intends to hold the securities for a portfolio and not for resale. Each unregistered certificate must be imprinted with a legend that warns the holder about distribution restrictions under the law. Because a private placement represents an exemption from the Securities Act of 1933, however, it is laden with numerous restrictions and requirements. It is not an option that is practical for every issuer.

Most corporate issuers opt instead for a public offering, in which the new issue is distributed directly to investors at large. (The process is described later in this chapter.) In a private placement, the issue is offered to a limited number of purchasers who are often institutional investors. In a private placement, the offering is sold directly by the issuer to the purchaser, often without the help of the invest-

ment banker, at a lower overall cost because such a placement avoids the expenses of a public offering.

The Investment Banker

Once the corporation has selected a securities dealer
to act as underwriter, the investment banker may act as
either principal or agent. As *principal*, it purchases the
issue from the firm, assumes the financial responsibility
for selling it, and resells it to the public. Regardless of its
success — or the lack of it — in selling the issue to the
public, the underwriter must pay the full contracted price
to the issuer. Generally, only the more reputable corporations whose securities have a proven history of success
enjoy such an arrangement. For making this commitment,
investment bankers receive a higher fee than they would if
they acted as agents. In fact, sometimes the commitment
is so risky that underwriters ask for a *market-out* clause —
an "escape hatch" provision that relieves them of their
obligations under certain conditions. When underwriters
make such a guarantee to the issuer, it is called a *firm commitment;* that is, they agree to sell all of the offering or retain
any securities that they cannot distribute, at the same time
guaranteeing the full proceeds to the issuer. In effect, they
absorb a loss for any undistributed securities.

As agent, an investment banker is committed to selling only as much of the issue as possible. It has no financial responsibility to the issuer for any part of the offering
not distributed. Naturally, the fees are lower for this kind
of service, known as a *best efforts* commitment. Small corporations with little or no track record must content themselves with this arrangement. In some cases, if a concern
cannot get a firm commitment, it may decide on an *all-or-
none offering;* that is if *all* the offering is not sold, then *none*
of it will be. The entire offering is then cancelled.

Investment bankers may also act as "standbys" in the
issuance of new securities by a *subscription privilege.* This
right or privilege enables present holders to purchase por-

tions of the new issue within a fixed period (usually 30 to 60 days) before the issue may be offered to the public. In such a case, the issuer may ask an underwriter to guarantee the distribution of any leftover shares or bonds not sold through the rights offering. In this case, the underwriter, acting as a principal, agrees to "stand by" until the rights period expires. Such an arrangement is called a *standby agreement*, or a *standby underwriting*.

After registering the security with the SEC, the issuer and underwriters have a number of additional obligations:

* The *preliminary prospectus* must be issued.
* The *due-diligence meeting* must be held.
* The issue must be "*blue skyed.*"
* The *agreement among underwriters* must be signed.
* An *agreement between the underwriters and the issuer* must be signed.

After these matters are attended to and the registration statement is scrutinized by the SEC, a final prospectus is issued for the public offering.

Let's take these steps one by one.

The Preliminary Prospectus

Solicitation of orders for new issues may not take place until the effective date, and the only offer in writing that may be made is by the prospectus. Yet the law allows underwriters to obtain *indications of interest* ("circle") from investors by sending them a preliminary prospectus. This prospectus, the *red herring*, alerts prospective buyers that the document is not final and that it is not a solicitation for an order. Although the red herring contains most of the pertinent information, often including the "maximum" offering price to give investors a general idea of the issue's value, that information is incomplete and possibly even inaccurate. Customers who indicate an interest in the new issue simple contact their broker/dealers, who often use this indication of interest to decide whether or not to participate in the underwriting group.

Due-Diligence Meeting

All syndicate participants and corporation officials must hold a "due-diligence" meeting sometime before the effective date. The purpose of this meeting is to review the items to be included in the formal agreement between them, such as what is to go into the registration statement, what is to go into the final prospectus (used to solicit orders), and points of negotiation for the underwriting agreement between the issuer and the investment bankers. Price may also be discussed, but it is not set until the night before or the morning of the effective date to allow for accommodation to prevailing market conditions.

In a competitive bidding situation, the competing groups do not discuss price with the corporation, only within their own group so that no group gains an unfair advantage. In this case, the due-diligence meeting is usually called an *information meeting.*

Blue-Skying the Issue

To be sure that the offering complies with state laws, attorneys for the underwriters check out the laws of each state where an offering will be made. This process is called *blue-skying the issue.* (When the Kansas state legislature passed the nation's first state securities law in the early 1900s, one of the lawmakers quipped, "Now Kansas citizens will have more of a basis for making investment decisions than merely by the shade of the blue sky.") If the legal maze makes the underwriters' involvement impractical, they will often cancel out of the deal.

Agreement Among Underwriters

Soon after the due-diligence meeting, the underwriters participating in the distribution draw up an agreement among themselves, which specifies, among other things, the responsibilities of the manager, including the following:

1. *Forming the Syndicate.* Once part of a syndicate, an investment banker may safely assume that its association with the group will continue for all future underwritings in which any one of them acts as manager. In fact, once established as a significant distributor of securities in such offerings, an investment banker becomes recognized as a "major-bracket" participant, and its name is publicized near the top of the group's tombstone. The percentage of its underwriting commitment ranks equally with other major-bracket firms. Other investment bankers in those syndicates may be classified as submajor-, middle-major- and minor-bracket underwriters, depending on their percentages of participation.

Once an underwriter has taken indications of interest and decides to participate in a group, it becomes subject to Rule 10b-6 of the Securities and Exchange Commission. This rule prohibits an underwriter from either buying a security in the marketplace for its own account or from inducing someone else to buy it while the distribution is pending.

2. *Appointing a Selling Group.* The manager also appoints other broker/dealers who agree to act as the underwriters' agents and to offer some of these securities to their customers. These firms make up what is known as "selling group." Each selling group member is allocated a portion of the issue to sell. Though selling group members abide by the terms and restrictions of the underwriting agreement, they do not receive the full underwriters' spread, because they assume no individual responsibility or financial liability to the issuing corporation. Their "*selling concession*" may range from 25% to 75% of the spread, depending on how difficult it is to sell the issue.

It is not unusual to see firms wearing two hats, acting as both underwriters and as members of the selling group. With a commitment as underwriters and an allocation as selling group appointees, their "double duty" enables them not only to enjoy greater participation in the offering, when the issue is popular, but also to better satisfy their clients. Even when the issue isn't that popular, underwriters use selling groups because members of today's selling group may be tomorrow's managing underwriters in other offerings.

3. *Establishing the Underwriters' Retention ("the Pot").* The manager holds back a part of the issue (often about 25%) for allocation to the selling group and to institutional purchasers, who deal in substantial quantities. This reserved allocation is called *the pot.* Since, in effect, each group member gets only 75% of its commitment, the manager's juggling of percentages is a touchy responsibility. Keeping everyone happy is the name of the game. Participants or customers want what they want, and the underwriters' rationale is easily understood: "If we must assume financial responsibility for the deal, we should enjoy the benefits of popular distributions and be able to satisfy our own customers first."

4. *Conducting Group Sales. Group sales* are not sales made by the selling group. Rather, they are sales made out of the pot. If an institutional investor wants, say, $100,000 worth of bonds, the manager fills the order out of the pot, rather than taking the securities from each of, say, ten underwriters. Unless the purchaser designates otherwise, all syndicate members benefit pro rata according to their percentages of participation. Group sales are good sales stimulators. When the manager announces, "The pot is clean!" sellers find that orders come in more quickly because investors realize that institutions consider the offering a good investment.

5. *Stabilizing the Market.* Either on the effective date or within a couple of days thereafter, the underwriters begin making their public offering. At about the same time, the security begins trading openly in the marketplace. This trading activity is called the *"aftermarket."* Since the un-

derwriters are bound to the terms of their agreement with company, they cannot allow the market price to go much below the public offering price. So unless the offering is an immediate sellout, the managing underwriter is empowered to maintain a bid in the aftermarket at or perhaps slightly below the public offering price, on behalf of the syndicate. This *syndicate bid* may be continued for as long as necessary, but it typically lasts no more than two weeks.

This is the one time when manipulating a market price is legal. Ordinarily anyone found manipulating the market prices of securities is subject to prosecution by the SEC under the terms of the Securities and Exchange Act of 1934. But stabilization to facilitate a bona fide distribution of securities is exempted from this restriction. Prompt notice, however, must be filed with the SEC and with the appropriate exchange.

When stabilizing aftermarket prices, the syndicate manager has no intention of repurchasing the entire issue. Often the manager notifies participating firms that the stabilizing bid is made with a penalty attached. In this case, their customers should not enter the aftermarket to sell this new security at the price of the stabilizing bid. Otherwise, the member firms either lose their spread or concession, are penalized so much per bond, or are not allowed to participate in future offerings.

A "penalty syndicate bid" is written into agreements between the underwriters and selling groups to ensure that participants strive to distribute the issue to investment portfolios and not to traders and speculators intent upon quick profits.

Although syndicate managers must make every attempt to maintain the public offering price, they have the authority to release members from that obligation if they see that the task has become hopeless. The security then fluctuates to its true level, as determined by market forces, even though the underwriters are still financially responsible to the issuer.

6. *Allocating Hot Issues.* Syndicate managers need not worry about maintaining the public offering price of "hot issues," which are securities that trade at an immediate premium in the aftermarket. This situation is a happy but delicate one. Using their business judgment, managers can legally oversell issues by up to 15% of the offering, because they will probably get that many cancellations.

Even if they do not, they can cover their short positions in one of two other ways: Managers can go into the aftermarket and purchase the securities. This alternative is not considered a stabilization effort because the syndicate pays the offering price or more. Any loss sustained in this process, like the losses sustained in stabilization, is apportioned pro rata to each member. That's one way.

Another way is for the corporation to grant the underwriters an option or warrant to purchase additional securities of the offering at a price below that of the public offering. This arrangement, called a "green shoe privilege," is usually exercisable within 30 days after the effective date at the underwriter's guaranteed price. This right, considered a new security, is registered with the SEC via an amendment to the original registration statement. The manager exercises the option, closes out the short position, and distributes the profit to each member pro rata.

7. *Agreement Between Underwriters and the Corporation.* This formal contract, called the "underwriting agreement" or the "purchase agreement," establishes firm prices. Signed the evening before or on the morning of the effective date, the contract is immediately filed with the SEC and becomes part of the registration statement via amendment.

The agreement also reflects the nature of the syndicate's responsibility to the issuer; that is, as a (Western) account or undivided (Eastern) account.

The Public Offering

Once the public offering is permitted to begin, underwriters start to solicit orders from investors, whether those investors saw the red herring or not. The only way that the underwriters may legally solicit orders is by means of a *final prospectus*, which is a condensation of the information in the updated, amended registration statement. At the very latest, the final prospectus must be sent to purchasers with their confirmation statements. This requirement is so strict that investors who make a purchase without having seen the final prospectus may cancel their orders, even after receiving their confirmation orders, without any penalty or loss.

(By the way, no margin may be extended by a participating distributor to purchasers of a new issue during the distribution and for up to 30 days thereafter.)

A tombstone advertisement is also published about this time.

Once the bonds have been fully distributed through the efforts of the underwriters' salespeople, the security starts trading in the secondary market along with the debt issues of the U.S. government, federal agencies, and municipalities.

TYPES OF CORPORATE BONDS

The lower rate of interest is particularly important to a corporate issuer because its reason for being is different from that of the U.S. government or municipalities. Whereas government at any level has to raise money to provide services, most corporations exist to make a profit. When they borrow money in any way, the interest becomes a cost of doing business. They must be able to earn profit at a greater rate than they incur expenses — including interest expenses. Using borrowed money to generate a greater return than the rate of interest paid out on the loan is called "leverage," and this is a characteristic more of corporate debt offerings than of Treasury or municipal issues.

Corporate bonds also differ from government issues in that the ability of the issuer to pay must be more closely scrutinized. Whereas Treasury or municipal securities are backed by taxing power, corporate debt needs to be secured in other ways. As a result, corporate bonds are usually categorized according to how they are collateralized. Bonds vary widely in this respect. If a company is financially strong, and if the amount of money needed is reasonable, a company may be able to issue a bond that is secured only by its general credit. On the other hand, if the issuer is not financially sound, investors will probably be interested only in bonds secured by tangible assets.

Mortgage bonds are secured (or collateralized) by a legal claim to specific assets of the issuer, such as real property like a factory. If the company defaults on payments due the bondholders, they have direct claims on the assets pledged.

If the bond indenture states that the agreement is "open-ended," the company can use the property pledged as collateral for these bonds for *additional* borrowing. Open-end mortgage bonds are normally issued in a series. All issues in the series give the holders the same claim to the common collateral, or equal "seniority," that is, no holder has a "senior" claim over the holder of another bond in the series.

Issues in a series can differ by having varying interest rates and other distinguishing features. One way in which issues differ is that their maturities are usually staggered according to a schedule set forth in the indenture. The issuing company's total long-term capital needs are met with the capital borrowed only as needed, and the debt is paid off in stages instead of in a lump sum.

If the bond is *closed-end,* the first lender has "senior status" (that is, first claim on the mortgaged property). Other loans can still be secured by the same property, but they are junior to the claims of the prior bondholders.

Sometimes, if a company undergoes reorganization or faces bankruptcy, it might ask first bondholders to surrender their status to a new class of creditors willing to lend capital; they, in turn, become senior bondholders. This new issue, called a "prior lien bond," is then regarded as a first mortgage, and the former issues become second mortgages.

A *debenture* is a bond that is backed only by the general credit of the issuer. Investors who purchase debentures become *general* creditors of the company. They are protected by the overall assets of the issuer, not by a particular asset, as are mortgage bondholders. Usually, only strong corporations with excellent credit are able to sell debentures, whereas financially weak corporations typically must resort to pledging specific assets as collateral.

Debentures can be senior or subordinated. A *senior* issue has first claim on company assets; a *subordinated* debenture by the same company has second claim.

An *equipment trust bond* is a specialized type of bond that is backed by specific types of equipment, such as trains, trucks, and airplanes. These bonds tend to be very safe because the bondholder is protected by the value of the equipment if the company defaults. Holders have an extra measure of protection in that the payback on equipment trust certificates is generally arranged to stay ahead of the depreciation on the equipment.

The typical equipment trust bond is arranged under what is known as the "Philadelphia plan," whereby the user of the equipment does the following:

* Pays a 20% down payment on the purchase price of the equipment.
* Gives title to the equipment to an independent trustee (a bank), which collects payments from the company and makes payments to the bondholders.

After the entire issue is retired, title to the equipment passes to the airline or transportation company that has been using the equipment. In effect, the user of the equipment pays for the equipment on the installment plan.

This type of issue is structured as a serial bond because it is self-liquidating. That is, it requires partial repayments of principal by means of a series of annual maturities. Smaller amounts often come due for redemption in the first few years, allowing time for the user to build revenues by making use of the new equipment. Over time the size of the repayments increases. This progressive increase in the size of payments is called a "balloon effect."

Income bonds are different in that they are not issued, but given in exchange for other bonds, usually in the case of impending bankruptcy. The company makes the promised interest payments only if it can afford to do so. If the company is losing money, it can omit making its interest payments. However, if the company is operating profitably, as defined in the bond indenture, it cannot omit making the interest payments.

If the company can't make the interest payments on its income bonds, the missed payments accrue at a predetermined interest rate and must be paid off before any dividends can be paid to the common shareholders. If a company misses an interest payment on any type of bond other than an income bond, the bondholders have the right to force the company into bankruptcy so as to protect their interests. Holders of income bonds, however, cannot force a company into bankruptcy for missing interest payments. In exchange for forfeiting this right, investors earn a higher rate of return on an income bond *when and if* the company makes interest payments.

PRICING CORPORATE BONDS

Like Treasuries, munis, and most other fixed-income instruments, corporate bond prices react to interest rate fluctuations and to changes in the inflation rate. However, the creditworthiness of the corporate issuer — its ability to pay — is much more of a factor in pricing. The ability to make interest payments and ultimately to repay the loan is indicated by a bond's rating. A highly rated bond, being less risky, commands a lower rate of interest than a bond with a low rating.

Bonds are rated on the relative probability of their issuer's defaulting. To reduce exposure to default as much as possible, bond investors watch bond ratings very closely. The two best known bond rating organizations are Standard & Poor's (S&P) and Moody's, whose ratings represent their current opinions as to the quality of most *large* corporate and municipal *bond* issues and of commercial paper.

The ratings provide a gauge of the relative ease with which a corporation can pay its bond interest. In evaluating a bond, the rating services are most interested in a company's health, as evidenced by its financial statements. Of course, because ratings are updated periodically, a bond's rating will change with the financial fortunes of the issuing corporation.

The rating notations of both services are similar. Standard & Poor's ratings range from AAA, AA, A, and so on to D. The corresponding ratings by Moody's are Aaa, Aa, A, and so on to D. Plus or minus signs are used by S&P to provide a finer calibration within a given category.

The first four categories, AAA (Aaa) through BBB (Baa), represent "investment grade" securities. Bonds reflecting the highest capability of the issuer to meet all obligations are rated AAA, whereas BBB securities indicate only "adequate" capability. Institutional investors usually confine their bond purchases to the top four categories of bonds.

Bonds with lower than investment-grade ratings — BB, B, CCC, CC — are considered to be "speculative," which means that the issuer's ability to meet obligations is less certain. These bonds are sometimes called "junk bonds" due to their high yield and high risk.

To improve the attractiveness of its bonds, a corporate issuer may institute several features that enhance either its creditworthiness or the appeal of the security itself.

One such enhancement is the sinking fund. In a sinking fund, the issuing company sets aside a portion of current earnings for the sole purpose of retiring an issue of

*Figure 8-3. Ratings of Bonds.**

Investment Bracket	Fitch	Moody's	Standard & Poor's
Top quality	AAA	Aaa	AAA
	AA	Aa	AA
	A	A	A
Medium quality	BBB	Baa 1-2-3*	BBB
Speculative	BB	Ba	BB
	B	B	B
Poor quality	CCC	Caa	CCC
	CC	Ca	CC
	C	C	C
Value is questionable	DDD		DDD
	DD		DD
	D		D

* The number 1 added to these ratings indicates the *high* end of the category — number 2 the *mid range* ranking — number 3 the *low* end.

bonds. Sinking funds offer great protection to the bond-holder. To reflect the additional security, the prices of bonds secured by sinking funds are higher than those of bonds without such funds, but the yields are lower.

Another enhancement is convertibility. A "convertible bond" may be exchanged for a specified number of common shares in the issuing corporation at a predetermined price. Such a bond offers holders not only income but also the option to share, through conversion, in the company's fortunes as owners of common stock. Convertible bonds usually yield less than equivalent bonds that are not convertible.

The issuing corporation states the conversion price of a convertible bond in the indenture. The "conversion price" is the price of the underlying common stock at which the bond may be converted. The price is set at such a level that bondholders do not benefit financially if they convert before the underlying stock reaches the conversion price. For example, a $1,000 convertible bond's indenture specifies a conversion price of $40 a share. When the issuer's common stock reaches that price, bondholders may convert each certificate into 25 shares ($1,000 face value divided by $25). Owners do not benefit financially by conversion, however, until the common stock reaches or exceeds $40 per share.

Generally, by the time the stock reaches the conversion price, the price of the bond has increased as well.

The number of shares that the holder of a convertible bond receives at conversion is determined by the "conversion ratio," which is calculated by dividing the face amount of the bond by the conversion price. In the preceding example, the conversion ratio is $1,000 divided by $40, or 25 shares of stock.

The conversion price must be adjusted downward in the event of stock dividends and splits. For instance, a bond has a conversion price of $40, and the stock has a two-for-one stock split. The $40 conversion price is adjusted to $20, and the number of shares to be received is doubled ($1,000 divided by $20, which results in 50 shares).

These adjustments protect bondholders against "dilution."

"Conversion parity" is the point at which the price of the convertible bond and that of the corresponding common stock are equal. Conversion parity is calculated by means of the following formula:

$$\frac{\text{Par value of bond}}{\text{Conversion price}} = \frac{\text{Market price of bond}}{\text{Market price of stock}}$$

Here's an example: A bond is convertible at $20 per share, and the common stock is selling at $35. The formula is then:

$$\frac{\text{Par value of bond}}{\text{Conversion price}} = \frac{\text{Market price of bond}}{\text{Market price of stock}}$$

$$\frac{\$1,000}{\$20} = \frac{\text{Market price of bond}}{\$35}$$

$$\$1,750 = \text{Market price of bond}$$

When the bond is trading at 175, or $1,750, it is worth the same as (that is, it is at "parity" with) the underlying stock at $35 per share.

If a discrepancy arises between the value of the stock and the value of a convertible bond, an investor could make a profit by simultaneously buying one security and selling the other on the bond and stock markets. This activity is called "arbitrage," and it is usually practiced only by professional traders called "arbitrageurs."

UNDERSTANDING BOND QUOTATIONS

The investor who wants to enter orders to buy or sell stock needs to know only the name and current price of the stock. Bond investors need additional information: namely, the rate of interest the bond is paying and its maturity.

Let's look at the IBM 9⅜04 in the left-hand column. The description "IBM9⅜04" means that the issuer of the bond is International Business Machines, that the bond has a 9⅜% coupon (or nominal) rate, and that it matures in 2004. Bond investors and brokers would refer to this bond as "nine and three-eighths of oh-four." This information tells you two things: First, that the bond will pay $93.25 in interest each year, in two semiannual payments of $46.625 each; second, that it will pay the holder of the face value of $1,000.

Skip the next column, labeled "Cur Yld" for now.

Figure 8-4. Reading the Bond Quotations

NEW YORK EXCHANGE BONDS

Tuesday, March 17, 1987

Total Volume $33,610,000

SALES SINCE JANUARY 1

1987	1986	1985
$2,085,513,000	$2,589,837,000	$1,841,393,000

	Domestic Tue.	Domestic Mon.	All Issues Tue.	All Issues Mon.
Issues traded	802	784	806	789
Advances	320	289	323	289
Declines	280	292	280	295
Unchanged	202	203	203	205
New highs	35	37	36	37
New lows	6	10	6	10

Dow Jones Bond Averages

–1985– High	–1985– Low	–1986– High	–1986– Low	–1987– High	–1987– Low		Tuesday –1987–		Tuesday –1986–		Tuesday –1985–	
83.73	72.27	93.65	83.73	95.51	93.43	20 Bonds	94.77	+0.06	89.89	–0.02	72.32	–0.11
82.88	68.62	95.79	81.85	98.23	95.64	10 Utilities	97.08	+0.19	90.43	–0.07	68.97	–0.20
84.58	75.61	91.64	84.82	93.10	91.21	10 Industrial	92.46	–0.07	89.36	+0.03	75.68	–0.02

Bonds	Cur Yld	Vol	High	Low	Close	Net Chg.
Hutton 12s05	11.3	24	106⅝	106	106	– ⅝
IBM Cr 9⅞88	9.7	10	102	102	102	+ ⅜
IBM Cr 9⅝90	9.3	140	103¾	103¾	103¾	...
ICN 12⅞98	12.7	30	101⅝	101	101	– ¾
IdelB 9¼00f	...	25	92	89	92	+ 3
IllBel 8s04	8.3	15	96¾	96¾	96¾	– 1½
IllPw 10½04	10.0	10	105½	105½	105½	+ ½
IllPw 8⅝06	8.9	1	97	97	97	– 1
IllPw 9⅜16	9.2	25	102	102	102	...
Inco 12⅜10	12.0	20	103	103	103	...
IndBel 8⅛11	8.5	15	96	96	96	– ¾
IndBel 8⅛17	8.5	10	95⅛	95⅛	95⅛	– 1⅜
Inexc 8½00	cv	32	91	90⅝	90⅝	...
InldStl 9½00	10.1	5	93⅞	93⅞	93⅞	+ 1¾
InldStl 7.9s07	10.3	36	76½	76½	76½	...
InldStl 11¼90	11.2	292	100¾	99⅝	100½	– 1½
ItgRs 10¾96	10.8	33	99½	99¼	99½	+ ¼
Intlgc 11.99s96	12.8	15	94	93⅞	94	+ ⅛
Intrfst 7¾05	cv	30	69	68½	69	...
IBM 9⅜04	8.9	111	105⅛	105	105	...
IBM 7⅞04	cv	414	122¼	121	122	+ ¾
IBM 10¼95	9.1	8	113	113	113	– 1
IPap 8.85s95	8.7	10	102	102	102	...
IntRec 9s10	cv	8	86	85	86	...
Intnr 10½08	cv	90	135	131½	135	+ 3¾
Intnr 11s95	10.2	10	108	108	108	+ 2¼
Ipco 5¼89	5.6	4	94½	94½	94½	

Bonds	Cur Yld	Vol	High	Low	Close	Net Chg.
Mobil 13.76s04	12.0	27	115⅛	115⅛	115⅛	...
Monog 10s99	11.0	10	91	91	91	...
Mons 8¾08	8.7	75	100¾	100¾	100¾	– ¼
MonW 4⅞90	5.2	57	93	92½	93	...
MonW 9⅜00	9.3	4	100½	100½	100½	+ ⅛
MntWC 6½87	6.5	2	99½	99½	99½	...
MntWC 9¼90	9.2	5	101	101	101	– ½
MntWC 9.6s95	9.1	15	105⅜	105⅜	105⅜	...
Morgn 4¾98	cv	10	234	234	234	...
MtSTl 9¾12	9.2	34	106	105½	106	+ ½
MtSTl 9⅝15	9.1	9	105¼	105¼	105¼	...
MtSTl 8⅝18	8.7	10	99¼	99¼	99¼	+ ¼
NBD 8¼10	cv	40	134	134	134	...
NBI 8¼07	cv	1	77	77	77	+ ½
NLInd 7½95	9.0	145	83	82	83	+ 2
NWA 7½10	cv	31	126	126	126	– 1
NConv 9s08	cv	15	90¾	90¾	90¾	– ¼
NtEdu 6½11	cv	30	115½	115	115	...
NEnt 4¾96	cv	3	58	58	58	+ 1
NtGyp zr04	...	757	61½	60	61½	+ 1
NMed 9s06	cv	113	114¾	114½	114⅝	+ ⅛
NMed 8s08	cv	187	103⅞	103½	103½	– ⅜
NMed 12¾99A	11.8	5	107⅞	107⅞	107⅞	+ 2⅝
NMed 12⅛99B	11.5	5	105⅛	105	105	– ⅛
NMEd 12s00	11.4	10	105	105	105	...
NMed 12½00	11.8	25	106½	106	106	– ½
NMed zr04	...	252	22¾	22¾	22¾	⅜

The column headed "Vol" tells you the number of IBM bonds traded that day. In this case, 111 bonds traded.

The "High," "Low," and "Close" columns provide a record of price fluctuations during the trading day. The highest price at which IBM traded for the day was 105⅛, and the lowest was 105 — the same price at which it closed.

Remember that bond quotations are not read the same as stock quotations. In stock trading, "95⅛" means "$95.125." In bond trading, "95⅛" means $951.25." In other words, a "point" in a stock price is $1, but a "point" in bond trading is $10.

The "Net Chg." (net change) column marks the change in the closing price from the last day's closing price. The IBM 9⅜04 did not change in price from yesterday. The IBM 7⅞04, on the next line down, went up ¾-point ($7.50), as indicated by the plus sign. So yesterday's closing was 121¼ (122 – ¾). The IBM bond below the 7⅞04 went down a full point ($10), so that yesterday's close was 114 (113 + 1).

Now let's go back to the "Cur Yld." (current yield) column. Because the price of the IBM 9⅜04 bond (105, or $1,050.00) is higher than the face value ($1,000), it is said to be trading at a *premium.* Because the seller has to pay more to own the bond, the yield on the investment is reduced. So if you apply the current yield formula to this bond, you will find that the current yield for the IBM 9⅜04 bond is 8.9% — just the figure shown in the column.

A bond that is selling for less than the face amount, such as the IntRec 9s10 a little farther down the column, is said to be trading at a *discount.* Because the discount in the price represents less of an investment outlay for the buyer, the percentage return is higher than if the bond were trading at *par*, that is, at its face value.

New issues of corporate bonds are brought to market almost always through a negotiated underwriting. When the issue is sold out and the syndicate disbanded, most corporate bonds — along with the debt securities of the U.S. government, federal agencies, and municipalities — are traded in the over-the-counter market. This part of the so-called "secondary market" is the subject of the next chapter.

Chapter 9

The Secondary Market

Once a bond — corporate, municipal, or Treasury — is brought to market, it begins to trade in the "secondary market." The syndicate, now disbanded, or the primary dealer, no longer plays a role in offering the securities. Instead, the bonds are bought and sold among investors, both individual and institutional.

Generally, buying or selling bonds in this market is easy and convenient. Most bonds, especially those issued by highly rated corporations and the government, are readily marketable and are traded on exchanges or over the

counter. Most bonds are therefore considered liquid investments — that is, readily convertible to cash.

The secondary market includes exchange and over-
the-counter trading and, in fact, some bonds are traded on
the New York Stock Exchange. The great preponderance of
bond trading, however, takes place in the OTC market. All
U.S. government securities, all federal agency issues, all
municipal bonds, and most corporate debt instruments are
traded OTC. So when we talk about bond trading, we have
to talk about the over-the-counter market.

THE BROKER-DEALERS

The over-the-counter market is not located in any one
place. Rather, it consists of thousands of broker/dealers
located throughout the country and transacting business
by telephone. Of the great variety of over-the-counter
firms, some engage only in OTC business and some specialize in particular types of securities, such as government or
municipal bonds. Some firms deal both on the exchanges
and in the over-the-counter market.

These firms are called broker/dealers because they
can buy or sell securities either as customer's brokers
(agents) or as dealers (principals). When acting as *agents*,
they buy and sell in behalf of their customers, who assume
the responsibility for losses and who benefit by profits. The
broker receives only a commission for executing the customer's orders. When acting as *principals*, they buy and
sell securities for their own inventories, not for their customers. They assume the risk of ownership. When they
sell the securities to customers or to other broker/dealers,
they make a profit (or lose money), depending on market
action. They receive no commission; instead, they charge
a markup on sales and a markdown on purchases.

On any one trade, broker/dealers may act as brokers
or as dealers, never as both. And they must also tell customers whether they are acting as agents or as principals.
As agents, they must disclose the amount of commission

charged. As principals, they must show the amount of markup or markdown on the confirmation statements sent to the customers.

Broker/dealers conduct all their over-the-counter business by telephone. When a customer calls the brokerage firm with an order, the broker/dealer can sell the bond to or buy it from the customer, if the firm is a market maker in the security. If the firm doesn't have the security in its inventory, it can go short the security to the customer, as long as its price is competitive with the best market in the street. Or it can negotiate a transaction with another firm that is a market maker in behalf of the customer.

Many broker/dealers "make markets" in securities, that is, they specialize in buying and selling the securities. These "market makers" are willing at all times to buy or sell the security at the quoted price and in multiples of the security's basic trading unit. For bonds the basic unit is 10 certificates.

Because transactions are effected this way, the OTC market is called a "negotiated" market. This contrasts with the way business is transacted on a stock exchange, which is an "auction" market. On an exchange, the shares are actually auctioned — the price of the stock is set by the highest bid or the lowest offer.

Broker/dealers acting as market makers may deal with many kinds of customers. Some are wholesalers and deal only with other dealers in what is often called the "inside market." Some deal only with large institutions, such as pension funds or insurance companies. Some smaller firms buy from wholesalers and sell to individual investors.

HOW AN OTC TRADE IS EXECUTED

Whether acting as agent or as principals, the traders in the trading department are supposed to make the firm's inventory of debt securities as profitable as possible. Like many businesses, brokerage firms finance their inventories; bonds in the firm's own account are costing the company money in the form of interest expense every day. Just holding inventory exposes the firm to interest-rate risk. (Sometimes, to hedge that risk on a large inventory, two or more dealers will hold the securities in a joint account.) The traders' job is to turn inventory — that is, buy and sell it — quickly and profitably.

A broker/dealer, whether receiving an order from a customer or trading for the brokerage firm's investors, locates the market makers in the security and the current price ranges of all over-the-counter securities by means of several information sources:

* The National Association of Securities Dealers Automated Quotations (NASDAQ) system
* The National Quotations Bureau (NQB) sheets

For municipal bonds, the trader can also get information from:

* *The Blue List*
* *Daily Bond Buyer*
* *Munifacts*

Created in 1971, the *NASDAQ system* is an electronic communications network with hookups for market makers, investors, and regulators. Market makers can enter their quotations for display on terminals throughout the system.

Three levels of service are available on NASDAQ. *Level one* is used by registered representatives; the terminal screens reflect the highest bids and the lowest offers available for NASD securities. *Level two*, used by retail traders, not only provides current quotations, but also identifies market makers. *Level three* is used by market makers. For each security, the system provides current quotes and identifies all market makers. Level three also allows users to enter, delete, or update quotations for securities in which they are making a market. To be an authorized subscriber to level three, an NASD member must meet certain net capital and other qualifications.

Broker/dealers may also use the National Quotations Bureau (NQB) sheets, or "yellow sheets," which contain information on corporate bond offerings.

Municipal bonds available for resale in the *secondary* market are listed by state in *The Blue List*, along with such information as the number of bonds offered, issuer, maturity date, coupon rate, price, and dealer making the offering. Ratings are *not* included. But there are sections on settlement dates of recent new offerings, prerefunded bonds, and miscellaneous offerings (some U.S. government and agency obligations, railroad equipment trust certificates, corporate bonds, and even preferred stocks). The dollar value of listings, referred to as the *floating supply*, gives an indication of the size and liquidity of the secondary municipal market.

The Daily Bond Buyer, in addition to important news, contains news of pending municipal offerings, official notices of sale, and such statistical information as:

* *20-Bond Index* — a sampling of medium-quality (Baa) to high-quality (Aaa) bonds with 20-year maturities, indicating a hypothetical composite "bid" by a dealer. If the index were at 6.25%, it would give an indication of the rate at which *new* issues rated A+ (the average rating of the 20 bonds) would have to be offered in order to compete with *outstanding* issues.

* *11-Bond Index* — contains only Aa-rated issues and thus has a higher rating and a lower yield than the 20-bond index.

* *Placement Ratio (Acceptance Ratio)* — the percentage of bonds sold of those offered for sale as new issues during the previous week. A high placement ratio (90% or more) indicates the public's ready acceptance of the new offerings and gives an insight into the underwriter's risk.

* *30-Day Visible Supply* — new offerings announced for sale within the next 30 days. This gives an idea of the supply "overhanging" the market at a given time. The visible supply does not include short-term offerings.

Munifacts is a subscription wire service provided by *The Bond Buyer,* similar to the Dow Jones or Reuter News services, but aimed at the municipal securities professional.

For all bond traders, however, the best source of information consists of their contacts in the business. Who among other firms' traders has a certain type of bond in inventory? Which of them owes a favor? Who quoted a favorable price on a certain bond just this morning? Who's trying to sell off a weak issue? And so on. Information like this is so specialized and often so fleeting that not even a highly automated quotation system like NASDAQ can capture it. This is the kind of information that is gathered during the course of countless phone calls and used at the precise time of its greatest effectiveness.

HOW BONDS ARE QUOTED

Corporate Bonds

When dealing in *corporate* bonds, traders for broker/dealers must specify:
*   The name of the issuer.
*   The months and dates when interest is paid.
*   The bond's coupon (its interest rate)
*   The year the bond matures.

For example, a corporate bond might be described as follows: "IBM-JJ15-7% of '010" This shorthand description indicates that the bond is issued by IBM corporation, pays its interest on January 15 and July 15 of each year, offers a 7% annual interest rate, and matures in the year 2010.

Let's look more closely at this description. Almost all corporate bonds pay their interest on either the first or the fifteenth of two months that are six months apart; that is, interest payments are semiannual. Thus there are only twelve possibilities:

Months Interest Is Paid	On the 1st *	On the 15th
January-July	JJ	JJ-15
February-August	FA	FA-15
March-September	MS	MS-15
April-October	AO	AO-15
May-November	MN	MN-15
June-December	JD	JD-15

*By convention, if interest is paid on the first of the month, the date is omitted.

Interest rate is always expressed as a percentage of the bond's $1,000 face value. The final component, the year the bond matures, is usually expressed without the first two digits. Thus 1991 is expressed as '91 and 2014 is expressed as '14.

If a corporate bond is trading in the market for a price other than par, its price is expressed in points and eighths of a point. Each point equals $10. For example, a price of 86⅜ means:

$$(86 \times \$10.00) + (\tfrac{3}{8} \times \$10.00) = \$860 + \$3.75 = \$863.75$$

And a price of 123⅛ means:

$$(123 \times \$10.00) + (\tfrac{1}{8} \times \$10.00) = \$1,230 + \$1.25 = \$1,231.25$$

The quotation itself in bond trading consists of a bid and an ask price, which is characteristic of OTC trading. For example, if the bid is 9.40% and the ask is 8.25%, the quoting dealer is willing to buy the bonds at 9.40% or sell them at 8.25%.

In the secondary market, the *spread* is not the difference between the underwriter's purchase and sales prices; it is the difference between the quoted bid and asked prices.

As such, the spread is based on issuer quality, time to maturity, supply and demand, and other market factors.

In practice, the spread on municipal bonds ranges from 1 to 3 points; on municipal notes, from ⅛ to ½ point.

The spread is also called the dealer's markup or markdown. In the OTC market, when a dealer buys a security from a marketmaker and sells it to a customer at a higher price, the difference in prices is called a *markup*. When the dealer buys from the customer and sells to a marketmaker at a higher price, the difference is a *markdown*. Either way, the markup or markdown determines the spread. Neither need be itemized on the customer's trade confirmation in principal transactions.

(When quoting bonds prices, traders often repeat themselves, to assure accurate communication. They even very commonly call back after a trade if they have any doubt about the terms.)

Municipal Bonds

Municipal bonds are similarly quoted, but there is no specific unit of trading. However, when professional muni traders say "one bond," they are saying "$1,000 face value." They use this term even though most municipal bonds are issued in denominations of $5,000. One certificate, bearing a $5,000 face value, would therefore be called "five bonds." Why? Up to the 1960s, munis were issued in $1,000 denominations, and old habits die hard. To the professional, "a bond" is still a $1,000.

Otherwise, the language used to describe a municipal bond is pretty straightforward. Take the following example: a "$5,000 State of Washington, 5% of April 1, 1988, at 5.75%." This is a muni bond with a face value of $5,000, issued by the State of Washington, with a coupon rate of 5%, maturing on April 1, 1988, and trading at a price to yield 5.75%.

Serial bonds are usually quoted on a yield-to-maturity basis with a dollar price added as a convenience. *Term bonds* are often quoted only as a percentage of face value. For example, the quotation of 92½ is a percentage. Hence it would mean a dollar value of $921.25 for a $1,000-par bond but $4,606.25 for a $5,000-par bond.

Larger purchases tend to have a "better price" than smaller purchases. Occasionally secondary market trades are quoted all-or-none (AON); in this case, the quote is firm only for the number of bonds given.

SHOPPING THE STREET

Once a broker/dealer identifies the market makers in a security, the next step is to call all the market makers to get the best price. The broker/dealer is said to be "shopping the street." While on the phone with the market maker, the broker/dealer may obtain one of several types of quotes:

1. *Firm* bids or offers are prices at which the quoting broker/dealer is committed to buy or sell at least a round lot of bonds, even though the broker/dealer requesting the quote is not obliged to do business. A firm bid or offer can be good for the moment that the quote is given or for a longer period. Also, unless otherwise stated, it is good for one unit of trading. In other words, the broker/dealer's commitment to buy or sell at the quoted price is limited to 10 bonds at the quoted price.

How does the second dealer know whether the quote — firm or not — is the best available? Generally, a dealer giving a quote allows the inquiring dealer up to one hour to make a transaction. If, during that hour, a third dealer wishes to take advantage of the quote, the original inquirer has usually five minutes to make a sale or forego the quote.

Let's look at an example. Dealer A calls dealer B, who is a marketmaker in Belliup County bonds, for a quote. Dealer B says, "Firm at 97½ for an hour, with five." (This accommodation is sometimes referred to as an option.) Dealer A hangs up and continues inquiring with other dealers, knowing that he or she has one hour to take advantage of that quote. The Belliup bonds are said to be "out firm."

Occasionally, the option has a "recall privilege" attached to it. For example, dealer C calls dealer B, hears the quote, and wants to do business right away. In that case, dealer B advises dealer A that he or she has five minutes to make a deal. Otherwise dealer C will be given the bonds.

The prices quoted in the yellow sheets and on NASDAQ are not firm quotes. The NASDAQ and the yellow sheets only make it easier for buyers and sellers to find each other and provide a good indication of price. Firm quotes, sometimes referred to as the "actual market," must be obtained verbally from the market maker, and all transactions are executed verbally by telephone.

2. If the broker/dealer gives a quote and says that it is *subject*, then the quote is "subject" to confirmation. Generally, the broker/dealer has to have more information before making the quote firm.

Subject quotes can be expressed in several ways:
*   "It is quoted [that is, *I'm* not quoting it] 85½."
*   "Last I saw, it was 85½."
*   "It is 85½, subject."

3. Sometimes the broker/dealer gives a quote with a very wide spread and follows it by the word "workout." A *workout quote* is not firm. Instead, it provides a range in which the dealer believes a price can be worked out. These quotes are typically used for infrequently traded securities.

Bid or Offer Wanted

Occasionally, a broker/dealer wants to buy or sell but receives no bids or offers. In these cases, the broker/dealer hangs something like a "for sale" sign on the security by advertising the would-be transaction in the National Quotation Bureau sheets. The phrase "bid wanted (BW)" tells other broker/dealers that the stock is for sale and that the advertising broker/dealer is looking for bids. "Offering wanted (OW)" means that the broker/dealer wants to buy the security and is soliciting offerings.

The bid-wanted business is a typical kind of work for the broker's broker. When dealers cannot get bids for a bond, they turn to a broker's broker, who seeks bids for them.

These brokers also buy certain types of bonds from a dealer at a specific offering price, because the dealer wants to keep the sale confidential. (Brokers do not reveal the identities of dealers without their permission.)

Perhaps the bond brokers' greatest service is their continuous contact with major dealers. They closely track who owns and who's buying or selling bonds. This view is known as a "picture" of the market. The dealers' anonymity makes them more willing to give out information. Often, the bond broker has access to more information than a dealer. When brokers make a trade, they usually earn ⅛ of a point per bond, or $1.25. For high-volume trades, the commission is frequently cut.

Executing OTC Orders

The most common types of order entered by customers in the over-the-counter market are market orders and limit orders. A *market order* must be executed as soon as possible and at the best possible price. A *limit order* specifies the price at which the security must be bought or sold. Limit orders may be entered for the day, in which case they become invalid if not executed by the close of trading. They can also be marked "good 'till cancelled (GTC)," which means that the order remains valid until it is executed by the broker or cancelled by the customer.

Other types of orders are available. *All-or-none* (AON) orders must be executed in full or not at all. A variation of the all-or-none order is the *fill-or-kill* (FOK) order, which is cancelled if it cannot be filled immediately.

Regardless of the type of order entered, the broker must always get the best possible price for the customer.

How a broker/dealer is compensated for transactions in the secondary market depends on whether the firm acted as agent or as principal. As the customer's agent, it may charge a commission. As a market maker, it may charge a markup or markdown.

When acting as a broker or *agent*, the NASD member must disclose to the customer the amount of the commission charged. The actual dollar amount charged must be printed on the confirmation.

Sometimes, a broker may receive orders from different customers for both the buy and sell side of a transaction. This is called a "riskless transaction," because the broker/dealer is not subject to any risk but has only to cross the two orders. In such a case, each customer sees only his or her part of the commission, markup, or markdown.

The amount of the commission charged by broker/dealers must be fair, reasonable, and in accordance with the NASD's 5% markup policy (which is explained shortly).

When trading from the firm's own account as a *market maker*, a broker/dealer makes a profit on either a markup or markdown. Unlike commissions, markups and markdowns (on non-National Market Systems stocks) do not have to be disclosed to customers. The only requirement is that the broker/dealer must tell the customer that the firm is acting as a principal in the trade.

The NASD's 5% guideline governs markups and markdowns. Its purpose is to assure that NASD members earn profits that are fair, equitable, and proportionate to current market prices. The 5%, however, is intended to be used as a guide, not as a rule. The key message is that markups and markdowns must not be unfair, regardless of the percentage. For example, a markup of over 5% would not be unfair if the dealer had owned the security for a long time and computed the markup on the basis of current market prices, rather than on cost. On the other hand, a 5% markup could be unfair if a broker/dealer buys a security for a customer by using the proceeds from the sale of another one of the customer's securities.

How does a broker/dealer know what is fair? The NASD board believes that, in determining fairness, NASD members and committees should consider the type of security, the availability of the security, its prices, the size of the transaction, the pattern of markups, and the nature of the member's business.

THE NATIONAL ASSOCIATION OF SECURITY DEALERS (NASD)

The National Association of Security Dealers (NASD) was organized under the Maloney Act, an amendment to the Securities Exchange Act of 1934. Although established by Congress and supervised by the SEC, the NASD operates not as a government agency but as an independent membership association.

The NASD's power to regulate lies in its ability to deny membership to any broker/dealer operating in an unethical or improper manner. Because only NASD members have the advantage of price concessions, discounts, and similar allowances, the loss of membership privileges all but prevents a firm from competing in the marketplace. In addition, NASD members are permitted to do business only with other members. Nonmembers are therefore severely restricted in the business they can do.

The NASD imposes its requirements on members through two sets of regulations: the Rules of Fair Practice and Uniform Code of Conduct. These regulations spell out the terms and conditions of everyday operation, as well as the classification, qualification, and responsibilities of its members.

Membership in the NASD is open to all properly qualified "brokers" and "dealers" whose regular course of business is transacting in any part of the investment banking or securities business in the United States. A *broker* is defined as a legal entity (individual, corporation, or partnership) that effects transactions for the accounts of others. A *dealer* is a legal entity that engages in the buying or selling of securities for its own account. By definition, banks are not broker/dealers and are therefore not eligible for NASD membership.

MUNICIPAL SECURITIES RULEMAKING BOARD (MSRB)

Since the Securities Act of 1934 did not cover municipal securities, they were left unregulated for over 40 years, until Congress passed the Securities Act Amendment of 1975. This act, called the Maloney Act, brought *self*-regulation to municipal trading in the form of the Municipal Securities Rulemaking Board. Funding is by initial and annual fees from broker/dealers, plus assessments on underwritings of new securities with maturities of two years or more.

Enforcement of MSRB rules belongs to the NASD if the member is a securities brokerage firm. If the member is a bank, rules are enforced by either the Federal Deposit Insurance Corporation (FDIC), the Federal Reserve Board, or the Comptroller of the Currency. Though there is no MSRB rule like the NASD's 5% markup/markdown policy, MSRB members must:

* Give and abide by fair quotations that reflect current market prices, that are fair and reasonable, and that are bona fide bids and offers (with the exception of "nominal" or informational quotes that may be published if clearly identified as such).
* Neither receive nor give gratuities in excess of $100 per year (an occasional theater or sports event ticket is legitimate).

BOND TRADING AND SETTLEMENT

Corporate Bonds

When two investors want to enter into a secondary market bond transaction, they have to agree not only on the price at which the transaction will occur, but also on when the actual exchange of bond certificates and cash will occur. Thus, if on a Monday two parties (in separate parts of the country) agree to enter into a bond transaction, they have to agree not only on the price at which the transaction will occur but also on which day the bonds and the cash will actually change hands. Tuesday? Wednesday? The following Monday? Perhaps the seller has to get the bonds out of a safe deposit box. Or the buyer may need to liquidate some money market investments before making payment.

By convention, the transaction may take place, or *settle*, in one of five common ways, each involving a different day. These dates are called the *settlement options*.

1. A *regular way trade* settles on the fifth business day after the trade date. Only business days are counted — no weekends or holidays. Usually this results in a trade that settles one calendar week after the trade. Regular way settlement is assumed for all corporate bond trades unless the parties specify a different settlement option at the time they enter into the trade.

2. A *cash settlement trade* settles on the same day on which the trade is made. Obviously, both parties have to agree to, and be prepared for, a cash settlement. By convention any cash trade that occurs at or before 2:00 P.M. settles at 2:30 P.M. Any trade that occurs after 2:00 P.M. settles one half-hour later.

3. A *next-day settlement* settles on the first business day after the trade date.

4. A *seller's option trade* settles *up* to 60 days after the trade date. This kind of settlement is usually chosen if the seller is not able to deliver the bonds within the time required by the other settlement options. For example, a seller may be on vacation when she wants to sell some bonds. If the bonds are in her safe deposit box at home, she has to opt for a seller's option settlement, "a seller's 60." When she returns home, she can deliver the bonds to the buyer at any time up to the 60-day limit, providing that she gives the buyer a one-day written notice of when the bonds will be delivered. Sellers who need to settle via this option usually get a slightly lower price from buyers than they would if they were able to use one of the other settlement options.

5. A *buyer's option delivery* gives the buyer the option to receive securities on a specific date.

Five-day, regular way delivery applies to most trades in over-the-counter securities and securities listed on an exchange. All corporate, municipal, and most federal agency securities trade the regular way. United States government securities may be delivered for cash, regular way, on the day following the trade, and the seller's option of not less than two nor more than 60 days.

After a trade, each broker/dealer sends the other a notice to confirm the details of the trade. If both parties recognize and acknowledge the trade, it is "confirmed" or "compared." Sometimes, however, the contrabroker (the broker/dealer with whom the trade was made) sends back a signed "DK," a "don't know," notice telling the confirming broker that the contrabroker does not "know" — or recognize — the trade.

If, when the confirmation is sent out, the contrabroker does not respond at all by the close of four business days from the trade date, then not later than the fifteenth calendar day after the trade date, the confirming member sends a DK notice to the contrabroker. The contrabroker then has four business days after receiving the notice either to confirm or DK the transaction. Failure to receive a response from the contrabroker by the close of four business days constitutes a DK, and the confirming member has no further liability.

Transfer of Ownership

Bonds are negotiable, in that they can be readily transferred from one owner to another. The method of transfer depends on the form of ownership, of which there are two: registered and bearer. Most bonds are in registered form, which means that the owner's name and address are printed on the bond certificate and registered on the issuer's books. Interest payments are sent directly to the bondholder. If a registered bond is sold, the broker sends the bond to a transfer agent who reissues the bond in the name of the new owner.

Bearer bonds are not really issued anymore, in this hi-tech time when registering bonds is not the time-consuming, labor-intensive task it was in the past. But there are still a few in circulation. Because these bonds were issued and distributed without registration, they are assumed to belong to the bearer. Consequently, they are fully negotiable, like cash. To be paid the interest amount, the bearer must cut (or "clip") coupons from the bond certificate and present them for payment as they come due. Each coupon represents one payment.

To assure clear ownership, the NASD requires "good delivery" in all transactions, that is, the security must be in proper form so that the record of ownership can be transferred. To facilitate transfer of ownership, the NASD defines the requirements of good delivery.

Municipal Bonds

The requirements for the settlement of municipal trades are very similar to those for corporates. While most muni s settle the regular way, some trade on a cash basis. Buyer's and seller's options also occur. In addition, "when, as, and if " trades may settle anywhere from six business days to the time stated in the confirmation.

Municipal bond settlement differs from corporate settlement, however, in that the legal opinion plays a key role. Without it, how do buyers know that all new issues offered are in accordance with the law? So important is this opinion that municipal bonds are not a good delivery if it is lacking. The opinion is printed on the bond certificate or, in the case of older issues, on a separate document.

Occasionally bonds are offered "ex-legal" (older issues missing the legal opinion). Provided the buyer agrees to accept delivery ex-legal before the trade is made, the ex-legal delivery is permissible. Otherwise, ex-legal deliveries are not acceptable. The expenses connected with obtaining a legal opinion are generally borne by the issuer.

If a bond or its coupons are mutilated (that is, if any part is unreadable), the broker/dealer must have the certificate validated by the trustee, registrar, transfer agent, paying agent, issuer, or an authorized agent of the issuer. A brokerage firm or one of its sales representatives *cannot* validate a mutilated certificate. Also, for a bond to be good delivery, all unpaid coupons must be attached (although a check for the coupon payment due within 30 days can replace that particular coupon).

Upon delivery to the buying broker/dealer by the selling broker/dealer, the buyer has the *right of rejection.* That is, the buyer may refuse to accept delivery should the certificate not be in good delivery form. If the securities have been delivered and then either dealer realizes that the certificate does not constitute a good delivery, either party has the *right of reclamation* (returning or demanding the return of the securities). Note that rejection takes place before acceptance of delivery, whereas reclamation takes place after acceptance of delivery.

The purchaser does not have to accept partial delivery. All municipals are assumed to be bearer securities, unless otherwise stated. The seller pays the shipping costs. The confirmation should be delivered to the contra broker/dealer the next business day with all pertinent information.

ACCRUED INTEREST

Sellers of bonds are entitled to any interest accrued on a bond up to the day before the settlement date. So if a bond is sold anytime between interest payment dates, some interest is due to the seller and the rest to the buyer. Yet the issuer's paying agent is going to issue only one check for the full interest amount to the holder of record on the payment date. How, then, do sellers get the accrued interest to which they are entitled? The answer is that the buyer of the bond pays the seller, and then takes the full interest amount on the next payment date.

The only thing remaining is to calculate the actual accrued amount. The regular way settlement date is the fifth business day after the transaction, but if the trade is for "cash" it is the same day as the transaction. In the event of same-day settlement, accrued interest is computed up through the *previous* business day.

Let's take an example. An Awac bond has a coupon rate of 10¾. The price of the bond is 98¾ — that is, $987.50. A buyer of this bond would have to pay the seller $987.50, plus any interest accrued since the last payment. Assume that the bond is purchased about midway between payment dates. Since each six-month interest payment is $53.75 (10 ¾% times $1,000 divided by two payments), the accrued interest for three months is about $27. The buyer would pay the seller $987.50 plus $27 ($1,014.50). On the next payment date, the entire coupon payment of $53.75 is paid to the buyer.

Naturally, not all bonds are sold conveniently at the midway point between payments. To calculate the exact amount of accrued interest, regardless of when the bond is sold, use the following formula:

$$\frac{\text{Accrued}}{\text{interest}} = \frac{\text{Annual}}{\text{interest}} \times \frac{\text{Days in holding period}}{360 \text{ days}}$$

For corporate and municipal bonds, all whole months are assumed to have 30 days, and the year is figured on the basis of 360 days. For example, bondholder Mathers received her last interest payment of $53.75 dollars on April 1. Her next check is due on October 1. In June, she sells the bond to buyer Ridgemount for 97½ (or $975) for settlement on June 28. Disregarding commissions and fees, Mathers has to pay Ridgemount $975, plus an amount for accrued interest:

$$\frac{\text{Accrued}}{\text{interest}} = \frac{\text{Annual}}{\text{interest}} \times \frac{\text{Days in holding period}}{360 \text{ days}}$$

$$= (2 \times \$53.75) \times \frac{(30 \text{ days} + 30 \text{ days} + 27 \text{ days})}{360 \text{ days}} *$$

$$= \$107 \times \frac{87 \text{ days}}{360 \text{ days}}$$

$$= \$25.88$$

* April and May count for 30 days each, and June for 27.

The check that goes to Ridgemount is for $1,000.88 ($975 purchase price plus $25.88 accrued interest).

Some bonds, such as income bonds and bonds in default, trade without any accrued interest. They are said to trade "flat."

This method for calculating accrued interest is valid for municipal and corporate bonds. *Government* bonds, however, are figured on an "exact days" basis, with the months being 28, 29, 30, or 31 days in length.

Heavy volumes of corporate, municipal and U.S. government securities trade every day in the secondary market. Yet, as large and active as the bond market is in the United States, it is only a part of the worldwide fixed-income trading arena, which includes the issues of overseas companies and governments. But that is a subject requiring another whole book.

Glossary

Accrued Interest. (1) The amount of interest due the seller, from the buyer, upon settlement of a bond trade. (2) Prorated interest due since the last interest payment date.

Active Bonds (The "Free Crowd"). A category of debt securities that the NYSE Floor Department expects to trade frequently and that are consequently handled freely in the trading ring in much the same manner as stocks. *See* Inactive Bonds.

Active Box. A physical location where securities are held awaiting action on them.

Adjustment Bonds. See Income (Adjustment) Bonds.

Aftermarket. A market for a security either over the counter or on an exchange after an initial public offering has been made. *See* Hot Issue; Stabilization; Withholding.

Agreement Among Underwriters. An agreement among members of an underwriting syndicate specifying the syndicate manager, his duties, and his privileges, among other things. *See* Underwriter's Retention; Underwriting Agreement.

All-or-None (AON) Offering. A "best-efforts" offering of newly issued securities in which the corporation instructs the investment banker to cancel the entire offering (sold and unsold) if all of it cannot be distributed.

All-or-None Order. An order to buy or sell more than one round lot of stock at one time and at a designated price or better. It must not be executed until both conditions can be satisfied simultaneously.

"And Interest". A bond transaction in which the buyer pays the seller a contract price plus interest accrued since the corporation's last interest payment.

AON Offering. See All or None (AON) Offering.

AON Order. See All-Or-None (AON) Order.

Arbitrage. The simultaneous purchase and sale of the same or equal securities in such a way as to take advantage of price differences prevailing in separate markets. *See* Bona Fide Arbitrage; Risk Arbitrage

Arbitrage Bonds. All bonds found in violation of federal arbitrage regulations as deemed by the Internal Revenue Service. If the IRS deems a bond an arbitrage bond, then the interest becomes taxable and must therefore be included in each bondholder's gross income for federal tax purposes.

Arbitrageur. One who engages in arbitrage.

As Agent. The role of a broker/dealer firm when it acts as an intermediary, or broker, between its customer and another customer, a market maker, or a contrabroker. For this service the firm receives a stated commission or fee. This is an "agency transaction." *See* As Principal.

As Principal. The role of a broker/dealer firm when it buys and sells for its own account. In a typical transaction, it buys from a market maker or contrabroker and sells to a customer at a fair and reasonable markup; if it buys from a customer and sells to the market maker at a higher price, the trade is called a mark-down. *See* As Agent.

Ask-Bid System. A system used to place a market order. A market order is one the investor wants executed immediately at the best prevailing price. The market order to buy requires a purchase at the lowest offering (asked) price, and a market order to sell requires a sale at the highest (bid) price. The bid price is what the dealer is willing to pay for the stock, while the ask price is the price at which the dealer will sell to individual investors. The difference between the bid and ask prices is the spread. *See* Bid-and-Asked Quotations.

At-the-Close-Order. An order to be executed, at the market, at the close, or as near as practicable to the close of trading for the day.

At-the-Market. (1) A price representing what a buyer would pay and what a seller would take in an arm's-length transaction assuming normal competitive forces; (2) an order to buy or sell immediately at the currently available price.

At-the-Money. A term used to describe a security option where the strike price and market price are the same.

At-the-Opening (Opening Only) Order. An order to buy or sell at a limited price on the initial transaction of the day for a given security; if unsuccessful, it is automatically cancelled.

Auction Marketplace. A term used to describe an organized exchange where transactions are held in the open and any exchange member present may join in.

Away from Me. When a market maker does not initiate a quotation, transaction, or market in an issue, he says it is "away from me."

Away from the Market. An order where the limit bid is below (or the limit offer is above) the quote for the security. For example, if a quote for a security is 20 to 20½, a limit order to buy at 19 is away from the market.

Baby Bond. A bond with a face value of less than $1,000, usually in $100 denominations.

Backing Away. The practice of an OTC market maker who refuses to honor his or her quoted bid-and-asked prices for at least 100 shares, or 10 bonds, as the case may be. This action is outlawed under the NASD Rules of Fair Practice.

Back Office. An industry expression used to describe non-sales departments of a brokerage concern, particularly a firm's P&S and cashier departments.

Balance Orders. The pairing off of each issue traded in the course of a day by the same member to arrive at a net balance of securities to receive or deliver. The net difference between buyers and sellers on the opening of the market allows the specialist to appropriately open the market.

Balloon Effect. A term used to describe a serial bond issue having lower principal repayments in the early years of its life and higher principal repayments in the later years.

BAN. See Bond Anticipation Note.

Bank Dealer. A bank engaged in buying and selling government securities, municipal securities, or certain money market instruments.

Bankers' Acceptances. Bills of exchange guaranteed (accepted) by a bank or trust company for payment within one to six months. Used to provide manufacturers and exporters with capital to operate between the time of manufacturing (or exporting) and payment by purchasers. Bids and offers in the secondary marketplace are at prices discounted from the face value.

Banks for Cooperatives (Co-op). An agency under the supervision of the Farm Credit Administration that makes and services loans for farmers' cooperative financing. The agency is capitalized by the issuance of bonds whose interest is free from state and local income taxes.

Basis Point. One one-hundredth of a percentage point. For example, if a Treasury bill yielding 7.17% changes in price so that it now yields 7.10%, it is said to have declined seven basis points.

Basis Price Odd-Lot Order. An odd-lot order executed on a fictitious round-lot price somewhere between the prevailing bid and offering, if (1) the issue doesn't trade throughout the day; (2) the spread is at least two full points; and (3) the customer requests such an execution.

Bearer Bond. A bond that does not have the owner's name registered on the books of the issuing corporation and that is payable to the bearer.

Bearer Form. Securities issued in such a form as not to allow for the owner's name to be imprinted on the security. The bearer of the security is presumed to be the owner who collects interest by clipping and depositing coupons semiannually.

Beneficial Owner. The owner of securities who receives all the benefits, even though they are registered in the street name of a brokerage firm or nominee name of a bank handling his or her account.

Best-Efforts Offering. An offering of newly issued securities in which the investment banker acts merely as an agent of the corporation, promising only his best efforts in making the issue a success but not guaranteeing the corporation its money for any unsold portion. *See* All-or-None (AON) Offering.

Bid-and-Asked Quotation (or Quote). The bid is the highest price anyone has declared that he/she wants to pay for a security at a given time; the asked is the lowest price anyone will accept at the same time. *See* Offer.

Bidding Syndicate. Two or more underwriters working together to submit a proposal to underwrite a new issue of municipal securities. *See* Syndicate.

Blowout. A securities offering that sells out almost immediately.

Blue-Sky Laws. State securities laws pertaining to registration requirements and procedures for issuers, broker/dealers, their employees, and other associated persons of those entities.

Blue-Skying the Issue. The efforts of the underwriters' lawyers to analyze and investigate state laws regulating the distribution of securities and to qualify particular issues under these laws.

Board of Governors. (1) The governing body of the NASD, most of whom are elected by the general membership; the remainder are elected by the board itself. (2) *See* Federal Reserve Board.

Bona Fide Arbitrage. Arbitrage transactions by professional traders that take profitable advantage of prices for the same or convertible securities in different markets. The risk is usually minimal and the profit correspondingly small. *See* Risk Arbitrage.

Bond. A certificate representing creditorship in a corporation and issued by the corporation to raise capital. The company pays interest on a bond issue at specified dates and eventually redeems it at maturity, paying principal plus interest due. *See* Bearer Bond; Collateral Trust Bond; Equipment Trust Bond; Income Bond; Mortgage Bond; Receiver's Certificate; Registered Bond; Serial Bond; Tax-Exempt Securities; United States Government Securities.

Bond Amortization Fund. An account in a sinking fund. The issuer makes periodic deposits of money eventually to be used to purchase bonds on the open market or to pay the cost of calling bonds.

Bond and Preferred Stock Companies. Investment companies that emphasize stability of income. In the case of the municipal bond companies, income exempt from federal taxation is the chief goal.

Bond Anticipation Note (BAN). A short-term municipal debt instrument usually offered on a discount basis. The proceeds of a forthcoming bond issue are pledged to pay the note at maturity.

Bond Broker. A member of the NYSE or any other exchange who executes orders in the bond room as a continuing practice.

Bonded Debt. The portion of an issuer's total indebtedness represented by outstanding bonds of various types.

Bond Fund. An investment company with a diversified portfolio of municipal securities. Unites or shares in the investment company are sold to investors. Unit investment trusts (UIT) and managed funds are the two basic types of bond funds.

Bond Interest Distribution. Bonds that are traded at a market price and interest require an adjustment for

the interest on the settlement date. The buyer therefore pays the seller the price plus interest accrued since
the last payment date, and the buyer is thereby entitled
to the next full payment of interest. The interest due
is calculated by multiplying Principal x Rate x Time.
See Ex-Dividend Date.

Bond Issue.   Bonds (1) sold in one or more series; (2)
authorized under the same indenture or resolution;
and (3) having the same date.

Bond Purchase Agreement. The contract between the issuer
and underwriter that sets down the final terms, conditions, and prices by which the underwriter purchases
an issue of municipal securities.

Bond Room. Formerly, the room at the New York Stock Exchange where bonds are traded.

Bought Deal. A commitment by a group of underwriters to
guarantee performance by buying the securities from
the issuer themselves, usually entailing some financial
risk for the underwriters (or syndicate).

Box. A section of a cashier department where securities are
stored temporarily. The department's responsibilities
are sometimes subdivided to monitor both an active
box and a free box for securities held by the firm.

Broker. An agent, often a member of a stock exchange firm
or the head of a member firm, who handles the public's
orders to buy and sell securities and commodities, for
which service a commission is charged. The definition
does not include a bank. *See* Agent; As Principal.

Broker's Broker. Also known as a municipal securities
broker's broker, a person who deals only with other
municipal securities brokers and dealers, not with the
general public.

BW. An abbreviation for "Bid Wanted," indicating that the
broker/dealer is soliciting buyers of the stock or bond.

Cabinet Crowd. See Inactive Bonds.

Cage (The). A slang expression used to describe a location where a brokerage firm's cashier department responsibilities are satisfied.

Call Feature. (1) A feature of preferred stock through which it may be retired at the corporation's option by paying a price equal to or slightly higher than either the par or market value. (2) A bond feature by which all or part of an issue may be redeemed by the corporation before maturity and under certain specified conditions.

Call Protection. A term used to describe a bond or preferred stock without a call feature or with a call feature that cannot be activated for a period of time.

Callable. See Call Feature.

Can Crowd. See Inactive Bonds.

Cash Contract. A securities contract by which delivery of the certificates is due at the purchaser's office the same day as the date of the trade. *See* Regular Way Contract; When Issued/When Distributed Contract.

Cash on Delivery (COD). See Delivery Versus Payment.

Cash Trade. A transaction involving specific securities, in which the settlement date is the same as the trade date.

Cashier Department. A department of a broker/dealer organization responsible for the physical handling of securities and money, delivery and receipt, collateral loans, borrowing, lending, and transfer of securities, and other financial transactions.

Catastrophe (Calamity) Call. An issuer's call for redemption of a bond issue when certain events occur, such as an accident at a construction site that severely affects the completion of the project.

CATS (Certificates of Accrual on Treasury Securities). Issues from the U.S. Treasury sold at a deep discount from their face value. They are called a *zero-coupon* securities because they require no interest payments during their lifetime, but they return the full face value at maturity. They cannot be called away. *See* Zero-Coupon Discount Security.

CD. See Certificate of Deposit (CD).

Central Bank. (1) A Federal Reserve Bank situated in one of twelve banking districts in the United States. (2) The Federal Reserve System.

Central Certificate Service (CCS). Former name of the Depository Trust Company.

Certificate. The actual piece of paper that is evidence of ownership or creditorship in a corporation. Watermarked certificates are finely engraved with delicate etchings to discourage forgery.

Certificates of Accrual on Treasury Securities. See CATs.

Certificate of Deposit (CD). A negotiable money market instrument issued by commercial banks against money deposited with them for a specified period of time. CDs vary in size according to the amount of the deposit and the maturity period, and they may be redeemed before maturity only by sale in a secondary market.

Certificate of Incorporation. A state-validated certificate recognizing a business organization as a legal corporate entity. *See* Charter.

Certificate of Indebtedness (CI). A federal bearer debt instrument in denominations of $1,000 to $500 million at a fixed interest rate, with maturities up to one year; they are fully marketable at a price reflecting their average rate of return.

Certified Security. A security whose ownership may be represented by a physical document. Also known as being available in "definitive form."

Charter. A document written by the founders of a corporation and filed with a state. The state approves the articles and then issues a certificate of incorporation. Together, the two documents become the charter and the corporation is recognized as a legal entity. The charter includes such information as the corporation's name, purpose, amount of shares, and the identity of the directors. Internal management rules are written by the founders in the *bylaws*. *See* Certificate of Incorporation.

Churning. A registered representative's improper handling of a customer's account: He or she buys and sells securities for a customer while intent only on the amount of commissions generated, ignoring the customer's interests and objectives.

Clean Opinion. See Qualified Legal Opinion.

Clearance. (1) The delivery of securities and monies in completion of a trade. (2) The comparison and/or netting of trades prior to settlement.

Clearing House Funds. (1) Money represented by a person's demand deposit account at a commercial bank. Withdrawals are accomplished by means of a check, which notifies the bank to transfer a sum to someone else's account, or to another bank. (2) Funds used in settlement of equity, corporate bond, and municipal bond settlement transactions. (3) A term used to mean next-day availability of funds. *See* Federal Funds.

Close. The final transaction price for an issue on the stock exchange at the end of a trading day.

Close-Out Procedure. The procedure taken by either party to a transaction when the contrabroker defaults; the disappointed purchaser may "buy in," and the rejected seller may "sell out" or liquidate.

Closing. A meeting of all concerned parties on the date of delivery of a new issue of municipal securities, usually including the representatives of the issuer, bond counsel, and the purchasers or underwriters. The issuer makes physical delivery of the signed securities, and the required legal documents are exchanged.

Closing Quotation. A market maker's final bid and asked prices for an issue as he or she ceases trading activities at the end of the business day.

Closing the Underwriting Contract. The finalizing of contractual terms between an issuing corporation and the underwriters. Usually one week after the effective date, the certificates are given over to the underwriters and payment in full is made to the corporation.

COD Trade. Cash on delivery. A general term to describe a transaction in which a seller is obliged to delivery securities to the purchaser or the purchaser's agent to collect payment.

COD Transaction. A purchase of securities in behalf of a customer promising full payment immediately upon delivery of the certificates to an agent bank or broker/dealer.

Collateral. Securities and other property pledged by a borrower to secure repayment of a loan.

Collateral Trust Bond. A bond issue that is protected by a portfolio of securities held in trust by a commercial bank. The bond usually requires immediate redemption if the market value of the securities drops below or close to the value of the issue.

Commercial Paper. Unsecured, short-term (usually a maximum of nine months) bearer obligations in denominations from $100,000 to $1 million, issued principally by industrial corporations, finance companies, and commercial factors at a discount from face value.

Commission. A broker's fee for handling transactions for a client in an agency capacity.

Comparison. A confirmation of a contractual agreement citing terms and conditions of a transaction between broker/dealers. This document must be exchanged by the contra firms shortly after trade date. *See* Confirmation.

Competitive Bidding. A sealed envelope bidding process employed by various underwriter groups interested in handling the distribution of a securities issue. The contract is awarded to one group by the issuer on the basis of the highest price paid, interest rate expense, and tax considerations.

Concession. (1) In a municipal bond offering, the underwriters may offer a dollar discount from the offering price to MSRB members who are not taking part in the underwriting but who buy for their own or customers' accounts. (2) In a corporate underwriting, the underwriters may extend a dollar remuneration for each share or bond to selling group members who market the securities successfully.

Confirmation. An announcement of transaction terms and conditions and other pertinent information that is prepared for customer trade activities. It serves as a bill for customer purchases and as an advisory notice for sales.

Consumer Credit. Credit extended to the ultimate users of goods and services.

Contrabroker. A term used to describe the broker with whom a trade was made.

Conversion. A bond feature by which the owner may exchange his or her bonds for a specified number of shares of stock. Interest paid on such bonds is lower than the usual interest rate for straight debt issues. *See* Conversion Parity; Conversion Price; Conversion Ratio.

Conversion Arbitrage. A transaction where the arbitrageur buys the underlying security, but then buys a put and sells a call, both of which options have the same terms. *See* Reversal Arbitrage.

Conversion Parity. The equal dollar relationship between a convertible security and the underlying stock trading at or above the conversion price.

Conversion Price (Value). In the case of convertible bonds, the price of the underlying common stock at which conversion can be made. The price is set by the issuing corporation and is printed in the indenture.

Conversion Ratio. The ratio indicating how many underlying shares may be obtained upon exchange of each convertible security. *See* Convertible Security.

Convertible Bond. Bond that can be exchanged for a specified number of another security, usually shares, at a prestated price. Convertibility typically enhances the bond's marketability.

Convertible (Security). Any security that can be converted into another security. For example, a convertible bond or convertible preferred stock may be converted into the underlying stock of the same corporation at a fixed rate. The rate at which the shares of the bond or preferred stock are converted into the common is called the conversion ratio.

Cooling-Off Period. See Twenty-Day (Cooling-Off) Period.

Co-Op. See Banks for Cooperatives.

Corporation. A business organization chartered by a state secretary as a recognized legal institution of and by itself and operated by an association of individuals, with the purpose of ensuring perpetuity and limited financial liability. *See* Certificate of Incorporation; Charter.

Coupon Bond. A bond with interest coupons attached. The coupons are clipped as they come due and are presented by the holders to their banks for payment. *See* Bearer Bond; Registered Bond.

Coupon Yield. See Nominal Yield.

Currency in Circulation. Paper bills and coins used by the general public to pay for goods and services.

Current Yield. The annual dollar interest paid by a bond dividend by its market price. It is the actual return rate, not the coupon rate. Example: Any bond carrying a 6% coupon and trading at 95 is said to offer a current yield of 6.3% ($60 coupon – $950 market price = 6.3%). Also sometimes referred to a current yield to maturity. *See* Nominal Yield.

Cushion Bond. A higher-than-current coupon debt instrument with a deferred call provision in its indenture offering a better current return and minimal price volatility (as compared with a bond without call protection). It normally trades with large premiums.

Dated Date. With regard to bonds and other debt instruments, the date from which interest is determined to accrue, upon the sale of the security. The buyer pays the amount equal to the interest accrued from the dated date to the settlement date and is reimbursed with the first interest payment on the security.

Day Order. A transaction order that remains valid only for the remainder of the trading day on which it is entered.

Day Trading. The act of buying and selling a position during the same day.

Dealer. An individual or firm in the securities business acting as a principal rather than as an agent. *See* As Agent; As Principal.

Dealer Bank. (1) A commercial bank's offering of a market in government or agency securities. (2) A bank department registered as a municipal securities dealer with the MSRB.

Dealer Book. A publication by *The Bond Buyer* issued semi-annually listing municipal bond dealers, municipal finance consultants, and bond attorneys within the United States. The book is colloquially referred to as the "red book" (the color of its cover), but it is really entitled *Directory of Municipal Bond Dealers of the United States.* Standard & Poor's Corporation prints a similar book entitled *Securities Dealers of North America,* which includes Canadian dealers.

Debenture. An unsecured debt offering by a corporation, promising only the general assets as protection for creditors. Sometimes the so-called "general assets" are only goodwill and reputation.

Debt Instrument. The document specifying the terms and conditions of a loan between a lender and a borrower.

Debt Security. Any security reflecting the loan of money that must be paid back to the lender in the future, such as a bill, note, or bond.

Deep Discount Bond. A bond, although issued at par, that is currently selling below 80 percent of its par value. *Not* a bond sold at an original issue discount. *See* Discount Bond.

Default. The failure of a corporation to pay principal and/or interest on outstanding bonds or dividends on its preferred stock.

Defeasance. (1) The substitution of a new debt for old debt. Specifically, a corporation replaces old, low-rate debt with securities having less face value but paying a higher interest. (2) A company could also have a broker/dealer buy up its bonds and convert them to a new issue of the company's stock, which is of equal value to the bonds. The broker can later sell the stock for a profit.

Delivery Versus Payment. The purchase of securities in a cash account with instructions that payment will be made immediately upon the delivery of the securities, sometimes to the contra broker but usually to an agent bank. Also known as "deliver against cash" (DAC). *See* COD Trade.

Demand Deposit. A loan or checking account that gives its owner the right to withdraw funds from a commercial bank at his or her own discretion.

Depository Trust Company (DTC). An independent corporation owned by broker/dealers and banks responsible for: (1) holding deposit securities owned by broker/dealers and banking institutions; (2) arranging the receipt and delivery of securities between users by means of debiting and crediting their respective accounts; (3) arranging for payment of monies between users in the settlement of transactions. The DTC is generally used by option writers because it guarantees delivery of underlying securities if assignment is made against securities held in DTC.

Depth. (1) The amount of general investor interest in the market, comparing the number of issues traded with the number of issues listed: the more that are traded, the greater the "depth" of the market. (2) The "depth" of a security depends on how large a buy or sell order it can absorb without its price changing greatly.

Designated Concession. An order for a number of securities given to a syndicate, that designates the concessions for the nonmembers of the account. For example, nonmember A gets 1,000 out of an order for 2,000 securities; nonmember B gets 750 and nonmember C, 250.

Discount. A term used to describe debt instruments trading at a price below their face values. For example, trading at 99 would mean that for $990 one could purchase a bond that would pay $1,000 principal at maturity.

Discount Bond. A bond that sells in the marketplace at a price below its face value. *See* Deep Discount Bond.

Discount Broker. A broker/dealer whose commission rates for buying and selling securities are markedly lower than those of a full-service broker. These brokers usually provide execution-only services.

Discount Note. A note, originally sold at par, selling below its par value. A note is usually a government security.

Discount Rate (The). A rate of interest associated with borrowing reserves from a central bank by member banks in the Federal Reserve district. The rate is set by the officials of that central bank.

Discount Security. A security sold on the basis of a bank rate discount. The investment return is realized solely from the accretion of this discounted amount to the security's maturity value. The most common type is a U.S. Treasury bill.

Discount Window. A teller-like cage at which member banks may borrow reserves from the Federal Reserve Bank upon pledge of acceptable collateral.

Distributor. See Underwriter.

Distribution. The sale of a large block of stock, through either an underwriting or an exchange distribution.

District Bank. One of the twelve Federal Reserve Banks acting as the central bank for its district.

District Business Conduct Committee. An NASD district subcommittee responsible for supervising and enforcing the Board of Governors' Rules of Fair Practice; it consists of the officials of the district committee itself.

District Committee. The governing body of each of the 13 districts of the NASD.

District Uniform Practices Committee. One of 13 district committee within the NASD whose function is the dissemination of information regarding the Uniform Practice Code.

Dollar Bonds. Corporate or municipal serial bonds that are denominated and that trade in currency values instead of as a percentage of face amount because of the relatively small amounts available for each maturity in the entire issue.

DNR. See Do Not Reduce (DNR) Order.

Do Not Reduce (DNR) Order. A limit order to buy, a stop order to sell, or a stop-limit order to sell that is not to be reduced by the amount of a cash dividend on the ex-dividend date because the customer specifically requested that it be entered that way.

Double-Barrelled Bond. Usually municipal revenue bonds, secured by both a defined source of revenue plus the full faith and credit of an issuer with taxing powers. *See* Overlapping Debt.

Downgrade. Lowering a bond rating by a rating service, such as Moody's or Standard & Poor's.

Draft. A debt instrument payable on sight, or at a specific future time, upon presentation to a paying agent, usually a bank.

DTC. See Depository Trust Company.

Due-Diligence Meeting. A meeting between corporation officials and the underwriting group to (1) discuss the registration statement, (2) prepare a final prospectus, and (3) negotiate a formal underwriting agreement.

Dutch Auction. Auction in which the sellers offer down for a purchase instead of the buyers bidding up. This term is often used incorrectly to describe the weekly T-bill auction.

DVP. See Delivery Versus Payment.

Easy Money. A situation in which the Federal Reserve System allows banks to accumulate enough funds to lower interest rates and make borrowing easier. Easy money fosters economic growth and inflation. *See* Tight Money.

Edge Act. A 1919 federal law allowing commercial banks the right to conduct international business across state lines.

Edge Act Corporation. A federal- or state-chartered subsidiary involved with foreign lending operations. *See* Edge Act.

Effective Date. The date on which a security can be offered publicly if no deficiency letter is submitted to the issuer by the SEC. It is generally no earlier than the twentieth calendar day after filing the registration statement.

Effective Sale. A round-lot transaction consummated on the floor of the New York Stock Exchange after entry of an odd-lot order by a customer. Its price is used to determine the execution price for the odd-lot order after consideration of the dealer's fee. *See* Differential.

Either/Or Order. See Alternative (Either/Or) Order.

Electing Sale. The round-lot transaction that activates (triggers) a stop order.

Equipment Trust Bond. A serial bond collateralized by the machinery and/or equipment of the issuing corporation.

Equity. The ownership interest in a company of holders of its common and preferred stock.

Equivalent Bond Yield. A percentage used to express the comparison of the discount yield of money market securities with the coupon yield of government obligations.

Execution. Synonym for a transaction or trade between a buyer and seller.

Ex-Legal. In municipals trading, the absence of a bond counsel's legal opinion usually connected with the delivery of the securities in the secondary market.

Face Value. The redemption value of a bond or preferred stock appearing on the face of the certificate, unless that value is otherwise specified by the issuing corporation. Also sometimes referred to as par value.

Fair and Reasonable. See Five Percent Guideline.

Fair Market Value. The price, based on the current market value determined by supply and demand, for which a buyer and seller are willing to make a transaction.

Fair Treatment. Under the NASD Rules of Fair Practice, members have a business relationship with their customers and a fiduciary responsibility in handling their accounts.

Fannie Maes. See Federal National Mortgage Association.

FANS. See Free Account Net Settlement.

Farm Credit Banks. Banks set up to deal with the specific financial needs of farmers and their businesses.

Farmers Home Administration (FHA). Agency set up by the Federal Department of Agriculture empowered to make loans to farm owners or tenants to help finance the acquisition or improvement of farm properties. The FHA also helps finance community facilities by making loans to qualified municipal issuers.

Fast Market. Term used to describe fast-paced activity in a class of listed options. If the exchange cannot control the market, new orders may be delayed.

Federal Funds. (1) The excess reserve balances of a member bank on deposit at a central bank in the Federal Reserve system. This money may be made available to eligible borrowers on a short-term basis. (2) Funds used for settlement of money market instruments and U.S. government securities transactions. (3) A term used to mean "same-day availability" of money. *See* Clearing House Funds.

Federal Funds Rate. A rate of interest associated with borrowing a member bank's excess reserves. The rate is determined by the forces of supply and demand.

Federal Home Loan Banks (FHLB). A government-sponsored agency that finances the home-building industry with mortgage loans from monies raised on offerings of bond issues; interest on these bonds is free from state and local income tax.

Federal Intermediate Credit Banks (FICB). An agency under the supervision of the Farm Credit Administration that makes loans to agricultural credit and production associations, with revenues derived from five-year bond issues. The interest on those bonds is free from state and local income tax.

Federal Land Banks (FLB). Government-sponsored corporations that arrange primary mortgages on farm properties for general agricultural purposes; interest on their bonds is exempt from state and municipal taxes.

Federal National Mortgage Association (FNMA). A publicly owned, government-sponsored corporation that purchases and sells mortgages insured by the Federal Housing Administration (FHA) or Farmers Home Administration (FHA); or guaranteed by the Veterans' Administration (VA). Interest on these bonds, called Fannie Maes, is fully taxable.

Federal Open Market Committee. See Open Market Operations.

Federal Reserve Bank. One of the banks forming the Federal Reserve system.

Federal Reserve Board (FRB). A United States government agency empowered by Congress to regulate credit in the country. Its members are appointed by the president of the United States.

Federal Reserve Requirements. Each commercial bank must set aside a certain percentage of its deposits, as determined by the Federal Reserve, in order to limit its potential credit-granting capability.

Federal Reserve System. A system of Federal Reserve banks in the United States forming 12 districts under the control of the Federal Reserve Board. These banks regulate the extension of credit as well as other banking activities.

FHLB. See Federal Home Loan Banks.

FICB. See Federal Intermediate Credit Banks.

Fill-or-Kill (FOK) Order. An order that requires the immediate purchase or sale of a specified amount of stock, though not necessarily at one price. If the order cannot be filled immediately, it is automatically cancelled (killed).

Firm Market (Price, Quote). In the OTC market, a quotation on a given security rendered by a market maker at which he or she stands ready and able to trade immediately.

Five Percent Guideline. A general guideline established by the NASD Board of Governors to define "fair" in a random trading transaction; it is not a rule or regulation and is used only as a rough criterion for markups, markdowns, and commissions.

Flat. When accrued interest is not added to the contract price of bonds (that is, most income bonds and all obligations for which interest has been deferred) in a transaction, the bonds are said to be trading "flat."

FLB. See Federal Land Banks.

Flower Bond. A type of treasury bond selling at a discount with a special privilege attached permitting redemption after the death of the owner at par value in satisfaction of federal estate taxes. These bonds were issued prior to April 1, 1971, and will be in circulation up to final maturity in 1998.

FNMA. See Federal National Mortgage Association (FNMA).

FOK Order. See Fill-or-Kill (FOK) Order.

Fourth Market. A term referring to the trading of securities between investors without the use of broker/dealers.

FRB. See Federal Reserve Board.

Free Box. A bank vault or other secure location used to store fully paid customer securities. The depositories of the NCC and DTC serve as free boxes for many member firm customers.

"Free" Crowd. See Active Bonds (The "Free" Crowd).

Full Disclosure Act. The Securities Act of 1933.

Fully Registered Bonds. Bonds registered as to both principal and interest.

Funded Debt. The aggregate of a corporation's liabilities with maturities exceeding five years.

General Obligation (GO) Bond. A tax-exempt bond whose pledge is the issuer's good faith and full taxing power.

Gilt-Edged. A security (bonds more often than stocks) that consistently pays dividends or interest.

Ginnie Maes. See Government National Mortgage Association.

Go-Around. A process by which the Federal Open Market Committee gathers bids and offers from primary bank and nonbank dealers.

Going Away. A term applied to the purchase of one or more serial maturities of an issue either by institution or by a dealer.

Going Private. Moving a company's shares from public to private ownership, either through an outside private investor or by the repurchase of shares. A company usually decides to go private when its shares are selling way below book value.

Going Public. A private company is "going public" when it first offers its shares to the investing public.

Good Delivery. Proper delivery by a selling firm to the purchaser's office of certificates that are negotiable without additional documentation and that are in units acceptable under the Uniform Practice Code.

Good Faith Deposit. An amount of money given by members of an underwriting syndicate to the syndicate manager to guarantee their financial performance under the syndicate agreement.

Good Money. Another term for federal funds.

Good-till-Cancelled (GTC or Open) Order. An order to buy or sell that remains valid until executed or cancelled by the customer.

Government National Mortgage Association (GNMA). An offshoot of the FNMA, a wholly owned government corporation (operated by the Department of Housing and Urban Development, HUD) that provides primary mortgages through bond issuances carrying no tax exemptions. GNMA securities are called "Ginnie Maes."

Green Shoe. In an underwriting agreement, a clause that allows the syndicate to purchase additional shares at the same price as the original offering. This lessens the risk for the syndicate.

Group Sales. Sales of securities by a syndicate manager to institutional purchasers from "the pot."

GTC. See Good-Till-Cancelled (GTC or Open) Order.

Guaranteed Bonds. Bonds issued by a subsidiary corporation and guaranteed as to principal and/or interest by the parent corporation.

Hedge. Any combination of long and/or short positions taken in securities, options, or commodities in which one position tends to reduce the risk of the other.

Hit the Bid. Term applied to the situation in which a seller accepts the buyer's highest bid. For example, if the ask price is 34¼ and the bid 34, the seller "hits the bid" by accepting 34.

Hot Issue. A security that is expected to trade in the after-market at a premium over the public offering price.

House. On the street, a firm or individual engaged in business as a broker/dealer or investment banker.

House Account. An account managed by a firm executive and/or handled at the firm's main office. No salesperson receives a commission or transactions in a house account.

Housing Authority Bond. A municipal bond whose payment of interest and/or principal is contingent upon the collection of rents and other fees from users of a housing facility built with the proceeds of the issuance of the bond.

Immediate or Cancel (IOC) Order. An order that requires immediate execution at a specified price of all or part of a specified amount of stock: the unexecuted portion has to be cancelled by the broker.

Inactive Bonds. Debt instruments that are expected by the NYSE Floor Department to trade only infrequently. All bids and offers, therefore, are filed in a "cabinet" or "can" (on cards colored to reflect effective lifetimes) until they are cancelled or executed.

Inactive Market. See Narrow Market.

Income (Adjustment) Bonds. In the event of bankruptcy, long-term debt obligations are offered in exchange for outstanding bonds by the court-appointed receiver. The interest requirement associated with such debt will be paid by the corporation only when, as, and if earned.

Indenture. A written agreement between corporation and creditors containing the terms of a debt issue, such as rate of interest, means of payment, maturity date, terms of prior payment of principal, collateral, priorities of claims, trustee.

Indenture Qualification Statement. For publicly offered debt instruments not subject to registration under the Securities Act of 1933 but subject to the Trust Indenture Act of 1939, the statement required to be filed with the SEC to comply with the latter act.

Indication of Interest. An expression of consideration by an underwriter's circle of customers for investment in a new security expected to be offered soon. It is not a binding commitment on the customer or the underwriter.

Industrial Development Bonds. Industrial revenue bonds issued to improve the environment and subject to certain Internal Revenue Service regulations with regard to the tax-exempt status of the interest payments.

Industrial Revenue Bonds. Municipal bonds issued for the purpose of constructing facilities for profit-making corporations. The tax-exempt feature of these bonds may be restricted by certain Internal Revenue Service regulations. The corporation, rather than the municipality, is liable for the payment of interest and principal.

Inflation. A general rise in prices.

Insider. An officer, director, or principal stockholder of a publicly owned corporation and members of their immediate families.   This category may also include people who obtain nonpublic information about a company and use it for personal gain.

Institution. A large organization engaged in investing in securities, such as a bank, insurance company, mutual fund, or pension fund. An *institutional broker* buys and sells securities for any of the above dealing in large volumes and charging a lower-than-usual per-unit commission. An *institutional investor* is any of the institutions above who buy and sell securities. An *institutional house* is any brokerage firm dealing with such institutions. *Institutional sales* are sales of any type of securities by such institutions.

Insubstantial Quantity. Under NASD interpretations regarding hot issues, $5,000 face value in bonds is considered an "insubstantial quantity." It may be allocated to certain restricted parties.

Interpositioning. An unethical and unfair practice by a broker/dealer of needlessly employing a third party between the customer and the best available market, so that the customer pays more on a purchase or receives less on a sale than he or she should.

In the Tank. Colloquial expression for a security or group of securities that is quickly losing value.

Intraday. Meaning "within the day," this term is most often used to describe daily high and low prices of a security or commodity.

Investment Advisor. A person, company, or institution registered with the SEC under the Investment Advisors Act of 1940 to manage the investments of third parties.

Investment Advisors Act of 1940. A federal law requiring those who charge a fee for investment advice to register with the SEC. Exceptions include banks, some brokers, and newspapers with broad-based readership.

Investment Banker. A broker/dealer organization that provides a service to industry through counsel, market making, and underwriting of securities.

Involuntary (Statutory) Underwriter. An individual or corporation that purchases an unregistered security and offers it in a public distribution without an effective registration statement. Such parties are subject to fine and/or imprisonment.

IOC Order. See Immediate or Cancel (IOC) Order.

Irredeemable Bond. (1)*See* Perpetual Bond. (2) A bond whose issuer does not have the right to redeem the bond before maturity.

Issue (Issuance). (1) Any of a company's class of securities. (2) The act of distributing securities.

Issuer. A corporation, trust, or governmental agency engaged in the distribution of its securities.

Jeeps. See Graduated Payment Mortgages (GPM).

Joint Account. An account including jointly two or more people.

Joint Tenants in Common. An account in which the two or more people participating have fractional interests in its assets. The interest percentage of the assets becomes part of each person's estate upon death.

Joint Tenants With Rights of Survivorship (W/R/O/S). An account in which two or more people have an ownership interest and whose assets are inherited by its survivors upon the death of any participant.

Junk Bond. Any bond with a Moody's or Standard & Poor's credit rating of BB or lower. Such bonds, usually issued by companies without long track records, can produce high yields.

Lead Manager. The member of an underwriting syndicate charged with the primary responsibility for conducting the affairs of the syndicate. *See* Syndicate.

Legal Delivery. A delivery of securities that is not good delivery because of the way in which registration of the certificates was carried out.

Letter Bonds. Privately sold bonds that are accompanied by an investment letter giving the investor the right to transfer or resell them.

Level Debt Service. A requirement in a municipality's charter that the annual debt service payment must be approximately equal — or "level" — each year. Its purpose is to effectively budget all tax revenues of that municipality.

Leverage. (1) In securities, increasing return without increasing investment. Buying stock on margin is an example. (2) In finance, the relationship of a firm's debt to its equity, as expressed in the debt-to-equity ratio. If the company earns a return on the borrowed money greater than the cost of the debt, it is successfully applying the principle of leverage.

Limit Price. A modification of an order to buy or sell. With a *sell* limit order, the customer is instructing the broker to make the sale at or above the limit price. With a *buy limit order, the customer is instructing the broker to make the purchase at or below the limit price.*

Liquidity. (1) The ability of the market in a particular security to absorb a reasonable amount of trading at reasonable price changes. Liquidity is one of the most important characteristics of a good market. (2) The relative ease with which investors can convert their securities into cash.

Listed Bond Table. A daily publication appearing in many newspapers showing a summary of transactions by exchange or, if OTC, by security.

Long Market Value. The market value of securities owned by a customer (long in his or her account).

Long Position. The ownership of securities.

Long-Term Debt. The debt of a company due and payable more than one year hence.

M. (1) Abbreviation for 1,000. For example, "5M" means 5,000; "25M" means 25,000. Usually used to denote the face value of a bond. (2) Preceding the name of a stock in the National Quotation Bureau's daily pink sheet, the security can be margined.

M 1. The nation's money supply, defined as total currency in circulation plus all demand deposits in commercial banks.

M 2. M1 plus savings and time deposits of less than $100,000 in commercial banks.

Major Bracket Participant. A member of an underwriting syndicate who will handle a large part of the issue in relation to other members of the syndicate.

Mandatory Redemption Account. See Bond Amortization Fund.

Manipulation. Making securiites prices rise or fall artificially, through aggressive buying or selling by one investor in connection with others. This is a severe violation of federal securities laws.

Markdown. The fee charged by a broker/dealer acting as a dealer when he or she buys a security from a customer and sells it, at a higher price, to a market maker. The fee, or markdown, is included in the sale price and is not itemized separately in the confirmation. *See* As Principal; Five Percent Guideline.

Marketable Security. (1) A security that may be readily purchased or sold. (2) A U.S. government bond freely traded in the open market. *See* Certificate of Indebtedness (CI); Treasury Bills; Treasury Bonds; Treasury Notes.

Marketability. How easily a security can be bought and sold. *See* Liquidity.

Market-If-Touched Order. An order allowable only on the CBOE. Such a buy order is activated when a series declines to a predetermined price or below. Such a sell order is activated when a series rises to a predetermined price or higher.

Market Maker. (1) An options exchange member who trades for his or her own account and risk. This member is charged with the responsibility of trading so as to maintain a fair, orderly, and competitive market. He or she may not act as agent. (2) A firm actively making bids and offers in the OTC market.

Market Not Held Order. An order to buy or sell securities at the current market with the investor leaving the exact timing of its execution up to the floor broker. If the floor broker is holding a "market not held" buy order and the price could decline, he or she may wait to buy when a better price becomes available. There is no guarantee for the investor that a "market not held" order will be filled.

Market Order. An order to be executed immediately at the best available price.

Market Price. (1) The last reported sale price for an exchange-traded security. (2) For over-the-counter securities, a consensus among market makers.

Market Tone. The "health" of a market. The tone is good when dealers and market markers are actively trading on narrow spreads. It is poor when trading drops off and spreads widen.

Market Value. The price that would be paid for a security or other asset.

Markup. The fee charged by a broker/dealer acting as a dealer when he or she buys a security from a market maker and sells it to a customer at a higher price. The fee, or markup, is included in the sale price and is not itemized separately in the confirmation. *See* As Principal; Five Percent Guideline.

Matched Sale/Purchase Transaction (Reverse Repurchase Agreement). A Federal Open Market Committee sale of Treasury bills or other government securities for cash settlement with a provision for repurchase at the same price plus interest on a specific date in the future.

Maturity (Date). The date on which a loan, bond, or debenture comes due; both principal and any accrued interest due must be paid.

Maturity Value. The amount an investor receives when a security is redeemed at maturity; not including any periodic interest payments. This value usually equals the par value, although on zero coupon, compound interest, and multiplier bonds, the principal amount of the security at issuance plus the accumulated investment return on the security is included.

Member Bank. A bank that is a member of the Federal Reserve System. Member banks must purchase stock in the Federal Reserve Bank in their district equal to 6 percent of their own paid-in capital.

Member Takedown. A situation in which a syndicate member buys bonds at the takedown (or member's discount) and then sells them to a customer at the public offering price.

Missing the Market. The failure by a member of the exchange to execute an order due to his or her negligence. The member is obliged to promptly reimburse the customer for any losses due to the mistake.

Monetary Supply. See M1; M2

Money. Coin or certificates generally accepted in payment of debts for goods and services.

Money Market. The market for dealers who trade riskless, short-term securities: T-bills, certificates of deposits, banker's acceptances, and commercial paper.

Money Market Fund. Name for an open-ended investment company whose portfolio consists of money market securities.

Money Market Instruments. Short-term debt (of less than one year to maturity) usually issued at a discount and not bearing interest. For example, Treasury bills, commercial paper, or banker's acceptances.

Money Supply. See M1; M2.

Moody's Investors Service. One of the best-known bond rating agencies, owned by Dun & Bradstreet. *Moody's Investment Grade* assigns letter grades to bonds based on their predicted long-term yield (M1G1, M1G2, etc). Moody's also rates commercial paper, municipal short-term issues, and preferred and common stocks. Another publication is a six-volume annual, with weekly or semiweekly supplements, giving great detail on issuers and securities. Publications include *Moody's Bond Record* and *Moody's Bond Survey.* Moody's investment ratings are considered the norm for investment decisions by fiduciaries.

Moral Suasion. An expression used to denote the Federal Reserve Board's ability to influence member bank financial policies by threatening to employ drastic powers in order to gain compliance with its own preferences.

Mortgage-Backed Certificate (Security). A security (1) that is issued by the Federal Home Loan Mortgage Corporation, the Federal National Mortgage Association, and the Government National Mortgage Association, and (2) that is backed by mortgages. Payments to investors are received out of the interest and principal of the underlying mortgages.

Mortgage Bond. The most prevalent type of secured corporate bond. The bondholders are protected by the pledge of the corporation's real assets evaluated at the time of issuance. *See* Open-End Provision.

Mortgage Pool. A group, or "pool," of mortgages on the same class of property, with the same interest rate and the same maturity date.

Mortgage REIT. A REIT primarily engaged in the financing of new construction.

MSRB. See Municipal Securities Rulemaking Board.

Municipal Bond (Security). Issued by a state or local government, a debt obligation whose funds either may support a government's general financing needs or may be spent on special projects. Municipal bonds are free from federal tax on the accrued interest and also free from state and local taxes if issued in the state of residence.

Municipal Securities Rulemaking Board (MSRB). Registered under the Maloney Act in 1975, the Board consists of industry and public representatives. It is designed to create rules and regulations for municipal bond trading among brokers, dealers, and banks. Its powers are similar to those of the NASD.

Munifacts. A private communications network originating in the New York offices of *The Bond Buyer.* It transmits current bond market information to subscribers.

Mutilation. A term used to describe the physical condition of a certificate, note, bond, or coupon when the instrument is no longer considered negotiable. The standards for determining what is mutilated are set forth in MSRB Rule G-12(e) (ix). Such missing items as the signature of the authorized officer, the serial number of the instrument, the amount or the payable date would cause the instrument to be considered mutilated. The issuing authority, or its agent, must be contacted to obtain certain documents needed to make the instrument negotiable again.

N. "Note" when used in lowercase with a U.S. government bid-asked quotation.

Narrowing the Spread. The action taken by a broker/dealer to narrow the spread between bids and offers, by bidding higher or offering lower than the previous bid or offer. Also called closing the market.

Narrow Market. Light trading and great price fluctuations with regard to the volume on a securities or commodities market. Also known as thin market and inactive market.

NASD. See National Association of Securities Dealers.

NASDAQ. See National Association of Securities Dealers Automated Quotations.

NASDAQ OTC Price Index. See National Association of Securities Dealers Automated Quotations Over-the-Counter Price Index.

NASD Code of Arbitration. Code governing the arbitration of controversies arising out of, and relating exclusively to, securities transactions. This code is available for disputes between members of the National Association of Securities Dealers or between customers and NASD members.

NASD Code of Procedure. Code prescribed by the Board of Governors of the National Association of Securities Dealers for the administration of disciplinary proceedings stemming from infractions of the Rules of Fair Practice.

National Association of Securities Dealers (NASD). An association of broker/dealers in over-the-counter securities organized on a nonprofit, non-stock-issuing basis. Its general aim is to protect investors in the OTC market.

National Association of Securities Dealers Automated Quotation System (NASDAQ). A computerized quotations network by which NASD members can communicate bids and offers.

> *Level 1* Provides only the arithmetic mean of the bids and offers entered by members.

> *Level 2* Provides the individual bids and offers next to the name of the member entering the information.

> *Level 3* Available to NASD members only, enables the member to enter bids and offers and receive Level 2 service.

National Association of Securities Dealers Automated Quotations Over-The-Counter Price Index. A computer-oriented, broad-based indicator of activity in the unlisted securities market, updated every five minutes.

National Clearing Corporation (NCC). An NASD affiliate organization responsible for arranging a daily clearance of transactions for members by means of a continuous net settlement process. Although its principal office is in New York City, it operates electronic satellite branches in major U.S. cities.

National Institutional Delivery System (NIDS). A system of automated transmissions of confirmation from a dealer to an institutional investor, and the affirmation and book-entry settlement of the transaction. MSRB rules state that NIDS must be used on certain transactions between dealers and customers. Also known as "Institutional Delivery," or ID for short.

National Quotation Bureau, Inc. (NQB). A subsidiary of Commerce Clearing House, Inc. that distributes to subscribers several lists a day of broker/dealers making bids and/or offerings of securities traded over-the-counter. Also known as pink sheets.

National Quotations Committee. A national committee of NASD that sets minimum standards for the publication of quotations furnished to newspapers, radio, or television.

Near Money. A bond whose redemption date is near.

Negotiability. In reference to securities, the ability to easily transfer title upon delivery.

Negotiable Paper or Instrument. An order or promise to pay an amount of money that is easily transferable from one person to another, such as a check, promissory note, or draft.

Negotiated Bid. A bid on an underwriting that is negotiated by the issuer and a single underwriting syndicate. *See* Competitive Bidding.

Negotiated Marketplace. The over-the-counter market, in which transactions are negotiated between two parties. The opposite of auction marketplace.

Negotiated Underwriting. The underwriting of new securities issues in which the spread purchase price and the public offering price are determined through negotiation rather than through bidding. *See* Negotiated Bid.

Net Interest Cost. The net cost to the issuer of a debt instrument, taking into account both the coupon and the discount or premium on the issue.

New Issue. (1) Any authorized but previously unissued security offered for sale by an issuer. (2) The resale of treasury shares.

New Money. The issue of new bonds with a greater par value than that of bonds being called or maturing.

New York Plan. A method of issuing equipment trust certificates (serial debt obligations issued by airlines, railroads, and other common carriers) to acquire equipment. *See* Philadelphia Plan.

Next-Day Contract. A security transaction calling for settlement the day after trade date.

NH. See Not Held (NH) Order.

Nominal Quotation. A quotation that is an approximation of the price that could be expected on a purchase or sale, and that is not to be considered firm in the event that a purchase or sale is consummated. *See* Numbers Only.

Nominal Value. See Face Value.

Nominal Yield. The annual interest rate payable on a bond, specified in the indenture and printed on the face of the certificate itself. Also known as coupon yield.

Normal Trading Unit. The accepted unit of trading in a given marketplace: For NASDAQ-traded securities, it is $10,000 par value for bonds. *See* Odd Lots; Round Lots.

Normal Yield Curve. A graph that plots the yield of equivalent securities with different maturities at any given point in time. A *normal yield curve* indicates that short-term securities have lower interest rates than long-term securities.

Not Held (NH) Order. An order that does not hold the executing member financially responsible for using his or her personal judgment in the execution price or time of a transaction. *See* Market Not Held Order.

Notice of Redemption. The announcement of an issuer's intention to call bonds prior to their dates of maturity.

Numbers Only. A dealer's response to a request for a quote with just numbers; the dealer is not obligated to make a transaction. *See* Nominal Quotation.

Odd Lot. An amount of stock less than the normal trading unit. *See* Round Lot.

Off-Board. An expression that may refer to transactions over the counter in unlisted securities or to transactions involving listed shares that were not executed on a national securities exchange.

Offer. The price at which a person is ready to sell. *See* Bid-and-Asked Quotation (or Quote).

Offering (Asked) Price. The lowest price available for a round lot.

Offering Circular. (1) A publication that is prepared by the underwriters and that discloses basic information about an issue of securities to be offered in the primary market. (2) Sometimes used to describe a document used by dealers when selling large blocks of stock in the secondary market.

Offering Date. When a security is first offered for public sale.

Offering Scale. The price, expressed in eighths of a point or in decimals, at which the underwriter will sell the individual serial maturities of a bond issue.

Offer Wanted (OW). Notation made, usually in the pink or yellow sheets, by a broker/dealer who wants another dealer to make an offer for a security.

Official Notice of Sale. An advertisement issued by a municipal issuer to solicit competitive bids for an upcoming municipal bond issue. It usually includes all the facts about the issue and appears in the *Daily Bond Buyer.*

Open Market Operations. The activity of the Federal Open Market Committee, in behalf of the Federal Reserve Banking System, to arrange outright purchases and sales of government and agency securities, matched sale/purchase agreements, and repurchase agreements in order to promote the monetary policy of the Federal Reserve Board.

Open Order. *See* Good-till-Cancelled (GTC or Open) Order.

Operating Income. Net sales less cost of sales, selling expenses, administrative expenses, and depreciation. The pre-tax income from normal operations.

Operations Department. A department of the NYSE responsible for (1) the listing and delisting of corporate and government securities, and (2) all trading activity and ancillary services.

Order Department. A group that routes buy and sell instructions to the trading floors of the appropriate stock exchanges and executes orders in the OTC market for trading accounts of both firms and customers.

OTC Margin Stock. A stock traded over-the-counter whose issuer meets certain criteria that qualify the stock for margined purchases or short sales, as governed by Regulation T.

Out for a Bid. In the municipal bond market, the securities are "out for a bid" when a dealer lends them to an agent who then attempts to sell them.

Outright Purchases or Sales. The net purchases or sales made by the Federal Open Market Committee, including buys and sells that may be partially offset by repo or reverse repo agreements.

Overlapping Debt. A bond having two issuers. *See* Double-Barrelled Bond.

Overnight Position. The investory in a security at the end of a trading day.

Over-the-Counter Option (OTC). A market, conducted mainly over the telephone, for securities made up of dealers who may or may not be members of a securities exchange. Thousands of companies have insufficient shares outstanding, stockholders, or earnings to warrant listing on a national exchange. Securities of these companies are therefore traded in the over-the-counter

market between dealers who act either as agents for
their customers or as principals. The over-the-counter
market is the principal market for U.S. government
and municipal bonds and for stocks of banks and insurance companies.

Overtrading. A practice in violation of NASD principles. A
broker/dealer overpays a customer for a security to
enable the customer to subscribe to another security
offered by that broker/dealer at a higher markup than
the loss to be sustained when the firm sells the
customer's first security at prevailing market prices.

Overvalued. In securities trading, a security whose market
price is higher than it should be in the opinion of fun-
damental analysts. *See* Fair Value; Undervalued.

OW. See Offer Wanted.

Paper. Relatively short-term debt securities.

Parity Bonds. Any two or more issues having the same
priority of claim or lien against pledged revenues.

Parking. The practice by a dealer of selling a security to
another dealer to reduce the seller's net capital. The
securities are sold back to the first dealer when a buyer
is found, and the second dealer recoups any carrying
charges.

Partial Delivery. A delivery of fewer securities than the
amount contracted for in the sales transaction.

Participate But Do Not Initiate (PNI) Order. On large orders
to buy or sell, an instruction given to a broker from institutional buyers or sellers not to initiate a new price,
but either to let the market create a new price or obtain a favorable price through gradual and intermittent
transactions. This allows the buyers or sellers to accumulate or distribute shares without disturbing the
market forces. This could also be done by institutions
that are not permitted by law to create an uptick or a
downtick in the market.

Pass-Through Security (P/T). A debt security representing an interest in a pool of mortgages requiring monthly payments composed of interest on unpaid principal and a partial repayment of principal. Thus the payments are passed through the intermediaries, from the debtors to investors.

Par (Value). The face or nominal value of a security. For preferred bonds, par value has importance in so far as it signifies the dollar value on which the dividend/interest is figured and the amount to be repaid upon redemption. Preferred dividends are usually expressed as a percentage of the stock's par value. The interest on bonds is expressed as a percentage of the bond's par value. *See* Face Value.

Pegging. Also known as stabilization. Keeping a security's offer price at a certain level by means of a bid at or slightly below the price. Pegging is legal only in underwriting.

Penalty Syndicate Bid. A series of restrictive financial measures written into agreements among underwriters with the purpose of discouraging resale of securities requiring stabilization. A monetary penalty helps insure distribution to investment portfolios and not to traders and speculators seeking short-term profits at the expense of the underwriters.

Perpetual Bond. A bond with no maturity date. Also called an annuity bond.

Philadelphia Plan. The issuance of equipment trust bonds in which the title to the leased equipment remains with the trustee until all of the outstanding serial maturities for the issue are retired. It would then pass to the leasing issuer of the securities. *See* New York Plan.

Pickup. The increased value (usually small) achieved by means of a swap of bonds with similar coupon rates and maturities at a basis price.

Picture. The prices at which a broker/dealer or specialist is ready to trade. For example, "The picture on XYZ is 18½ to 19, 1,000 either way."

Pink Sheets. A list of securities being traded by over-the-counter market markers, published every business day by the National Quotations Bureau. Equity securities are published separately on long pink sheets. Debt securities are published separately on long yellow sheets.

Pledged Revenues. Monies needed for — that is, pledged to — the payment of debt service and other deposits required by a bond contract. A *net pledge* or *net revenue pledge* is a pledge that all funds remaining after certain operational and maintenance costs are paid will be used for payment of debt services. A *gross pledge* or *gross revenue pledge* states that all revenues received will be used for the debt service prior to any deductions for costs or expenses.

PNI Order. See Participate But Do Not Initiate (PNI) Order.

Point. Since a bond is quoted as a percentage of $1,000, it means $10. For example, a municipal security discounted at 3½ points equals $35. It is quoted at 96½ or $965 per $1,000.

Pool. A group of debt instrument in which undivided interest is represented by another security.

Portfolio. Holdings of securities by an individual or institution. A portfolio may include preferred and common stocks, as well as bonds, of various enterprises.

POS. See Preliminary Official Statement.

Position. (1) The status of securities in an account — long or short. (2) To buy or sell a block of securities so that a position is established.

Pot, The. A pool of securities, aside from those distributed among individual syndicate members, that is allocated by the manager for group or institutional sales. When "the pot is clean," the portion of the issue reserved for institutional (group) sales has been completely sold.

Pot is Clean. See Pot, The.

Preliminary Agreement. An agreement between an issuing corporation and an underwriter drawn up prior to the effective date and pending a decision by the underwriter on the success potential of the new securities. *See* Indication of Interest.

Preliminary Official Statement (POS). Also known as the preliminary prospectus, the preliminary version or draft of an official statement, as issued by the underwriters or issuers and subject to change prior to the confirmation of offering prices or interest rates. It is the only form of communication allowed between a broker and prospective buyer before the effective date, usually to gauge the interest of underwriters. Offers of sale or acceptance are not accepted on the basis of a preliminary statement. A statement to that effect, printed in red, appears vertically on the face of the document. This caveat, required by the Securities Act of 1933, is what gives the document its nickname, "red herring."

Preliminary Prospectus. See Preliminary Official Statement (POS).

Premium. The amount by which the price paid for a preferred security exceeds its face value. The market price of a bond selling at a price above its face amount.

Presold Issue. A completely sold-out issue of municipal or government securities prior to the announcement of its price or coupon rate. This practice is illegal with regard to registered corporate offerings, but it is not illegal in the primary distribution of municipals or Treasuries.

Primary Distribution (Offering). The original sale of a company's securities. The sale of authorized but unissued shares of stock is a primary sale, while the resale of treasury shares is a secondary sale.

Primary Market. (1) Organized stock exchanges. (2) The new issue market as opposed to the secondary market.

Prime Rate. The interest rate charged by a bank on loans made to its most creditworthy customers.

Principal. See As Principal.

Principal Trade (Transaction). Any transaction in which the dealer or dealer bank effecting the trade takes over ownership of the securities.

Principal Value. The face value of an obligation that must be repaid at maturity and that is separate from interest. Often called simply "principal."

Prior Issue. (1) Term applied to an outstanding issue of bonds when they are to be refinanced by a refunding. (2) Previous bond issues that normally possess a first, or senior, lien on pledged revenues.

Prior Lien Bond. A bond that takes precedence over all other bonds from the issuer because they hold a higher-priority claim. These bonds are usually issued as a result of reorganizations arising from bankruptcy proceedings.

Prospectus. A document that contains material information for an impending offer of securities (containing most of the information included in the registration statement) and that is used for solicitation purposes by the issuer and underwriters.

Prudent Man Investing. Investing in a fashion that is exemplified by the conduct of a conservative person managing his or her own assets. In certain cases this type of investing is limited to "legal list." Some states use the "prudent man" rule as a legal guideline for investing others' money.

Public Offering (Distribution). The offering of securities for sale by an issuer.

Purchase Group. Investment bankers who, as a group, purchase a new issue for resale to the public. The purchase group (or syndicate) differs from the selling group, another group of investment bankers whose function is distribution. *See* Syndicate; Underwriting Agreement.

Qualified Legal Opinion. A conditional affirmation of a security's legality, which is given before or after the security is sold. An unqualified legal opinion (called a *clean opinion*) is an unconditional affirmation of the legality of securities.

Quotation or Quote. See Bid-and-Asked Quotation (or Quote).

RAN. See Revenue Anticipation Note.

Range. A set of prices consisting of the opening sale, high sale, low sale, and latest sale of the day for a given security.

Rate of Return. See Current Yield.

Rating Agencies. Organziations that publicly rate the credit quality of securities issuers, the most often cited being Moody's Investor's Service, Inc. and Standard & Poor's Corporation.

Receiver's Certificates. Short-term (90- to 120-day) debt obligations issued by a receiver for a bankrupt corporation to supply working capital during the receiver's inquiry. These obligations take priority over the claims of all other creditors.

Reciprocal Immunity Doctrine. A court decision that neither the federal government nor states can tax income received from securities issued by the other. A state cannot tax income from Treasury securities or federal agency obligations, and the federal government cannot tax income from state-issued securities.

Red Book. See Dealer Book.

Redemption. For bonds, the retirement of the securities by repayment of face value or above (that is, at a premium price) to their holders.

Redemption Notice. A publicly issued notice stating an issuer's intent to redeem securities.

Redemption Provision. See Catastrophe (Calamity) Call.

Red Herring. See Preliminary Official Statement (POS).

Rediscount. A situation in which a member bank of the Federal Reserve System borrows funds from the Federal Reserve using eligible collateral. This collateral, in turn, came from one of the bank's borrowers.

Refunding (Refinancing). The issuance of a new debt security, using the proceeds to redeem either older bonds at maturity or outstanding bonds issued under less favorable terms and conditions.

Registered as to Interest Only. Bonds that are registered as to interest and on which interest checks are sent to the registered owner, but that are payable to the bearer at maturity.

Registered as to Principal Only. Bonds that are registered and that are payable at maturity to the registered holder, but that have coupons attached that must be presented by the bearer periodically for payment.

Registered Bond. An outstanding bond whose owner's name is recorded on the books of the issuing corporations. Legal title may be transferred only when the bond is endorsed by the registered owner.

Registered Representative. See Account Executive.

Registered Security. (1) A certificate clearly inscribed with the owner's name. (2) A bond that is registered with the SEC at the time of its sale. If such an initial registration does not take place, then the term also includes any security sold publicly and in accordance with the SEC's rules.

Registration Statement. A document required to be filed with the SEC by the issuer of securities before a public offering may be attempted. The Securities Act of 1933 mandates that it contain all material and accurate facts. Such a statement is required also when affiliated persons intend offering sizable amounts of securities. The SEC examines the statement for a 20-day period, seeking obvious omissions or misrepresentations of fact.

Regular Way Contract. The most frequently used delivery contract. For stocks and corporate and municipal bonds, this type of contract calls for delivery on the fifth business day after the trade. For U.S. government bonds and options, delivery must be made on the first business day after the trade.

Regulation G. A Federal Reserve Board regulation requiring any person, other than a bank or broker/dealer, who extends credit secured directly or indirectly with margin securities, to register and be subject to Federal Reserve Board jurisdiction.

Regulation Q. The Federal Reserve Board's interest rate on time deposits.

Regulation T. A Federal Reserve Board regulation that explains the conduct and operation of general and special accounts within the offices of a broker/dealer firm, prescribing a code of conduct for the effective use and supervision of credit.

Regulation U. A Federal Reserve Board regulation that regulates the extension of credit by banks when securities are used as collateral.

Regulation W. The regulation of the Federal Reserve Board pertaining to installment loans.

Regulation X. A set of rules established by the Federal Reserve Board that places equal burdens of responsibility for compliance with Regulations G, T, and U on the borrower as well as the lender.

Reoffering Sale. Listed by date of maturity, the prices and yields of securities offered by the underwriters.

Reopening an Issue. The offering by the Treasury of additional securities in an issue that's been already offered and sold. The new securities have the same terms and conditions, but they sell at the prevailing prices.

Repo. See Repurchase Agreement.

Representations to Management. When any member of the NYSE or person associated with a member wishes to represent a corporation or its stockholders, that person must meet certain rules established by the exchange.

Repurchase Agreement (Repo). (1) A Federal Open Market Committee arrangement with a dealer in which it contracts to purchase a government or agency security at a fixed price, with provision for its resale at the same price at a rate of interest determined competitively. Used by dealers in government and municipal securities to reduce carrying costs. This transaction is not legal for nonexempt securities. (2) A method of financing inventory positions by sale to a nonbank institution with the agreement to buy the position back.

Reserve City Bank. A commercial bank with its main office in a city where a central bank or branch is located that has net demand deposits exceeding $400 million.

Reserve Requirement. The obligation of a commercial bank to set aside and refrain from lending a percentage of its available currency. This is a form of protection for depositors.

Retention. The portion of an underwriter's takedown for sale to its customers. The syndicate manager holds back the balance of the takedown for institutional sales and for allocation to selling group firms that are not syndicate members.

Retirement of Debt Securities. The repayment of principal and accrued interest due to the holders of a bond issue.

Return. See Yield (Rate of Return).

Revenue Anticipation Note (RAN). A short-term municipal debt instrument usually offered on a discount basis. Proceeds of future revenues are pledged as collateral to the payment of the note at maturity.

Revenue Bonds. Tax-exempted bonds whose interest payments are dependent upon, secured by, and redeemable from the income generated by a particular project financed by their issuance.

Reverse a Swap. The transaction following a bond swap that reinstates the original portfolio position — reversing the swap.

Reversal Arbitrage. A riskless arbitrage involving the sale of the stock short, the writing of a put, and the purchase of a call with the options all having the same terms. *See* Conversion Arbitrage.

Reverse Repurchase Agreement (Repo). (1) For Federal Open Market Committee transactions, synonymous with matched sale/purchase agreements. (2) A transaction by which a broker/dealer provides funds to customers by means of purchasing a security with a contract to resell it at the same price plus interest.

Risk Arbitrage. A purchase and short sale of potentially equal securities at prices that may realize a profit. *See* Bona Fide Arbitrage.

Round Lot. A unit of trading or a multiple thereof. On the NYSE, stocks are traded in round lots of 100 shares for active stocks and 10 shares for inactive ones. Bonds are traded in units of $1,000. *See* Normal Trading Unit; Odd Lot.

Rules of Fair Practice. A set of rules established and maintained by the NASD Board of Governors regulating the ethics employed by members in the conduct of their business.

Run. A market maker's list of offerings, including bid-offer prices (and, for bonds, par values and prices).

Run on a Bank. A situation in which a substantial number of depositors, fearing for the safety of their funds, seek withdrawal of their balances in currency.

Running Through the Pot. In a distribution, the syndicate manager can take securities back from the group members and put them into "the pot" for institutional sales. Usually this is done if institutional sales are doing better than retail sales. *See* Pot, The.

Savings Bank. A state-chartered institution that accepts both time and demand deposits. Usually organized as a stock or mutual company, it uses its deposits to invest in mortgages, real estate, government bonds, and so on.

Savings Bond. Bond issued through the U.S. government at a discount and in face values from $50 to $10,000. The interest is exempt from state and local taxes, and no federal tax comes due until the bond is redeemed. *See* Series EE (Savings) Bond; Series HH (Current income) Bond.

Savings Deposit. An interest-earning deposit in a commercial bank subject to immediate withdrawal.

Scale. When serial bonds are initially offered, the scale designates the various maturity dates, the coupon rates, and the offering prices.

Scale Orders. Multiple limit orders entered by investors at various prices but at the same time. The purpose is to obtain an overall, or average, favorable purchase or sale price. Multiples of round lots may be either *bought* at prices scaled down from a given value or *sold* at prices scaled up from a given value.

Scalper. A market maker who puts heavy markups or markdowns on transactions. *See* Five Percent Guideline.

Seasoned Issue. An issue, once distributed, that trades actively and that has great liquidity.

Secondary Market. (1) A term referring to the trading of securities not listed on an organized exchange. (2) A term used to describe the trading of securities other than a new issue.

Secured Obligation (Bond/Debt). A debt whose payment of interest and/or principal is secured by the pledge of physical assets.

Securities Act of 1933. Federal legislation designed to protect the public in the issuance and distribution of securities by providing to prospective purchasers full and accurate information about an issue.

Securities and Exchange Commission (SEC). A government agency responsible for the supervision and regulation of the securities industry.

Securities Exchange Act of 1934. Federal legislation designed to protect the public against unfair and inequitable practices on stock exchanges and in over-the-counter markets throughout the United States.

Securities Industry Association (SIA). An association devoted to instructing member employees and to lobbying for the members' interests.

Securities Industry Automation Corporation (SIAC). A corporation owned two-thirds by the New York Stock Exchange and one-third by the American Stock Exchange. The corporation is under contract to receive trade information from the two exchanges and from their members for the purpose of assisting in final settlement. Data is also supplied to the Consolidated Tape Association (CTA), the Consolidated Quotation System (CQS), the National Security Clearing Corporation (NSCC), and the Intermarket Trading System (ITS). To perform this function, SIAC issues balance orders and continuous net settlement information to the members.

Securities Investor Protection Corporation (SIPC). Formed by the Securities Investors Protection Act of 1970, a government-sponsored, private, nonprofit corporation that guarantees repayment of money and securities to customers in amounts up to $500,000 per customer in the event of a broker/dealer bankruptcy. SIPC covers up to a maximum of $500,00, only $100,000 of which may be for cash. If you have, for example, $100,00 in cash and $100,000 in securities in your account, your are covered for $200,000 ($100,000 of which is cash). If you have $200,000 in securities and $200,000 in cash, you are covered for $300,000 ($200,000 in securities plus $100,000 in cash). If you have $500,000 in securities and $100,000 in cash, you are covered for $500,000, the maximum.

Security. A transferable instrument evidencing ownership or creditorship, such as a note, stock or bond, evidence of debt, interest or participation in a profit-sharing agreement, investment contract, voting trust certificate, fractional undivided interest in oil, gas, or other mineral rights, or any warrant to subscribe to, or purchase, any of the foregoing or other similar instruments.

Security Districts. Thirteen administrative districts throughout the United States established by the NASD.

Each district is governed by a district committee and represented on the association's Board of Governors.

Security Ratings. Ratings set by rating services, such as Moody's, Standard & Poor's, or Fitch, denoting evaluations of the investment and credit risk attached to securities.

Seek a Market. Look to make or buy a sale.

Selling Group. Selected broker/dealers of the NASD who contract to act as selling agents for underwriters and who are compensated by a portion of the sales charge (selling concession) on newly issued stocks. They assume no financial liability for the unsold balance, but they do not share in profit from syndicate residuals.

Sell Stop Order. A memorandum that becomes a market order to sell if and when someone trades a round lot at or below the memorandum price.

Serial Bond. An issue that matures in relatively small amounts at stated periodic intervals.

Serial Issue. An issue of bonds with maturity dates spread out over several years.

Series EE (Savings) Bonds. Nontransferable U.S. government bonds that are issued in denominations of $50 to $10,000 at a discount from their face values and that mature at their face values.

Series HH (Current Income) Bonds. Nontransferable U.S. government bonds that pay interest semiannually. Since 1982, available only in exchange for Series EE bonds.

Shop/Shopping the Street. (1) "Shop" is slang for the broker/dealer's office. (2) "Shop" or "shopping the street" means a broker/dealer's gathering quotations from OTC market makers to form a basis for negotiating a transaction. *See* Firm Market; Subject Market; Workout Market.

Short Sale. The sale of a security that is not owned at the time of the trade, necessitating its purchase some time in the future to "cover" the sale. A short sale is made with the expectation that the stock value will decline, so that the sale will be eventually covered at a price lower than the original sale, thus realizing a profit. Before the sale is covered, the broker/dealer borrows stock (for which collateral is put up) to deliver on the settlement date.

Short-Stop (Limit) Order. A memorandum that becomes a limit order to sell short when someone creates a round-lot transaction at or below the memorandum price (electing sale). The short sale may or may not be executed since the rules then require that it be sold at least one-eighth above the electing sale as well as high enough in value to satisfy the limit price.

Simple Interest. Interest calculated only on the original principal.

Simultaneous (Riskless) Transaction. A transaction in which the broker/dealer takes a position in a security only after receipt of an order from a customer, and only for the purpose of acting as principal so as to disguise his or her remuneration from the transaction.

Sinker. Slang for a bond with a sinking fund. *See* Sinking Fund.

Sinking Fund. (1) An annual reserve of capital required to be set aside out of current earnings to provide monies for retirement of an outstanding bond issue and, sometimes, preferred stock. Such a feature has a favorable effect on the market value of that issue. (2) A separate account in the overall sinking fund for monies used to redeem securities by open-market purchase, by request for tenders or call, or in accordance with the redemption schedule in the bond contract.

Soft Market. The market for securities with low demand.

Sold to You. Term used by over-the-counter traders to confirm the acceptance of their offer.

Special Assessment Bond. A municipal general obligation bond whose debt service is paid by a special tax or assessment on users of the facility.

Special Bond Account. An account in which a customer may favorably finance a purchase of (1) exempted securities or (2) nonconvertible bonds traded on registered stock exchanges in the United States. The account is defined in Regulation T.

Special Convertible Security Account. An account used to finance activity in debt securities that are traded on a registered stock exchange and that (1) are convertible into a margin stock or (2) carry a warrant or right to subscribe to a margin stock. The account is defined in Regulation T.

Special Obligation Bond. A bond secured by a specific revenue source.

Special Tax Bond. A municipal bond whose payment of interest and/or principal is contingent upon the collection of a tax imposed against those who will benefit from the use of the funds obtained from the issuance of the bond.

Split Offering. (1) An offering combining both a primary and secondary distribution. (2) A municipal bond offering, part of which consists of serial bonds and part of which is made up of term bonds.

Split Rating. A term used to describe the situation in which a corporation has been given different credit ratings by different services.

Sponsor. See Underwriter.

Spread. (1) The difference in value between the bid and offering prices. (2) Underwriting compensation.

Stabilization. The syndicate manager is empowered by the members of his group to maintain a bid in the after-market at or slightly below the public offering price, thus "stabilizing" the market and giving the syndicate and selling group members a reasonable chance of successfully disposing of their allocations. This practice is a legal exception to the manipulation practices outlawed by the Securities and Exchange Act of 1934.

Stagflation. The combination of sluggish economic growth, high unemployment, and high inflation.

Stagnation. (1) A period of low volume and inactive trading on a securities market. (2) The economic doldrums resulting from retarded economic growth.

Standard & Poor's (S&P) Corporation. A source of investment services, most famous for its *Standard & Poor's Rating* of bonds and its composite index of 425 industrial, 20 transportation, and 55 public utility common stocks, called *Standard & Poor's Index.*

Standby Commitment. See Standby Underwriting Agreement.

Standby Underwriting Agreement. An agreement between an investment banker and a corporation whereby the banker agrees for a negotiated fee to purchase any or all shares offered as a subscription privilege (rights offering) that are not bought by the rights holders by the time the offer expires.

Statutory Underwriter. See Involuntary (Statutory) Underwriter.

Stickering. Changing the official statement of a new issue by printing the altered information on adhesive-backed paper and "stickering" onto the statement.

Sticky Deal. An underwriting that, for one reason or another, will be hard to market.

Stop Limit Order. A memorandum that becomes a limit (as opposed to a market) order immediately after a transaction takes place at or through the indicated (memorandum) price.

Stop Loss Order. A customer's order to set the sell price of a stock below the market price, thus locking in profits or preventing further losses.

Stop Order. A memorandum that becomes a market order only if a transaction takes place at or through the price stated in the memorandum. Buy stop orders are placed below it. The sale that activates the memorandum is called the electing (activating or triggering) sale. *See* Buy Stop Order; Market Order; Sell Stop Order.

Stop-Out Price. The lower dollar price at auction for which Treasury bills are sold.

Stopped Out. An expression reflecting a broker's unsuccessful attempt to improve upon the price of a transaction after having been guaranteed an execution price by the specialist.

Street. "Wall Street" — that is, the New York financial community, as well as the exchanges throughout the country. The term is becoming somewhate archaic, given the global nature of trading today.

Subject Market (Price, Quote). In the OTC market, a range of buying or selling prices quoted by market makers at which they are unable to trade immediately. Such prices are subject to verification by the parties whose market they represent.

Subordinated Debt Instruments. A debt instrument requiring that repayment of principal may not be made until another debt instrument senior to it has been repaid in full.

Substitution (Swap). The sale of one security in an account to use the proceeds to pay for the purchase of another security on the same trade date. *See* Switch (Contingent or Swap) Order.

Suitability. The appropriateness of a strategy or transaction, in light of an investor's financial means and investment objectives.

Sweetener. A special feature in a securities offering, such as convertibility, that encourages the purchase of the security.

Switch (Contingent or Swap) Order. An order to buy one security and then sell another at a limit, or to sell one security and then to buy another at a limit. The transaction may also be called a proceeds sale if, as is usually the case, the proceeds of the sell order are applied against the expenses of the buy order.

Syndicate. A group of investment bankers who purchase securities from the issuer and then reoffer them to the public at a fixed price. The syndicate is usually organized along historical or social lines, with one member acting as *syndicate manager*, who insures the successful offering of a corporation's securities.

Take a Position. (1) To hold bonds, in either a long or short position. (2) To purchase securities as a long-term investment.

Takedown. (1) In a municipal underwriting, the price that syndicate members pay when they take bonds from the account. (2) In an underwriting, the number of securities that a syndicate member is supposed to sell.

Take Delivery. In securities, accepting a receipt of stock or bond certificates after they have been purchased or transferred between accounts.

TAN. See Tax Anticipation Note.

Tape. A financial news service that reports the prices and sizes of transactions. Although this information was once reported on a paper tape from a "ticker tape" machine, it is now displayed on electronic screens. The name "tape," however, persists.

Tax Anticipation Bills (TAB). Treasury bills with maturity dates fixed several days after a major tax payment date with a proviso enabling their holders to tender them at face value in satisfaction of their tax requirement and earn a little extra interest in the process.

Tax Anticipation Note (TAN). A short-term municipal note usually offered on a discount basis. The proceeds of a forthcoming tax collection are pledged to repay the note.

Tax-Exempted Securities. Obligations issued by a state or municipality, or a state or local agency, whose interest payments (but not profits from purchase or sale) are exempted from federal taxation. The interest payment may be exempted from local taxation, too, if purchased by a resident of the issuing state. The term does not include U.S. government obligations. *See* General Obligation (GO) Bond; Revenue Bonds.

Tennessee Valley Authority (TVA). A government-sponsored agency whose bonds are redeemable from the proceeds of the various power projects in the Tennessee River area. Interest payments on these bonds are fully taxable to investors.

Ten Percent Guideline. Formula used in municipal debt issues analysis. The total bonded debt of a municipality shouldn't exceed 10 percent of the market value of the real estate within the municipality.

Term Bond. (1) A U.S. Treasury bond with a call privilege that becomes effective generally five years prior to maturity. (2) A large municipal bond issue with all the bonds maturing on the same date.

Term REPO. A repurchase agreement whose life extends beyond the normal overnight agreement.

Thin Market. See Narrow Market.

Thirty-Day Visible Supply. Calendar published each Thursday by the *Daily Bond Buyer* listing new negotiated and competitive municipal securities that will come to market within the next 30 days.

Three-Handed Deal. Colloquial expression for a municipal security issue underwriting consisting of serial maturities with two term maturities.

Thrift Institutions. Savings banks, savings and loans, or credit unions. Also known as thrifts.

Throwaway Offer. A nominal (approximate) bid or offer that should not be considered final.

Tight Market. An active, vigorous market with narrow bid-offer spreads.

Tight Money. An economic condition characterized by scarce credit, generally the result of a money supply restricted by the Federal Reserve. *See* Easy Money.

Time Deposit. An account containing a currency balance pledged to remain at that bank for a specified, extended period in return for payment of interest.

Tombstone. The type of newspaper advertisement used for public offering. The ad simply and durably lists all the facts about the issue. Also called the offering circular.

Trade Date. The date a trade was entered into, as opposed to settlement date.

Trader. A person or firm engaged in the business of buying and selling securities, options, or commodities for a profit.

Treasury Bill. A federal bearer obligation issued in denominations of $10,000 to $1 million with a maturity date usually of three months to one year. It is fully marketable at a discount from face value (which determines the interest rate). *See* Tax Anticipation Bill.

Treasury Bond. A federal registered or bearer obligation issued in denominations of $500 to $1 million with maturities ranging from five to thirty-five years, carrying a fixed interest rate and issued, quoted, and traded as a percentage of its face value. *See* Flower Bond; Term Bond.

Treasury Note. A federal registered or bearer obligation issued in denominations of $1,000 to $500 million for maturities of one to ten years, carrying a fixed rate of interest. These notes are issued, quoted, and traded at a percentage of their face value.

Treasury Securities. Debt obligations that the U.S. government issues and that the Treasury Department sells in the form of bills, notes, and bonds.

Turkey. A security that is not doing an investor any good.

TVA. See Tennessee Valley Authority.

Twenty-Day (Cooling-Off) Period. A period of twenty calendar days following the filing of a registration statement with the SEC, during which (1) the SEC examines the statement for deficiencies; (2) the issuing corporation negotiates with an underwriting syndicate for a final agreement; and (3) the syndicate prepares for the successful distribution of the impending issue. The final day of the period is normally considered the effective date.

Twenty-Five Percent Rule. In municipal securities analysis, a rule of thumb that an issuer's bonded debt should not exceed 25 percent of its annual budget.

Twenty-Five Percent Cushion Rule. In the analysis of municipal revenue bonds, a rule of thumb that the revenue from the facility built with the bond issue's proceeds should exceed the cost of operations, maintenance, and debt service by 25 percent.

Undervalued. A term used to describe a security that is trading at a lower price than it should. *See* Overvalued.

Underwriter. Also known as an "investment banker" or "distributor," a middleman between an issuing corporation and the public. The underwriter usually forms an underwriting group, called a syndicate, to limit risk and commitment of capital. He or she may also contract with selling groups to help distribute the issue — for a concession. In the distribution of mutual funds, the underwriter may also be known as a "sponsor," "distributor," or even "wholesaler." Investment bankers also offer other services, such as advice and counsel on the raising and investment of capital.

Underwriter's Retention. The percentage of total issue to which each member of an underwriter's group is entitled and which he or she distributes to customers. The retained amount is usually equal to about 75 percent of the member's total financial commitment. The syndicate manager decides, on behalf of the other members, how to distribute the rest of the issue, (or "the pot") and how it is to be sold to institutional investors (group sales) or reversed for handling by selling groups. *See* Philadelphia Plan; Western Account.

Underwriting Agreement. The contract between the investment banker and the corporation, containing the final terms and prices of the issue. It is signed either on the evening before or early in the morning of the public offering date (effective date).

Underwriting Compensation (Spread). The gross profit realized by an underwriter equal to the difference between the price he paid to the issuing corporation and the price of the public offering.

Undivided Account. In an underwriting agreement, an arrangement for the sharing of liability in which each member of the syndicate is liable for any unsold portion of an issue. The degree of liability is based on each member's percentage participation. *See* Syndicate.

Uniform Practice Code ("the Code"). A Code established and maintained by the NASD Board of Governors that regulates the mechanics of executing and completing securities transactions in the OTC market.

Uniform Practice Committee. An NASD district subcommittee that disseminates information and interpretations handed down by the Board of Governors regarding the Uniform Practice Code.

United States Government Securities. Debt issues of the U.S. government (Treasury Department), backed by the government's unlimited power of taxation, such as Treasury bills, notes, bonds, and Series EE and Series HH bonds.

Unlisted Security. A security that is not traded on an exchange. Usually called an over-the-counter security.

Unqualified Legal (Clean) Opinion. An unconditional affirmation of a security's legality, rendered either before or after the security is sold. *See* Qualified Legal Opinion.

Unsecured Obligation (Bond). A debt instrument whose repayment is backed solely by the creditworthiness of the issuer. No specific property is pledged as security. Also called a "debenture."

Upgrade. Raising a security's rating by improving the credit quality of the issuer or issuer.

Uptrend. Any generally upward movement in a security's price.

Variable Rate. Interest rate on a security that is subject to change, commonly in connection with the rates paid on selected issues of Treasury securities. Also called floating rate.

Vault Cash. All the cash in a bank's vault.

Velocity (of Money). The number of times a dollar changes hands in one year. Given a fixed money supply, increased velocity is usually a sign to the Federal Reserve that an increase in the money supply is needed.

Visible Supply. See Thirty-Day Visible Supply.

Volume. Number of bonds or shares traded during specific periods, such as daily, weekly, or monthly.

Voluntary Underwriter. An individual or corporation that purchases a security from an issuer or affiliated person and offers it for public sale under an effective registration statement.

Weak Market. A market characterized by a greater number of sellers than buyers, which creates a general downtrend in prices.

Western Account. An agreement among underwriters regarding liability, in which each member of the syndicate is liable only for the amount of its participation in, but not for the unsold portion of, the issue. *See* Syndicate.

When Issued/When Distributed Contract. A delivery contract involving securities (stocks or bonds) that have been proposed for distribution but not yet issued. The date of delivery is set for some time in the future by the NASD Uniform Practice Committee or the appropriate stock exchange, as the case may be.

Wholesaler. See Underwriter

Whoops. Securities of the Washington Public Power Supply System (WPPS).

WI. See When Issued.

Window Settlement. Transactions that are not cleared through the SCC or NCC and that are completed in the office of the purchasing firm by means of certificate delivery versus immediate payment.

Workout Market. In the OTC market, a range of prices quoted by a market maker who is not certain that a market is available, but who feels he or she can "work one out" within a reasonable period of time.

Yankee CD. A dollar-denominated, foreign-issued time deposit that is registered for sale in the U.S.

Yankee Bond. A dollar-denominated, foreign-issued bond that is registered for sale in the U.S.

Yellow Sheets. A daily publication of the National Quotation Bureau giving markets in corporate debt securities. *See* Pink Sheets.

Yield (Rate of Return). The percentage return on an investor's money in terms of current prices. It is the annual dividend/interest per share or bond, divided by the current market price of that security.

Yield Curve. Graph depicting the relation of interest rates to time: time is plotted on the *x*-axis, and yields on the *y*-axis. The curve shows whether short-term interest rates are higher or lower than long-term rates. A *positive yield curve* results if short-term rates are lower, and a *negative yield curve* results if short-term rates are higher. A *flat yield curve* results if long- and short-term rates do not differ greatly. Generally, the yield curve is positive because investors tie up their money for longer periods and are rewarded with better yields.

Yield to Maturity. The calculation of an average rate of return on a bond (with a maturity over one year) if it is held to its maturity date and if all cash flows are reinvested at the same rate of interest. It includes an adjustment for any premium paid or discount received. It is a calculation used to compare relative values of bonds.

Zero Coupon Discount Security. A debt security that *offers no payments of interest* — only payment of full *face value at maturity* but that is used at a deep discount from face *value.*

Index

Mortgage-backed pass-through securities
  (MBSs), 83-88, 234-35
  definition of, 83-84
  growth of, 83
  issuance method, 87-88
  issuers of, 84
  market for, 84
  pools of, 84
  settlement, 86-88
    delivery, 86-87
    dollar roll, 87
    pairing off transactions, 86
  TBA confirmation, 84-85
  twelve-year average life assumption, 85
Mortgage-backed securities, 70, 234-35
Mortgage-based securities desk, 109
Mortgage bonds, 172, 235
Mortgage-credit agencies, 74-83
  Federal Home Loan Bank, 74-76
  Federal National Mortgage Association
    (FNMA), 76-80
  Government National Mortgage Associa-
    tion (GNMA), 80-83
Municipal bonds
  categories of, 135
    general obligation (GO) bonds, 135-
      36
    revenue bonds, 135-37
  definition of, 131, 235
  history of, 131
  interest rates, 132-33
  municipal bond dealers, 134-35
  nongovernmental purpose bonds, 132
  offering date, 153
  private activity bonds, 132
  public purpose bonds, 132
  quotations, 188-89
  settlement, 197-99
  taxation of, 131-33
  Tax Reform Act of 1986 and, 132
  triple exemption, 133
  when, as and if issued, 153
Municipal debt, 130-56
  competitive underwriting, 148-56
  municipal bonds, 131-34
  municipal securities dealers,
    workings of, 146-48
  primary market, 134-46
  See also specific topics.
Municipal Finance Officers Association
  (MFOA), 155
Municipal notes, 29-30
  definition of, 29
  types of, 30
Municipal securities dealers, 146-55
  municipal research, 147
  operations, 147-48
  public finance group, 147
  sales force, 146-47
  traders, 146
  underwriting area, 146
Municipal Securities Information Document Central Repository, 155
Municipal Securities Rulemaking Board
  (MSRB), 194
Munifacts, 184, 186
Mutilated certificates, 198

N

National Association of Securities Dealers
  Automated Quotations (NASDAQ) system, 184, 190
  levels of service, 184
National Association of Security Dealers
  (NASD), 192-94
  delivery and, 197
  history of, 193
  membership in, 193-94
  power of, 193
National Quotations Bureau (NQB) sheets,
  184, 190
Negotiated bidding
  syndicates, 141, 143, 144, 146, 238
  versus competitive bidding, 154
Negotiated markets, 183
Negotiated underwriting, 158-71
  agreement among underwriters, 166-70
  blue-skying the issue, 166
  cooling-off period, 159-64
  due-diligence meeting, 166
  investment bankers, 158, 164-65
  preliminary prospectus, 165
  See also specific topics.
Net interest cost, 149, 150, 238
Next-day settlement, 195, 239
Nominal rate, 3
Nominal yield, 7, 239
Nongovernmental purpose bonds, 132
Normal scale, municipal bonds, 138
Normal yield curve, 65, 239

O

October 1987 Crash, effect on investors, ix
  x
Offering date
  definition of, 240
  municipal bonds, 153
Offering wanted (OW), 191
Official statement, 149, 151-52, 155
Open-end mortgage bonds, 172
Open market operations
  Federal Reserve, 38, 240
    manager, 41-42
Open market purchases, 7
Operations department, municipal
  securities dealers, 147-48, 241
Options
  definition of, 91
  theoretical value of, 92
  See also Interest rate options.
Original issue discounts (OIDs), 65
Out-of-the-money, 94
Over-the-counter (OTC) market
  bond trading in, 182
  brokers/dealers, 182-83
  OTC trading execution, 183-86

P

Parity, 178
Partial delivery, 198-99, 242
Par value, 3
Pass-through securities. *See* Mortgage-
  backed pass-through securities.

W

Wasting assets, *See* Interest rate options;
  Options.
Western account, syndicates, 141, 170,
  266
When-issued (WI) bills, 58, 129
WI bills, *See* When-issued (WI) bills.
Workout quotes, 190

Y

Yellow sheets, 184
Yield, 7-10, 267
    coupon yield, 7, 239
    current yield, 7-8, 215
    maximum yield, Treasury bonds, 61
    taxable equivalent yield, 64
    Treasury bills, 54
        calculation of, 54-55
    yield to maturity (YTM), 8-10, 15-16,
      64-65, 267
Yield curve, 17-22, 64-65, 267
    definition of, 18
    descending yield curve, 21-22
    expectations theory, 19-20
    indifference curve, 19
    normal curve, 65, 239
    upward-sloping yield curve, 20
Yield to maturity (YTM), 8-10, 15-16, 64-
  65, 267
    calculation of, 9-10, 15-16
    definition of, 8
    Treasury bonds, 64-65
    versus total return, 16
YTM, *See* Yield to maturity.

Z

Zero coupon issues, 65-66, 267-68
    original issue discounts (OIDs), 65
    stripped issues, 65-66
    Treasury bonds, 65